# Vicious Evil! Virtuous God?

# VICIOUS EVIL! VIRTUOUS GOD?

Answers for Our Pain and Suffering

LEE THAI, MD

FOREWORD BY
Randal Roberts

RESOURCE *Publications* · Eugene, Oregon

VICIOUS EVIL! VIRTUOUS GOD?
Answers for Our Pain and Suffering

Copyright © 2024 Lee Thai. All rights reserved. Except for brief quotations in critical publications or reviews, no part of this book may be reproduced in any manner without prior written permission from the publisher. Write: Permissions, Wipf and Stock Publishers, 199 W. 8th Ave., Suite 3, Eugene, OR 97401.

Resource Publications
An Imprint of Wipf and Stock Publishers
199 W. 8th Ave., Suite 3
Eugene, OR 97401

www.wipfandstock.com

PAPERBACK ISBN: 979-8-3852-0254-6
HARDCOVER ISBN: 979-8-3852-0255-3
EBOOK ISBN: 979-8-3852-0256-0

VERSION NUMBER 04/22/24

All Scripture quotations, unless otherwise indicated, are taken from the New American Standard Bible® (NASB), Copyright © 1960, 1962, 1963, 1968, 1971, 1972, 1973, 1975, 1977, 1995 by The Lockman Foundation. Used by permission. www.Lockman.org

Scripture quotations marked (NIV) are taken from the Holy Bible, New International Version®, NIV®. Copyright © 1973, 1978, 1984, 2011 by Biblica, Inc.™ Used by permission of Zondervan. All rights reserved worldwide. www.zondervan.com The "NIV" and "New International Version" are trademarks registered in the United States Patent and Trademark Office by Biblica, Inc.™

Scripture quotations marked (KJV) are taken from the KING JAMES VERSION, public domain.

# Contents

*Foreword by Randal Roberts* | vii
*Introduction: Where is God when it hurts?* | ix

**Part One: Answers for Our Pain and Suffering in This Fallen Realm.**

1. What does God do for his suffering children in this evil world? | 3
2. How does God use the evils on this earth for his greater purposes? | 24
3. Why doesn't God create humans with free will who never commit evil? | 39
4. Where do the evils in our lives come from? | 47
5. Will the evils and sufferings be redeemed in heaven? | 76
6. What are some practical means to manage the evils in our lives and help others in their suffering? | 94

**Part Two: A Novel Solution to the Problem of Evil**

7. Evil, an insurmountable problem? | 127
8. What is God's response to people who deny him and commit evil? | 138
9. Why does God not intervene to prevent all moral evils? | 147
10. Why does God not intervene to prevent all natural evils? | 168

11. Can a good God coexist with evil? | 180
12. Is there a way of escape from this world full of evil and suffering? | 191

Conclusion: Vicious evil! Virtuous God? | 207

*Bibliography* | 211
*Name and Subject Index* | 229

# Foreword

NOT MANY AUTHORS MAKE their debut into the Christian publishing world by tackling the knotty problem of how God's sovereignty relates to human free will. Fewer still follow that initial volume with another that examines the problem of evil in its various forms and how the existence of sin and suffering relates to the wisdom, providence, and goodness of the triune God.

But Dr. Lee Thai is not your typical author. An experienced anesthesiologist who also spends considerable time doing medical research, Dr. Thai has demonstrated that he is also a very competent theologian. When the fruit of his acute biblical research skills (informed by both extensive reading and rigorous logic) leads to a conclusion that he believes is supported by Scripture, even when it deviates from some popular theological paradigms, Dr. Thai isn't afraid to make that case; and you will find this freedom from inhibition on ample display in this volume.

Such fresh thinking is especially profitable when grappling with an issue as complicated, confounding, and controversial as the relationship of evil and suffering to the purposes and character of God. For a failure to resolve—at least to a reasonable degree—the various tensions that accompany that relationship has been a frequent stumbling block to both believer and unbeliever alike. That intellectual, emotional, and spiritual dilemma becomes especially acute when significant suffering enters a person's life (as it inevitably will, sooner or later). So those of us who have embraced the Christian faith need a biblically sound framework by which we can process this dynamic so that it strengthens our faith rather than weakens it. Those who have not yet trusted in the one true God and His authoritative written revelation would similarly profit from a candid, constructive, and credible explanation of how sin and suffering function in a world governed by the biblical God.

It is this kind of pastoral concern that characterizes Dr. Thai's work. While many of the issues associated with the co-existence of evil/suffering and a good/omnipotent/wise God are inevitably complex, Dr. Thai makes a considerable effort to make his case accessible to the typical reader rather than employ the technical vocabulary understood only by the Christian scholar. To that end, we find not just an abundance of illustrative anecdotes scattered throughout the text, but also a cornucopia of illuminating quotations ranging from remarkably diverse sources, both expected (e.g., Charles Spurgeon, C. S. Lewis, and N. T. Wright) and unexpected (e.g., Hugh Hefner, Jean Paul Sartre, and Ted Turner).

Similar abundance is found in the exhaustive citation of Scripture to back up his assertions. This not only gives the reader an appreciation of what biblical text is shaping Dr. Thai's conclusion, but also models a firm determination to allow biblical data to exercise its appropriate authority over one's theological methodology. Similarly, I appreciate Dr. Thai's resolve to discern an underlying harmony in the biblical treatment of the topics rather than prematurely resort to the concept of inexplicable "mystery."

So, I urge you as a reader to join me in engaging this book and its "Tough Love Theodicy" with both an open mind and an open Bible, prayerfully seeking light from our Lord so that we might correctly interpret His word. And even if you don't find yourself arriving at the same conclusion on every point as Dr. Thai, you will still benefit from the process of being exposed to his thinking and, like him, consciously and conscientiously submit your worldview to the unique wisdom and transcendent authority of Scripture.

May the Lord grant you the faith and wisdom needed to both trust and praise Him throughout all the vicissitudes of this life while we together persevere in eager anticipation of the consummation of His Christ-centered plan and its accompanying redemption, restoration, and renewal.

Randal Roberts, D. Min.
President Emeritus
Western Seminary (Portland, OR)

# Introduction: Where Is God When It Hurts?

> *Go to Him when your need is desperate, when all other help is vain and what do you find? A door slammed in your face, and a sound of bolting and double bolting on the inside. After that, silence. You may as well turn away.*
>
> —C. S. Lewis[1]

I COMPLETED MY RESIDENCY in Chicago, married my beloved wife, and accepted an anesthesiology position in Phoenix. We bought a two-story house near a mountain preserve and settled into an idyllic existence. Life was beautiful!

We were soon blessed with a son, Daniel, our pride and joy. Our little universe revolved around taking Dan to the nearby park (Roadrunner Park, although I have never seen a roadrunner there) where he would often fall asleep in the swings. Evening outings in our quiet neighborhood with Dan warmly nestled in his baby stroller, and trips to the lakes surrounding our "valley of the sun," filled our lives with happiness and thanksgiving. We still have a treasured picture of our chunky cherubim (well nurtured by his mom) resting contentedly in her embrace by the setting sun. God is good all the time!

One day, we noticed that Dan was falling behind in his speech and vocabulary milestones. However, the medical exams did not uncover any obvious issues and we were told that we needed to be patient and that he

---

1. C. S. Lewis, *A Grief Observed*, 7.

would eventually "outgrow" it. Unfortunately, he did not outgrow it and things took an ominous turn for the worse!

Soon after, Dan started to lose weight and fell off the growth charts. Also, he did not seem to have as much stamina as the other children in the playground. During outings, he frequently squatted down to rest after running for just a short distance.

Our dreamy existence was then disrupted by the unwelcome discovery of a heart murmur on a routine doctor's visit. Being an experienced physician, I quickly pulled out my trusty stethoscope to double check on such a preposterous claim! There was no heart murmur, even after a long and extensive auscultation of Dan's heart, thankfully made easier by his calm temperament. Nevertheless, being the careful person that I am, I decided to be present at the next check-up.

> Pediatrician (after carefully listening to Dan's heart): Hmm! He is behind in height and weight! And the murmur is still there!
>
> Me (worried): Are you sure?
>
> Pediatrician (confident): Yes! Do you want to listen to it?
>
> Me (eager): Sure! (Taking the stethoscope handed over by the pediatrician).
>
> Honestly, there is nothing there! Everything sounds normal. However, it would not be polite and professional to forcefully disagree with a fellow physician. Probably, it would be best to be conciliatory!
>
> Me (cool and collected): Yeah, maybe there is a little flow murmur there! (For my non-medical readers, a flow murmur is not significant).
>
> Pediatrician (hesitant): Well, we will see him back at the next check-up!
>
> Me: Good idea! (Relief! Let us go back to our blissful existence!).

Somewhat reluctantly, the pediatrician let us go home. Probably, she did not want to contradict me either!

I was working at the hospital when my boy had his next check-up. My wife called me there in tears and anguish, saying that the murmur had gotten worse and that she was told to take our son to a pediatric cardiologist at once. Later, the cardiologist contacted me and reported that my child had a large hole in his heart and a leaky valve that would require cardiac catheterization and open-heart surgery!

Panic-stricken, I felt waves of fear washing over me, causing me to be nauseous and lightheaded. As a physician, I knew the risks involved in a major heart surgery for such a little toddler in poor health. The symptoms of the heart condition were all there. My son was losing weight; he tired easily; he could not keep up with his peers at the playground.

Heartbroken and guilt-ridden, I knew that I had failed doubly in my duties as a father and a physician. Instead of acting swiftly on the early findings of the pediatrician, I had allowed my emotions (denial?) to delay a proper evaluation of Dan's condition, possibly aggravating his illness. Yes, I had been taught in medical school that one should never diagnose or treat one's own family. However, I had disregarded that cardinal rule and, after listening to my beloved child's heart, mistakenly opined that there was no heart murmur!

Unfortunately, there was nothing that I could do to turn back the clock. I was angry with God for not protecting my son and terrified by the disastrous outcome caused by my incompetence. The prospect of making further wrong decisions that might result in my child's demise horrified me.

The day came for Dan to have his cardiac catheterization in preparation for surgery. It was Friday, January 20, 1989, for the television in the waiting room of the hospital was broadcasting the inauguration of our 41st President, George H. W. Bush. I had been praying day and night that God would somehow heal Dan and that he would be spared from a life-threatening operation. Racked with guilt, I had begged God for his grace, mercy, and favor, and asked for a miracle. The cardiac catheterization procedure was supposed to take only one hour. An hour went by, then two without any news. By this time, I was confident that God had answered my prayers and the reason for the delay was that the cardiologist could not find any abnormality and was taking his time to double check the unexpected result!

Finally, the physician came out with the report. The hole was still there. The mitral valve still needed to be fixed. An open-heart operation was still required. God, why did you not do anything? Do you not care about my two-year-old boy, my only child? Have I not been a good Christian and a loyal follower? Why do you not answer my fervent prayers and our church's heartfelt pleadings?

But, after further thoughts, I realized the sheer foolishness of railing at the one who forgave my sins and genuinely loved me with an everlasting love! Was he not the one who had, many times before, rescued me in my desperate hours (medical school admission, loneliness, residency problems . . .) and the only one who could remedy our precarious situation?

So, I went to God again in feverish prayer, asking that, somehow, he would still take care of Dan's condition (and absolve me of my faults), even at that late hour. Surely, he healed all diseases and even resurrected people from the dead. What are holes in the heart and valve problems to him? However, it was not to be. Our efforts to feed Dan, increase his weight, and improve his health failed miserably! Through all this, God was silent.

Heartbroken, my wife and I were resigned to preparing Dan for surgery. We contacted the most highly recommended pediatric cardiac surgeon in town who, fortuitously, had just taken some special training on the type of valve surgery that Dan would need. I packed the operating room with the best nurses, the best anesthesiologist, the best heart pump technician . . .

The day of the heart operation came too quickly! At 6:30 am, the nurses came to take my son to surgery. I can still remember him dressed in a short, yellow patient's gown, so little, so skinny, so confused by the austere environment of the surgical suite. I can still see my grief-stricken wife give him a last goodbye kiss before tearing her soul and entrusting him to the waiting hands of the solemn nurses. Though we could not imagine life without our sweet, innocent little boy, my distraught wife and I tearfully gave him back to God to whom he belonged! Yes, children are gifts from the Lord,[2] yet God reserves the right to demand them back lest they become our idols (e.g., Abraham and Isaac).[3] Lord, let your will be done! I don't know why it must be this way but let your will be done!

Dan did make it through the open-heart surgery, with many blood transfusions, two chest tubes, and a post op infection. It broke our hearts to see him in great pain and hear him beg the nurses and doctors to go away by crying "All done! All done!" every time they entered his room. While he did recover from the ordeal, there is still some valve leakage that requires yearly follow-up.

2. Ps 127:3
3. Gen 22

## INTRODUCTION: WHERE IS GOD WHEN IT HURTS?

Why does God let calamity, pain, and evil happen to innocent little children? Does he not care? Why does he not intervene? These thoughts have haunted me for over thirty years. Besides my personal trial, I have seen sufferings and deaths daily in the hospitals where I worked. I have witnessed fear, anguish, despair, and agony on the faces of waiting relatives when I had to share the unwelcome news of a serious disease, or worse, the passing of their loved ones. In search for answers, I have read countless books and talked to numerous people about evil and suffering.

Unfortunately, the standard response to the question, "Why doesn't a virtuous God prevent vicious evils?" is "It's a mystery inaccessible to human minds."[4] This may not be particularly helpful to me or my fellow sufferers, as we are tormented and confused by our never-ending pains, griefs, and fears, desperately trying to understand, agonizingly searching for an explanation, a reason for our horrendous miseries on this earth! Nor is "mystery" a very convincing reply to non-theists who question God's existence in the presence of evil. Dr. Erickson asserted: "We must go as far as we can with our human reasoning and understanding before we label something a mystery."[5]

In agreement, I have thought long and hard on the issue and finally wrote a PhD dissertation on the subject. This work is the fruit of that exhausting quest for solution to one of the most painful human enigmas, what philosophers and theologians call "the problem of evil."

Part one of the book will answer the questions of Christians experiencing the many evils in this fallen realm.

1. What does God do for his suffering children in this evil world?
2. How does God use the evils on this earth for his greater purposes?
3. Why doesn't God create humans with free will who never commit evil?
4. Where do the evils in our lives come from?
5. Will the evils and sufferings be redeemed in heaven?
6. What are some practical means to manage the evils in our lives and help others in their suffering?

---

4. "The mystery of evil remains." Kenneth Keathley, *Salvation and Sovereignty*, 13.
5. Millard Erickson, *Christian Theology*, 330n14.

Part two will provide believers (and non-believers) with a novel solution to the problem of evil—the Tough Love Theodicy[6]—an explanation they can give to fellow sufferers who question the existence of a good and virtuous God in the presence of vicious evils in the world.

7. Evil, an insurmountable problem?
8. What is God's response to people who deny him and commit evil?
9. Why does God not intervene to prevent all moral evils?
10. Why does God not intervene to prevent all natural evils?
11. Can a good God coexist with evil?
12. Is there a way of escape from this world full of evil and suffering?

Dear fellow pilgrims, this work is written to answer our urgent and heart-wrenching questions in this "vale of suffering," bring us comfort in our many tribulations, provide us with some practical means to help others in their afflictions, and equip us to make a defense for the hope that we share in Christ.[7] Gloria Deo!

---

6. Theodicy is a word coined by the German philosopher Gottfried Leibniz from the Greek theos (God) and dike (justice). "A theodicy replies to an argument from evil by giving a justifying reason for the existence of the evil." William Hasker, "An Open Theist View," 61.

7. 1 Pet 3:15

# PART ONE

Answers for Our Pain and Suffering in This Fallen Realm

# 1

# What Does God Do for His Suffering Children in This Evil World?

*God does not give us everything we want, but He does fulfill His promises, leading us along the best and straightest paths to Himself.*

—Dietrich Bonhoeffer[1]

GEORGE WAS A CHARISMATIC partier who loved the four Bs—Beer, Bourbon, and B&B (Brandy and Benedictine). At the age of 20, he was arrested for disorderly conduct after he and some friends had "a few beers" and stole a Christmas wreath from a hotel.[2] When he was 26, he drunkenly drove to his parents' home and smashed into their neighbor's garbage can, dragging it down the street.[3] Four years later, he was arrested for driving under the influence. He had his driver's license suspended for two years.[4]

At the age of 31, George married a shy librarian and had twin daughters. Following in his father's footsteps, he operated a small oil exploration company in Texas. Unfortunately, oil prices cratered, causing his company to fall into debt. He bitterly bemoaned, "I am all name and

---

1. Dietrich Bonhoeffer, *Letters and Papers from Prison*, 206.
2. https://archive.nytimes.com/www.nytimes.com/library/politics/camp/061900wh-bush.html
3. https://www.cnn.com/ALLPOLITICS/time/2000/11/13/ride.html
4. https://archive.seattletimes.com/archive/?date=20001103&slug=4051081

no money."[5] Due to his excessive drinking, his marriage was in trouble, and he faced the prospect of losing his children.

In 1985, George was counseled by Billy Graham and began studying the Bible. He finally gave up drinking after waking up with a bad hangover from his 40th birthday celebration. "That's it. I'll take God. I'll beat drinking. I keep Laura and the girls; that simple. I will never take a drink again the rest of my life. Done."[6] He became a born-again Christian and, with God's help, turned his life around. George W. Bush, the 43rd President of the United States, acknowledged: "I quit drinking in 1986 and haven't had a drop since then . . . because I heard a higher call."[7]

It is never too late for people to turn to the Lord. There is no situation so dire or so desperate that he would throw up his hands and give up on his creatures as nothing is too difficult for him.[8] Help for George Bush and for anyone is available *if* they are willing to respond to their Creator's calls to return to him.

The holy God, in love, helps his followers escape from their seemingly "hopeless" situations. Their sins are forgiven, and their penalties of death taken by Jesus. They are "children of God,"[9] "fellow heirs with Christ,"[10] and recipients of his many blessings[11] and miracles.[12]

Yet, Dr. Keller argued: "It is unjust for God to perform miracles for some people and not for others."[13] However, one can hardly expect God to treat believers and non-believers the same way as "there is now no condemnation for those who are in Christ Jesus."[14] While God loves all his creatures,[15] he "will render to each person according to his deeds, to those who by perseverance in doing good seek for glory and honor and

---

5. https://www.washingtonpost.com/wp-srv/politics/campaigns/wh2000/stories/bush073099.htm

6. https://www.pbs.org/wgbh/pages/frontline/shows/jesus/president/spirituality.html

7. https://www.latimes.com/archives/la-xpm-2000-nov-01-mn-45190-story.html

8. Jer 32:27

9. John 1:12

10. Rom 8:17

11. Eph 1:3

12. Gal 3:5

13. James Keller, *Problems of Evil*, 60.

14. Rom 8:1

15. John 3:16

immortality, eternal life; but to those who are selfishly ambitious and do not obey the truth, but obey unrighteousness, wrath and indignation."[16]

Hence, believers are the beneficiaries of God's great love and concern. "He (God) has granted to us (believers) his precious and magnificent promises, so that by them you may become partakers of the divine nature."[17] Children of God can expect many good gifts from their Father in heaven. "If you then, being evil, know how to give good gifts to your children, how much more will your Father who is in heaven give what is good to those who ask Him!"[18] In this world replete with horrendous evils, believers, like George Bush, can look forward to much help and goodness from their benevolent Lord!

## God's Intimate Presence with His Children

In God's grace, believers are declared righteous (right with God as the penalty for sins has been charged to the substitute, Jesus Christ). "He (God) would be just and the justifier of the one who has faith in Jesus."[19] The theologian Albert Barnes affirmed:

> God retained the integrity of his character as a moral governor; that he had shown a due regard to his Law, and to the penalty of the Law by his plan of salvation. Should he forgive sinners without an atonement, justice would be sacrificed and abandoned ... A full compensation, an equivalent, has been provided by the sufferings of the Savior in the sinner's stead, and the sinner may be pardoned.[20]

As the believers' sins are forgiven, they are no longer separated from the holy God[21] and may have a close relationship with him through the gift of the Holy Spirit. "In him, you also, after listening to the message of truth, the gospel of your salvation—having also believed, you were sealed in him with the Holy Spirit of promise."[22] All Christians receive God's

16. Rom 2:5-8
17. 2 Pet 1:4
18. Matt 7:11
19. Rom 3:26
20. Albert Barnes, *Notes, Explanatory and Practical, on the Epistle to the Romans*, 89-90.
21. Rom 8:38-39
22. Eph 1:13

Holy Spirit, a privilege not given to many (only to sons and daughters). "The Spirit you received brought about your adoption to sonship. And by him we cry, 'Abba, Father.'"[23]

The Holy Spirit dwells inside believers[24] and gives them the power to carry out their tasks. "You will receive power when the Holy Spirit has come upon you; and you shall be My witnesses both in Jerusalem, and in all Judea and Samaria, and even to the remotest part of the earth."[25] The Holy Spirit "will teach you all things,"[26] "He will guide you into all the truth."[27] "I will dwell in them and walk among them; and I will be their God, and they shall be my people."[28]

The Holy God's intimate presence brings comfort and healing to his grieving children in their suffering. Pastor Rick Warren, the author of *The Purpose Driven Life,* pondered the problem of evil while reminiscing about the suicide of his 27-year-old son Matthew.

> *When Matthew died, I took a four-month grief sabbatical. I did not preach, I did not teach, so I spent eight hours a day alone with Jesus. I'm not the same man I used to be. I've got the same personality, the same flaws, but I'm just not the same guy I was. You can't spend four months alone in reflection, in the Bible, with scripture and with Jesus and it not change you [sic], deepen you and sensitize you to the pain of other people. When things happen to you, they become part of your life message. It doesn't replace my life message; it just adds to the mosaic. It's another piece that's been added . . . All the 'why' questions . . . But explanations never comfort. What you need in tragedy is not an explanation, you need the presence of God . . . Surrender is when you say I'd rather live and walk with God and have my questions unanswered than have all my questions answered and not walk with God.*[29]

Like Pastor Warren who experienced God's comforting presence in his private time "with Jesus," believers are not left alone as orphans in this world. The triune God (Father, Son, and Holy Spirit) dwells

---

23. Rom 8:15 NIV.
24. 1 Cor 3:16
25. Acts 1:8
26. John 14:26
27. John 16:13
28. 2 Cor 6:16
29. https://www.premierchristianity.com/Blog/Rick-Warren-My-son-s-suicide-and-God-s-garden-of-grace

intimately with his people,[30] and walks with them through their many tribulations in this fallen realm. "Even though I walk through the valley of the shadow of death, I fear no evil, for You are with me. Your rod and Your staff, they comfort me."[31] In faithful love, "God has said, 'Never will I leave you; never will I forsake you.'"[32] "The Lord himself goes before you and will be with you; he will never leave you nor forsake you. Do not be afraid; do not be discouraged."[33]

**God Answers His Children's Prayers**

God promises faithful believers[34] that he will answer their prayers. He encourages them to pray to him and ask him for whatever they need. "Ask, and it will be given to you; seek, and you will find; knock, and it will be open to you. For everyone who asks receives, and he who seeks finds, and to him who knocks it will be opened."[35] We are exhorted to ask, sometimes to receive even more than what we request. "Now to him who is able to do far more abundantly beyond all that we ask or think, according to the power that works within us, to him be the glory in the church and in Christ Jesus to all generations forever and ever."[36]

She was born in Baltimore, the youngest of four siblings. On July 30, 1967, misjudging the depth of the waters while diving into Chesapeake Bay, she suffered a neck fracture and became a quadriplegic.

She begged God to heal her and was convinced that God would do so. "I followed every scriptural injunction: I was anointed with oil, I went to the elders, I confessed sin."[37] She went to faith healing services without much success, wondering: "Something is wrong with this picture. What

---

30. John 14:23, 1 Cor 3:16

31. Ps 23:4

32. Heb 13:5 NIV.

33. Deut 31:8 NIV.

34. "For the one who doubts is like the surf of the sea, driven and tossed by the wind. For that man ought not to expect that he will receive anything from the Lord" (Jas 1:6-7). "You ask and do not receive, because you ask with wrong motives, so that you may spend it on your pleasures" (Jas 4:3). "If I regard wickedness in my heart, the Lord will not hear" (Ps 66:18).

35. Matt 7:7-8

36. Eph 3:20-21

37. https://www.christianitytoday.com/women/2017/july/joni-eareckson-tada-fifty-years-wheelchair-walk-jesus.html

kind of Savior? What kind of rescuer, what kind of healer, what kind of deliverer would refuse the prayer of a paralytic?"[38]

Fifty years later, after a mastectomy for stage 3 breast cancer, chemotherapy, and chronic pain, she reminisced on her life and her long-ago desperate request for healing: "God is interested in a *deeper* healing. There really are more important things in life than walking. There are more important things in life than having the use of your hands. And that is having a heart that's free of the grip of sin and pride and self-centeredness."[39] "I believe I have been healed—just not in the way that others expect."[40]

At a "Joni and Friends" family retreat in Alabama, a volunteer

> *gestured at the crowd and asked, "Miss Joni, do you ever think how none of this would be happening were it not for your diving accident?" ... She's right ... how did I get here? It has everything to do with God and his grace—not just grace over the long haul, but grace in tiny moments, like breathing in and out, like steppingstones leading you from one experience to the next. The beauty of such grace is that it eclipses the suffering until one July morning, you look back and see five decades of God working in a mighty way.*[41]

The loving and benevolent God kept his promise, answered Joni's prayer, and gave her much more than what she had asked. Joni Eareckson Tada's quadriplegia is an integral part of her ministry and allows her to minister to many previously unreached people. "Now, every day when I wheel into the Joni and Friends International Disability Center, I try to squeeze every ounce of ministry effort from my quadriplegic body. This summer, Joni and Friends will hold 27 Family Retreats in the United States and 23 in less resourced nations, reaching thousands of special-needs families for Christ."[42] Is that not a "more abundant" answer to the prayer of a faithful and steadfast believer?

So, we can boldly come to God to present our requests, knowing that he will give us what we need (and even more) to carry out his design

---

38. https://www.gty.org/library/sermons-library/TM13-2

39. https://www.christianitytoday.com/women/2017/july/joni-eareckson-tada-fifty-years-wheelchair-walk-jesus.html

40. http://content.time.com/time/arts/article/0,8599,2016484,00.html

41. https://www.thegospelcoalition.org/article/reflections-on-50th-anniversary-of-my-diving-accident/

42. Ibid.

on earth.[43] With unceasing faithfulness, "the Spirit also helps our weakness; for we do not know how to pray as we should, but the Spirit himself intercedes for us with groanings too deep for words."[44] Furthermore, Christ "is at the right hand of God and is also interceding for us,"[45] that God may reward "those who earnestly seek him."[46] With the Holy Spirit's and Christ's intercessions on our behalf, we can "confidently say, 'The Lord is my helper, I will not be afraid. What will man do to me?'"[47]

**God's Pledge to His Children**

Christians are given a great pledge by God in this age of evil. "And we know that God causes all things to work together[48] for good to those who love God, to those who are called according to his purpose."[49] All things (even evil things like cancer and accidents) can work together for our good. No gratuitous evil (i.e., evil not necessary for a greater good,[50] evil without an accompanying greater good) can happen to faithful believers.[51] Dr. Grudem affirmed: "It should be our great confidence and a source of peace day by day to know that God causes all things to move us toward his ultimate goal for our lives, namely, that we might be like Christ and therefore bring glory to him."[52]

The youngest of three siblings, Beth was raised in a Christian family and accepted Christ at the age of five.

On October 13, 2005, Beth's father Tom was scheduled for surgery on his knee. At five a.m. that day, Beth decided to go surfing. "Have a

---

43. "Abba! Father! All things are possible for You; remove this cup from Me; yet not what I will, but what You will." (Mark 14:36). "Your will be done, on earth as it is in heaven." (Matt 6:10).

44. Rom 8:26

45. Rom 8:34 NIV.

46. Heb 11:6 NIV.

47. Heb 13:6

48. The Greek word is "sunergeo," meaning "work together." https://biblehub.com/greek/4903.htm "Sunergeo" is the root of the English "synergy." https://www.etymonline.com/word/synergy

49. Rom 8:28

50. or evil not necessary for "the prevention of an evil at least as bad." Nick Trakakis, "The Evidential Problem of Evil."

51. However, unfaithful believers can bring gratuitous calamities on themselves by disobeying God.

52. Wayne Grudem, *Systematic Theology*, 232.

good time, honey . . . Remember, my surgery's today. Keep me in your prayers.' 'Duh, Dad. You're always in my prayers. Gotta go!'"[53]

A little after seven a.m., Tom was at the hospital receiving a spinal anesthetic. "Just then the door to the operating room flew open. A doctor stuck his head in . . . 'We gotta have this OR right now! We've got a shark attack victim.'"[54] Tom was wheeled out of the OR to make space for his daughter whose left arm was bitten off by a shark. "'I was praying to God to rescue me and help me,' Bethany said. 'And then, I had this one pretty funny thought, I think. I was thinking, 'I wonder if I'm going to lose my sponsor.'"[55]

Bethany Hamilton survived the ordeal and went back to competitive surfing with much success. She later reminisced about her accident. "Because of where Jesus brought me, I have no regrets of the adversities God has allowed me to go through . . . As you look at me, you could think, 'Wow, have pity on her, she lost her arm to a shark.' But I look it [sic] as something beautiful. God has taken something awful and turned it into something incredibly amazing."[56] "I see that God is able to use my story to help others. Once a girl came up and told me that she had had cancer. When she learned my story, it made her realize that she didn't need to give up. I think that if I can help other people find hope in God, then that is worth losing my arm for."[57]

"Consider it all joy, my brethren, when you encounter various trials, knowing that the testing of your faith produces endurance. And let endurance have its perfect result, so that you may be perfect and complete, lacking in nothing."[58] Even amid difficulties, we know that we are not alone for Christ has said, "I am with you always, even to the end of the age."[59] God promises us his *eternal* love[60] and continued help in taking "something awful" (e.g., a shark attack, a jail sentence) and turning "it into something incredibly amazing."

---

53. https://www.guideposts.org/better-living/positive-living/surfer-bethany-hamiltons-strong-faith-after-shark-attack

54. Ibid.

55. http://abcnews.go.com/2020/story?id=124360&page=1

56. https://www.deseretnews.com/article/865603326/Surfer-Bethany-Hamilton-attributes-success-happiness-to-God.html

57. http://www.dove.org/soul-surfer-bethany-hamilton/

58. Jas 1:2-4

59. Matt 28:20

60. Ps 136:1, Jer 31:3

Furthermore, the Lord declares: "I will make up to you for the years that the swarming locust has eaten."[61] "Through repentance all which had been lost by sin, is restored . . . God, through Christ, restores the sinner, blots out sin, and does away with its eternal consequences."[62] Therefore, we can assert:

> *If a person returns, God promises to forgive, restore, and make all things work together for good for that person (1 John 1:9, Rom 8:28, Isa 55:7).*

In love, God pledges to help faithful believers and cause all things (good and evil) to work together for their good, *without* excusing, condoning, or whitewashing the evils.[63]

## God Provides a Way of Escape for His Children

In times of temptation, believers are provided with ways of escape so that they do not fall into sin. "No temptation has overtaken you, but such as is common to man, and God is faithful, who will not allow you to be tempted beyond what you are able, but with the temptation will provide the way of escape also, so that you will be able to endure it."[64] Queen Victoria's Royal Chaplain W. Teignmouth Shore affirmed: "We have in this verse, perhaps, the most practical and therefore the clearest exposition to be found of the doctrine of free-will in relation to God's overruling power. God makes an open road, but then man himself must *walk* in it. God controls circumstances, but man uses them. That is where *his* responsibility lies."[65] No believer must sin or cannot resist sin. If he does sin and fall, it is because he willingly chooses not to take the way of escape that God provides.

Jack "grew up very, very poor in Jumping Branch, West Virginia . . . 'We never had a car. We didn't have TV until later in life.'"[66] At the age of fourteen, Jack started a construction company that slowly grew

---

61. Joel 2:25
62. Edward Pusey, *The Minor Prophets*, 126.
63. "When we forgive evil, we do not excuse it." Dr. Lewis Smedes. https://www.news-journalonline.com/story/news/2014/02/22/if-god-does-not-forgive-per-revelation-why-should-we/30658029007/
64. 1 Cor 10:13
65. W. Teignmouth Shore, "The First Epistle to the Corinthians," 92.
66. http://abcnews.go.com/2020/powerball-winner-cursed/story?id=3012631

and eventually employed over 100 people. By 2002, he had 17 million dollars in assets. He claimed concerning his faith: "I'm (a) Christian, and a Christian is supposed to tithe 10% of what they [sic] get . . . I've been doing that my whole life."[67]

Jack did not play the lottery regularly, only buying tickets when the jackpot was over 100 million dollars. On Christmas Day 2002, his 100-dollar wager brought in 314.9 million. He was on top of the world, rich, famous, with a loving wife (Jewell whom he met when he was fourteen) and a doting granddaughter, Brandi.

Considering that he was worth 17 million dollars even before winning the lottery, should Jack give the windfall to charity?

> On Aug. 5, 2003, thieves stole $545,000 from his car in a West Virginia strip club parking lot while he was inside . . . On Jan. 25, 2004, robbers once again broke into his car, stealing an estimated $200,000 in cash that was later recovered. And a string of personal tragedies followed. On Sept. 17, 2004, his granddaughter's boyfriend was found dead from a drug overdose in Whittaker's home. Three months later, the granddaughter (Brandi) also died of a drug overdose. Her mother, Ginger Whittaker Bragg, died five years later, on July 5, 2009. Whittaker himself is alleged to be broke—a claim he made as early as January 2007 . . . He's also being sued by Caesars Atlantic City casino for bouncing $1.5 million worth of checks to cover gambling losses. "I wish I'd torn that ticket up," he sobbed to reporters at the time of his daughter's death.[68]

In 2005, three years after the big win, Whittaker's wife filed for divorce, ending nearly 42 years of marriage. This began a long, drawn-out fight for Whittaker's winnings.[69]

Jack Whittaker remarried and owned "two businesses that 'haven't been doing very good. I'm still working and I'm 68 years old.' Whittaker still dreams of winning the lotto again. Every week, he spends about $600 buying lottery tickets."[70] He died in 2020 at the age of 72.

No one is doomed to sin and ruin his/her life. The faithful and benevolent Lord takes pains to warn his followers of the dangers in this world (gambling, strip club . . .). In love, God provides them with many

---

67. http://articles.latimes.com/2002/dec/30/local/me-pastor30

68. http://newsfeed.time.com/2012/11/28/500-million-powerball-jackpot-the-tragic-stories-of-the-lotterys-unluckiest-winners/slide/andrew-jack-whittaker/

69. http://www.euro-millions.org/america/180/

70. http://money.cnn.com/2015/02/10/pf/lottery-winners-losers/index.html

ways of escape (not gambling at casinos, staying away from strip clubs . . .) so that they may not fall into sin. However, the decision to take the way of escape is theirs alone!

The bishop was an old man when the soldiers came to arrest him. The governor gave him two choices, "recant your Christian faith and live" or "persist in your belief and die." Considering the cleric's advanced age, the governor tried to persuade him to take the path of life. "Respect your age, swear by the divine power of Caesar, change your mind . . . I have wild animals. I'll throw you to them . . . I'll have you burned alive if you don't change your mind . . . Take the oath (to Caesar) and I'll let you go. Curse Christ." In times of temptation to recant our faith, we are free to take the way of escape or not.

Polycarp, bishop of the church in Smyrna, answered the governor: "Eighty-six years I have served him, and he never did me any wrong. How can I blaspheme my King who saved me?"[71] Polycarp was burned alive at the stake for that memorable declaration of faith and his choice of taking the way of escape[72] provided by his loving Lord. "I am the resurrection and the life; he who believes in Me will live even if he dies."[73] May we follow our forefathers' examples of undying faithfulness to our Lord who gave himself for us![74]

## God Forgives His Children's Sins

When believers sin, God promises that the transgressions, once confessed, will be forgiven. "If we confess our sins, He is faithful and righteous to forgive us our sins and to cleanse us from all unrighteousness."[75] Since we are cleansed from all unrighteousness after confession, we can resume our close fellowship with the holy God and continue to rely on his help and counsel. Furthermore, as we are forgiven by God for our sins, we must also forgive others for their trespasses against us.[76]

Born in 1958 in Turkey, Mehmet was a petty criminal and a gang member in his youth. He smuggled heroin between Turkey and Bulgaria

---

71. https://wau.org/resources/article/the_martyrdom_of_polycarp_1/
72. God's way of escape/path of life is often the opposite of the way of this world.
73. John 11:25
74. Gal 2:20
75. 1 John 1:9
76. Eph 4:32

14   PART ONE: ANSWERS FOR OUR PAIN AND SUFFERING IN THIS FALLEN REALM

and "became a member of the Grey Wolves, a Turkish neo-fascist nationalistic terrorist organization that may have relied on the financial backing of the Turkish mafia."[77] Mehmet later moved to Syria and received training in weaponry and terrorism.

In May 1981, he went to Rome to carry out a secret mission. Whether he acted independently or was a part of a larger conspiracy is still unknown. On May 13, he waited for Pope John Paul II to arrive at St. Peter's Square. When the Pope passed by, Mehmet opened fire, hitting the pontiff in his left hand, right arm, and lower intestines.

To cover Mehmet's escape, an accomplice was tasked with a diversionary explosion but did not fulfill the assignment. Consequently, Mehmet was caught and sentenced to life in prison. The Pope was severely injured but survived.

"Four days after the attempt on his life, the Pope made a public statement forgiving (Mehmet) Ağca and asking the world to pray for him."[78]

> In 1983, John Paul II visited his would-be assassin. They had a private conversation and emerged as friends. The Pope stayed in touch with Ağca's family during the latter's incarceration, and in 2000 requested that he be pardoned. The request was granted. Ağca was released and deported to Turkey, where he was imprisoned for the life sentence he had fled decades prior.[79]

Mehmet Ağca renounced the Muslim faith, converted to Christianity, and was released in 2010. In 2014, he returned to the Vatican and laid white roses on the Pope's tomb in St. Peter's Basilica.[80]

In a message to the Church, Pope John Paul II declared: "As Scripture bears witness, God is rich in mercy and full of forgiveness for those who come back to him . . . God's forgiveness becomes in our hearts an inexhaustible source of forgiveness in our relationships with one another, helping us to live together in true brotherhood."[81]

God is quick to forgive believers (and non-believers) who confess their sins and repent from their misdeeds. However, forgiveness does not

---

77. https://www.atlasobscura.com/articles/the-unsolved-case-of-the-attempted-assassination-of-pope-john-paul-ii

78. Ibid.

79. http://mashable.com/2015/09/30/pope-john-paul-ii-assassin/#5NGn_xLK9uq4

80. https://www.dailymail.co.uk/news/article-2888550/Man-tried-kill-Pope-John-Paul-II-puts-roses-tomb.html

81. https://w2.vatican.va/content/john-paul-ii/en/messages/peace/documents/hf_jp-ii_mes_08121996_xxx-world-day-for-peace.html

mean the removal of natural consequences of one's actions (e.g., diseases from drug abuse), nor does it guarantee a cancellation of earthly discipline (e.g., jail time for murders). God's love and compassion are always balanced by his justice, as they are all part of God's nature.

## God Matures His Children through Suffering

Why do believers appear to suffer the same as non-believers? Should we not expect that believers would receive a better deal from God, as far as sufferings are concerned?

Unfortunately, this is not the case. Christians encounter the same vicissitudes of life as non-Christians since God does not want his people to follow him for selfish motives (e.g., a hope for less suffering). "Truly, truly, I say to you, you seek Me, not because you saw signs, but because you ate the loaves and were filled. Do not work for the food which perishes, but for the food which endures to eternal life.'"[82] The outcome of the sufferings may be different ("God causes all things to work together for good" for believers) but the amount, kind, severity, or duration of the sufferings may be similar. Hence, non-believers are not bribed to adopt Christianity in exchange for some "guaranteed" promises of "health and wealth" upon conversion, followed by a blissful paradise in the life to come.

Also, Christians should expect to suffer more than their non-Christian brethren. "If you were of the world, the world would love its own, but because you are not of the world, but I chose you out of the world, because of this the world hates you."[83] Besides the common sufferings in this evil realm (e.g., cancer, thefts), Christians are faced with ostracisms for their belief in many parts of the world.

"As a young boy, the Australian [Graham] became a pen friend of one Santanu Satpathy of Baripada (India) with whom he shared his birthday."[84] In 1965, Graham visited India and decided to stay as a missionary. Working among the tribal poor, he started a home to care for the ostracized leprosy patients. He taught them to make mats out of rope, items they could sell to earn a living. While working with these diseased outcasts, Graham met his wife Gladys, a nurse, whom he

---

82. John 6:26-27
83. John 15:19
84. http://www.ibsresources.org/articles/staines.shtml

married in 1983. They had three children, a daughter, Esther, and two sons, Philip and Timothy.

Despite Graham's evangelistic efforts, and "contrary to general perceptions . . . the religious map of Orissa has not changed."[85] Nevertheless, some local groups claimed that he had lured many Hindus into Christianity. Tensions between the majority Hindus and the minority Christians steadily rose. "There were at least 60 attacks on churches in Orissa between 1986 and 1998, the highest number in any state."[86]

On January 22, 1999, Graham and his two boys aged seven and ten attended a Christian gathering in Manoharpur village. They were sleeping in their station wagon when a mob of fifty people armed with axes attacked and set their vehicle on fire. Graham, Philip, and Timothy Staines were burned alive. "Even in death they were inseparable. Charred beyond recognition and reduced to fragile frames of ashes, the three bodies lay clinging to each other in what must have been a vain attempt to protect each other and escape the mob."[87]

Ten years later, Gladys, Graham's widow, reminisced:

> I cannot express how I felt when I got the news of my husband and sons being burnt alive. I told my daughter Esther that though we had been left alone, we would forgive, and my daughter replied, 'Yes, we will'. . . . I feel sad that I do not get to see my sons growing up. Christ has been my companion, but at times I miss the support of my husband. God gives me great support, and the prayers of people has [sic] been a source of great consolation, and this is the solidarity I share with the widows of Kandhamal. It is Jesus who is the source of every consolation and support. God gives us the strength to be able to carry our cross and to live in His will. Our life and our work here on earth has [sic] to go on according to His holy will.[88]

Believers grow in Christlikeness through suffering as they are not spared from gruesome evils in this fallen realm.[89]

Besides the normal difficulties of life and the persecutions for being believers in a non-believing world, Christians can also expect God's

---

85. Ibid.

86. Ibid.

87. Ibid.

88. https://www.asianews.it/news-en/Widow-of-Graham-Staines:-Do-not-give-up-hope,-pray-for-India-14257.html

89. Jas 1:2-4

loving discipline when they disobey (e.g., Jonah). "For those whom the Lord loves, He disciplines."[90] God loves his sons and daughters too much to let them go astray and destroy themselves in the process. The Lord's discipline of his children is for their benefit, though it may be painful during the tribulation.

We need to recognize that suffering is necessary and that it will not last forever. "In this you greatly rejoice, even though now, for a little while, if necessary, you have been distressed by various trials, so that the proof of your faith, being more precious than gold which is perishable, even though tested by fire, may be found to result in praise and glory and honor at the revelation of Jesus Christ."[91] The benevolent God aims for the maturation of his children through suffering!

### Letter From the Father

My dear beloved child,

I know that you are hurting.[92] I empathize with you[93] and share your sufferings[94] as you share in mine.[95] My precious child, "Do not fear, for I am with you; do not anxiously look about you, for I am your God. I will strengthen you, surely, I will help you, surely, I will uphold you with my righteous right hand."[96] You are not alone in your pains and afflictions. "I am with you,"[97] we are all here with you[98] and we will help you through this difficult trial.[99] Trust me[100] and you will overcome for "you are from God, little children, and have overcome them; because greater is He who is in you than he who is in the world."[101]

90. Heb 12:6
91. 1 Pet 1:6-7
92. Ps 18:6
93. Heb 4:15
94. 1 Cor 12:26-27, Col 1:18, Isa 53:4
95. 2 Cor 1:5
96. Isa 41:10
97. Matt 28:20
98. John 14:23, 1 Cor 3:16
99. Is 41:13
100. Prov 3:5-6
101. 1 John 4:4

There are angels ministering to you.[102] There are prayers from the Church on your behalf.[103] Rest assured that your Lord and the Holy Spirit are actively interceding for you[104] in your sufferings. You are not left alone[105] in your fight against the powers of this world, for your "struggle is not against flesh and blood, but against the rulers, against the powers, against the world forces of this darkness, against the spiritual forces of wickedness in the heavenly places."[106] Though you do not see me,[107] I am here to help you.[108] Let me in to be with you[109] in your time of need.[110]

I understand that you are grieving.[111] I am aware of your sufferings.[112] I keep track of your tears in a bottle.[113] Talk to me, "come and pray to me and I will listen to you,"[114] for my ears are attentive to your prayers.[115] I listen to your cry, I am not deaf to your weeping.[116] Call to me from the ends of the earth when your heart is faint[117] and I will comfort you,[118] for I am near to the brokenhearted and save those who are crushed in spirit.[119] I heal them and bind up their wounds.[120] So, "come to Me, all who are weary and heavy-laden, and I will give you rest."[121]

As to your question, "Why am I suffering? Why me? Why us?" you know that you live in a broken world, enslaved to corruption,[122]

---

102. Heb 1:14
103. Jas 5:16
104. Rom 8:34, Rom 8:26
105. 2 Ki 6:17
106. Eph 6:12
107. John 1:18
108. Ps 46:1
109. Rev 3:20
110. Heb 4:16
111. Ps 22:24, Ps 31:10, 22
112. Exo 3:7
113. Ps 56:8
114. Jer 29:12
115. 1 Pet 3:12
116. Ps 39:12
117. Ps 61:2
118. 2 Cor 1:3-4
119. Ps 34:18
120. Ps 147:3
121. Matt 11:28
122. Rom 8:21

suffering,[123] and death[124] under the dominion of the evil one.[125] All those who follow me will have to suffer in this hostile realm[126] bent on rebellion.[127] You are aliens and strangers[128] here, subject to the twisted wills of evil people[129] and the ravages of a fallen creation.[130] Nevertheless, do not fear them, for they cannot harm your souls,[131] nor can they separate you from my love. "Neither death, nor life, nor angels, nor principalities, nor things present, nor things to come, nor powers, nor height, nor depth, nor any other created thing, will be able to separate us from the love of God,"[132] for "I have loved you with an everlasting love."[133]

My child, I know that your pains are often unbearable, and your sufferings are excruciating like your Lord's crucifixion[134] and your forefathers' martyrdoms. "They were stoned, they were sawn in two, they were tempted, they were put to death with the sword."[135] Follow their examples, "do not be surprised at the fiery ordeal among you, which comes upon you for your testing, as though some strange thing were happening to you; but to the degree that you share the sufferings of Christ, keep on rejoicing."[136] My dear child, this painful trial is for your good,[137] if you take it in the right spirit of trust and acceptance.[138] Or do you want to leave me because of it?[139] "Blessed is the one who perseveres under trial because, having stood the test, that person will receive the crown of life that the Lord has promised to those who love him."[140] Your inheri-

123. John 16:33
124. Heb 2:14, Heb 9:27
125. 1 John 5:19
126. Acts 14:22
127. Ps 14:1
128. 1 Pet 2:11
129. 2 Tim 3:12
130. Rom 8:20-22
131. Matt 10:28
132. Rom 8:38-39
133. Jer 31:3
134. Luke 23:33
135. Heb 11:37
136. 1 Pet 4:12-13
137. Rom 8:28
138. Matt 6:10
139. John 6:66-67
140. Jas 1:12

tance is waiting for you in heaven,[141] "therefore, do not throw away your confidence, which has a great reward."[142]

As to how long these pains and sufferings are going to last, your tribulations will not be long. "For a little while, if necessary, you have been distressed by various trials."[143] Even a lifetime is not long when you consider a future eternal life[144] without suffering or death.[145] Yes, it does *feel* long when you are in pain and mired in helplessness. But my child, you are not helpless. I am here to help you.[146] I will not fail you or forsake you.[147] Trust[148] and hope in me. "Those who hope in the Lord will renew their strength. They will soar on wings like eagles; they will run and not grow weary, they will walk and not be faint."[149] Keep praying, do not give up.[150] Draw near to me and I will draw near to you.[151] "Weeping may last for the night, but a shout of joy comes in the morning."[152]

You also ask, "What can I do amid my pain and suffering?" If you are in bedrest with no physical strength, you can pray for yourself and for others.[153] If you have time and strength, go out to use your gifts "to serve one another, as good stewards of God's varied grace."[154] Whether in prayer or in service, you are my "workmanship, created in Christ Jesus for good works, which God prepared beforehand so that we should walk in them."[155] You know that "each man's work will become evident; for the day will show it because it is to be revealed with fire, and the fire itself will test the quality of each man's work. If any man's work which he has built on it remains, he will receive a reward."[156] My child, it is yet day but "night

141. 1 Pet 1:4
142. Heb 10:35
143. 1 Pet 1:6.
144. John 3:16
145. Rev 21:4
146. Isa 41:10
147. Deut 31:6
148. Ps 28:7
149. Is 40:31
150. Luke 18:1
151. Jas 4:8.
152. Ps 30:5
153. Jas 5:16
154. 1 Pet 4:10
155. Eph 2:10
156. 1 Cor 3:13-14

is coming, when no one can work."[157] So, "work out your salvation with fear and trembling; for it is God who is at work in you, both to will and to work for His good pleasure."[158] "The Lord will give strength to His people; the Lord will bless His people with peace."[159]

When you finish your work in this wretched realm, "I will come again and will take you to myself, that where I am you may be also."[160] You will be my "good and faithful servant! You have been faithful with a few things; I will put you in charge of many things. Come and share your master's happiness!"[161] I "will wipe away every tear from their eyes, and there will be no more death or mourning or crying or pain, for the former things have passed away."[162] "Death is swallowed up in victory,"[163] for "I am the resurrection and the life; he who believes in Me will live even if he dies."[164] "I am the Alpha and the Omega who is and who was and who is to come, the Almighty."[165] "I am the Lord, the God of all flesh."[166] "What I have said, that I will bring about; what I have planned, that I will do."[167]

Keep fighting the good fight, finish the course, keep the faith for in the future there is laid up the crown of righteousness, which the Lord, the righteous Judge, will award "to all who have loved His appearing!"[168] "'For I know the plans I have for you,' declares the Lord, 'plans to prosper you and not to harm you, plans to give you hope and a future.'"[169]

My beloved child, "I have told you these things, so that in me you may have peace. In this world you will have trouble. But take heart! I have overcome the world."[170] Remember, "the Lord is my light and my salvation; whom shall I fear? The Lord is the defense of my life; whom

---

157. John 9:4
158. Phil 2:12
159. Ps 29:11
160. John 14:3
161. Matt 25:21
162. Rev 21:4
163. 1 Cor 15:54
164. John 11:25
165. Rev 1:8
166. Jer 32:27
167. Isa 46:11
168. 2 Tim 4:7-8
169. Jer 29:11, Rom 8:28
170. John 16:33

shall I dread?"[171] So, "be strong and courageous! Do not tremble or be dismayed, for the Lord your God is with you wherever you go!"[172] Rest in the "shadow of the Almighty"[173] for "I am with you always, even to the end of the age."[174]

Your loving[175] abba[176] Father[177]

## Summary

In answer to our first question, "What does God do for his suffering children in this evil world?" we affirm that God gives his faithful followers much needed comfort and many precious promises in this fallen realm.

Through the Holy Spirit,[178] God dwells intimately with his children and provides them with everything they need to flourish and mature.[179] In love, he always answers their prayers and often gives them more than what they ask.[180] He pledges that everything will turn out for their good and benefit.[181] In his mercy, he provides them with advice and ways of escape[182] so that they will not fall into sin. He forgives their trespasses,[183] encourages them to forgive others[184] and live at peace with everyone.[185] Thus, believers shall proclaim: "The Lord is my strength and my shield; my heart trusts in Him, and I am helped; therefore, my heart exults, and with my song I shall thank Him."[186]

171. Ps 27:1
172. Josh 1:8
173. Ps 91:1
174. Matt 28:20
175. 1 John 4:8
176. Rom 8:15
177. Matt 6:9
178. 1 Cor 12:11
179. Eph 4:11-13
180. Eph 3:20
181. Rom 8:28
182. 1 Cor 10:13
183. 1 John 1:9
184. Col 3:13
185. Rom 12:18
186. Ps 28:7

Yet, we sometimes wonder: "Does our loving Lord *cause* people to commit evil to fulfill his ultimate plans (e.g., Joseph's brothers sold him into slavery, resulting in many lives saved from starvation, Gen 50:20)?" Does our Father *need* the evils in this fallen realm (e.g., COVID-19) to bring about good? How does God use the evils in this world for his greater purposes (our second question)?

# 2

# How Does God Use the Evils on This Earth for His Greater Purposes?

*So great and boundless is God's wisdom that he knows right well how to use evil instruments to do good.*

—John Calvin[1]

In 1972, he came to the US as a 17-year-old foreign student and became a refugee when South Vietnam fell to the communists in 1975. His father died in the debacle, leaving him an orphan without a country as he had already lost his mom to suicide (over his dad's adultery). That Christmas in Texas, in the deserted dormitory, he desperately cried out to Buddha for help, but his forlorn pleas went unanswered!

Looking out of a window near the top of the high-rise dorm, he contemplated the deep snow and wondered if that would muffle the sound of his fall. In that fateful moment of truth, he finally understood what his mother had done long ago, for a time comes when life is a living hell, mere existence is an excruciating torture, and the future apocalypse is now!

By "happenstance," a friend saw him alone in the dorm and invited him home for Christmas. Hearing about this Jesus who offers love and protection to his people, the kid decided to change religion as Buddha had done nothing to alleviate his sufferings.

Subsequently, he earned a master's degree and applied to various PhD programs. Wonder of wonders, he was accepted by MIT with a full

---

1. John Calvin, *Institutes of the Christian Religion*, 1.17.5

scholarship! However, of what use would be a PhD in microbiology in Vietnam where research was non-existent? Would he dare hope that his new God would secure him a spot in medical school? But does the God of the Bible really exist?

Summoning his training, he decided to apply science to religion: set up an experiment that would unequivocally rule out a pure coincidence, leaving the only alternative as the work of God. The disadvantage of such an attempt was that, if God does not exist (or if he refuses to participate), the consequence might be painful for the experimenter. Nevertheless, the kid realized that he could not live in a perpetual uncertainty for he was expending considerable time and effort at church, all of which would be wasted if God only exists as a figment of one's imagination!

So, he told God what he was about to do. He would turn down MIT (and his full ride scholarship) and apply to medical school the following year. The crux of the experiment was that his chance of acceptance was zero without God's intervention! He was a foreigner without any legal paper. He had no money and no family that could use connections to push his application. He would have to compete with native English speakers for the few scarce slots in medical school.

Without much hope, he applied to Harvard, Yale, Johns Hopkins . . . and all the schools in Texas. Soon after, the rejection letters came quickly from the out-of-state private schools. Furthermore, the state schools advised him that they reserved their slots for Texas residents only. This turn of events forced him to "help God out" by endeavoring to get the all-important "green card" (permanent residency) within three months to meet the admission deadlines.

His first step was to contact the overworked US immigration office. After a long wait in a sweltering room packed with worried applicants, he was finally accorded five minutes with the immigration officer. The bored bureaucrat barely listened and summarily dismissed the kid with the comment that "nothing could be done." In truth, the orphan boy did not expect much from this meeting. He just wanted to say to God (if he exists) that he did his part and that he *expected God to do his.*

In the same spirit, he asked the office of his congressman for help. However, upon hearing that he could not vote, the secretary said she would "relay the message."

A friend suggested joining the Texas National Guard to get American citizenship. Of course, the kid was thrilled and immediately called the recruiting officer. Unfortunately, they were soon at cross purposes since the recruiter needed the kid's "green card" to sign him up and he wanted to enlist to get a "green card." This perfect storm of problems was way over anyone's capacity to solve. Of course, the kid already knew that his chance of success was nil, but *it still hurt to be right!*

Unbeknownst to him, a bill was working its way through congress, passed by the House on September 27, 1977, approved by the Senate on October 10, and signed by President Jimmy Carter on October 28. It was called "an act to authorize the creation of a record of admission for permanent residence in the cases of certain refugees from Vietnam, Laos, or Cambodia." The exceptional part of this act was its retroactive nature (uncommon for laws), for "the attorney general shall establish a record of the alien's admission for permanent residence as of March 31, 1975, or the date of the alien's arrival in the United States, whichever date is later."[2]

In December 1977 (it took a while for the kid to learn about the law through the congressman's secretary who "happened" to keep his contact information rather than file it in the wastebasket), he found out that, legally, he had been a permanent resident of the United States since March 31, 1975. With no time to spare, he quickly informed the Texas medical schools of his status of "Texas resident" and was subsequently accepted by several institutions!

Coincidence or the hand of the omnipotent God? If all these events were due to mere chance, I am extremely glad that they always fell my way! I believe the experiment demonstrates beyond a reasonable doubt that God exists and is the omnipotent and omnibenevolent (all-good) Creator of the universe, capable of influencing both the House and the Senate, as well as the President for the sake of *one* of his followers.

Yet, God often endeavors to exercise "divine hiddenness" (to avoid undue coercion[3] on non-believers)[4] when he intervenes on behalf of those who acknowledge his existence and ask for his help. Such interventions are cloaked under the mantle of "coincidences," giving people

---

2. https://www.govinfo.gov/content/pkg/STATUTE-91/pdf/STATUTE-91-Pg1223.pdf

3. "In the life of the people of God, as it has made its pilgrim way through the vicissitudes of human history, there has at times appeared a way of acting that was hardly in accord with the spirit of the Gospel or even opposed to it. Nevertheless, the doctrine of the Church that no one is to be coerced into faith has always stood firm." Pope Paul VI, *Dignitatis Humanae*, 12.

4. "If God is directly present to me in all his power, glory, and love, my intellect compels my assent to the proposition that he exists; there is no room for free assent." William Rowe, "Paradox and Promise," 115.

complete freedom to *interpret the facts as they see fit*. The French theologian François Fénelon observed:

> *God works in a mysterious way in grace as well as in nature, concealing his operations under an imperceptible succession of events, and thus keeps us always in the darkness of faith. He not only accomplishes his designs gradually, but by means that seem the most simple, and the most competent to the end, in order that human wisdom may attribute the success to the means, and thus his own working be less manifest; otherwise every act of God would seem to be a miracle, and the state of faith, wherein it is the will of God that we should live, would come to an end.*[5]

Hence, non-theists have total freedom to believe in God or to uphold their independence. They can claim that events in this world (e.g., passage of a retroactive law for refugees) are just random coincidences of an aimless universe.[6]

In contrast, Christians believe that their heavenly Father cares for them and can work secretly in inscrutable ways[7] to bring good out of evil.[8]

If goods ensue from the evils, it is not because the evils are necessary for the (greater) goods.[9] Rather, God works to *redeem* the evils,[10] turning human misdeeds into good for the sake of his followers (e.g., Joseph),[11] without condoning the wrongs. Evil is not a functional good,

---

5. François Fénelon, *Spiritual Progress (Avis Chrétiens)*, 70.

6. "So inclined is the heart of man to blindness and delusion, that it is prone to even atheism itself." Jonathan Edwards, *The Works of President Edwards*, 28.

7. Rom 11:33

8. Rom 8:28

9. "A central contention in most theodicies, including for example Leibniz (1710) in his 'best of all possible worlds' theodicy, is that evil does play an important, even necessary role in advancing greater good." Michael Levine, "The Positive Function of Evil?" 149. "The 'greater good' principle . . . states that each and every instance of evil is a means to a greater good . . . that *even God could not obtain without there being that evil*." William Hasker, "The Open Theist Response," 155. In contrast, the Tough Love Theodicy affirms that evils are *not* necessary for greater goods.

10. The "redemption" concept is different from the "defeat" concept advocated by Adams and Chisholm (i.e., evil can be part of an overall good, the overall beauty of God's canvas). Marilyn McCord Adams, *Horrendous Evils*, 205. Roderick Chisholm, "The Defeat of Good and Evil," 53–68. In the Tough Love Theodicy, evil only detracts from the beauty of God's canvas.

11. Gen 50:20

"somehow rational and fitting in God's economy, thus distorting its true theological significance as needless and harmful."[12]

While God does not *need*[13] evils (adultery, suicide, war, refugees, COVID-19 . . .), as they are not necessary[14] to accomplish his purpose, he can use them to bring his creatures into a deeper relationship with him. Heavens and earth were created "very good," without resorting to any evil,[15] as "no evil dwells with" God.[16] The Lord abhors evil,[17] and cherishes righteousness.[18]

Yet, we may wonder, "Does God *cause* people to commit evil to fulfill his ultimate plans and bring the greater good?"

## Does God Cause People to Commit Evil to Bring the "Greater Good"?

Arguing against the claim that God causes evil (e.g., drunk driving) to bring about a "Greater Good," Dr. Bishop contended: "If theists are reduced . . . to pleading that God causes evil that good may come, the logical Argument from Evil[19] has been rebutted only at the cost of compromising distinctively theist morality."[20] In other words, the justification that "God causes evil to bring a greater good," is contrary to Christian ethics and morality.

In God's economy, the (good) end never justifies the (evil) means.[21] The apostle Paul declared: "And why not say (as we are slanderously reported and as some claim that we say), 'Let us do evil that good may

---

12. Michael Peterson, "Introduction," 9.

13. Acts 17:24-25. "God does not need us or the rest of creation for anything." Wayne Grudem, *Systematic Theology*, 190.

14. Of course, trials that are necessary for the believer's growth are not evil as they are meant for good (1 Pet 1:6).

15. Gen 1:31

16. Ps 5:4

17. Prov 15:9

18. Ps 45:7

19. "In a world in which there is evil, it is logically impossible . . . that God exists." Nick Trakakis, "The Evidential Problem of Evil." Theists often argue that a good God and evil (logically) coexist since evil is necessary for the greater good.

20. John Bishop, "On Identifying the Problem of Evil," 50.

21. Rom 6:1-2

come'? Their condemnation is just."[22] Evil is never caused, condoned, or endorsed by God to bring a greater good. Trespasses and sins are strictly humans' handiwork, a course of action they choose against God's holy standards.

God does not induce humans to perpetrate wrongdoing to fulfill God's plans and purposes. God's work must be done God's way,[23] and that does not include making people commit evil.

For example, God did not entice Joseph's brothers to sell Joseph into slavery as this practice was forbidden in Exodus 21:16, "He who kidnaps a man, whether he sells him or he is found in his possession, shall surely be put to death." God did not cause the brothers to sin to bring about the "greater good" of Genesis 50:20,[24] for God "does not tempt anyone" to transgress his commandments.[25] He could have accomplished his plan and purpose without causing anyone to do evil. Joseph and his brothers could have been instructed by God to go to Egypt to trade. While they were there, God could have caused Pharaoh to seek Joseph's help in interpreting the dreams. Joseph could have been elevated to power and saved many lives without the need for wrongdoings by his brothers. The kidnapping and selling into slavery were totally unnecessary and expressly forbidden. In his compassion and justice, God *redeemed* the evil for the sake of his faithful follower Joseph *without* condoning the brothers' sin.

Furthermore, God does not want his people to sin just to show that God can forgive and bring good out of evil. He clearly commands his followers: "Abstain from every form of evil."[26]

> *Evangelical Christians have developed a rather confusing habit when it comes to sharing testimonies. We have a tendency to prefer telling dramatic stories about dark, reckless pasts turned around at a sudden moment to grab the attention of the crowd and stir their emotions rather than describe the ebb and flow of real-life faith stories . . . This practice can seemingly justify delinquent*

---

22. Rom 3:8

23. In contradiction to God's way, King David transported the ark on a cart. Despite David's good intentions, this unsanctioned method resulted in Uzzah's death (1 Chr 13:10).

24. "You meant evil against me, but God meant it for good in order to bring about this present result, to preserve many people alive" (Gen 50:20).

25. Jas 1:13

26. 1 Thess 5:22

*behavior that occurs after the conversion experience and eliminates the Christian sin factor.*[27]

Rather than emphasizing faithfulness and lifelong loyalty to the Lord, we magnify our sinful lapses to dramatize God's abounding grace and forgiveness. However, "are we to continue in sin so that grace may increase? May it never be! How shall we who died to sin still live in it?"[28] Sin and evil, whether by believers or non-believers, are never caused or condoned by God.

## God Can Use Evil as a Tool in This World

While God never approves of sins and wrongdoings, he sometimes uses the existing evils in this world as tools to bring about good (i.e., God redeems the evils without excusing them). "And we know that God causes all things to work together for good to those who love God."[29] The "all things" can include good and evil things. Augustine asserted: "For the Omnipotent God, whom even the heathen acknowledge as the Supreme Power over all, would not allow any evil in his works, unless in his omnipotence and goodness, as the Supreme Good, he is able to bring forth good out of evil."[30] Aquinas concurred: "This is part of the infinite goodness of God, that He should allow evil to exist, and out of it produce good."[31]

For non-theists who do not acknowledge God's existence, the evils they experience may fulfill the purpose of bringing them back to their Creator, a good outcome that the Lord desires for all his creatures.[32]

Jeff was the son of a hypochondriac mother who suffered from depression, even to the point of attempting suicide. The family moved frequently as his father struggled with college and work. In his childhood, Jeff developed a bizarre obsession with dead animals, preserving their bodies in jars of formaldehyde that he hid in a nearby hut.

---

27. Becca Vandekemp. "What We Get Wrong about 'Giving Our Testimony.'" https://relevantmagazine.com/god/what-we-get-wrong-about-giving-our-testimony

28. Rom 6:1-2

29. Rom 8:28

30. Augustine, *Enchiridion on Faith, Hope, and Love*, 3.11

31. Aquinas, *Summa Theologica*, 1.2.3

32. 1 Tim 2:4, 2 Pet 3:9

When Jeff turned eighteen in 1978, his parents divorced, and he was left alone in the family home. That was when he killed his first victim, a 19-year-old hitchhiker, and dissolved the body in acid. His crime spree continued until he was caught in 1991 and convicted of fifteen counts of first-degree murders, necrophilia, cannibalism, and preservation of body parts. Found sane, he was sentenced to life in prison without parole.

At the maximum-security prison, Jeff was at first kept in solitary confinement, as the warden was concerned for his safety. However, he was later transferred to the general jail population.

The police detective who took his confession gave him a Bible, and Jeff became a born-again Christian in prison. Concerning his baptism, he proclaimed: "I know it washes away my sins. If anyone needed to have his sins washed away, it is me!"[33]

When Jeff was viciously assaulted in prison, his mother was greatly distressed and worried. He replied: "It doesn't matter, Mom. I don't care if something happens to me."[34] To his minister, he wondered: "Am I sinning against God by living? Should I have been dead, and should I find some way of making myself dead because by living I am somehow going against God?"[35]

Four months later, Jeffrey Dahmer was murdered by another inmate. He was cremated and his ashes were given to his parents.

As with the thief on the cross who repented,[36] the evils done by Dahmer were redeemed by Jesus' substitutionary death, fulfilling God's purpose of reconciliation with his wayward creature.[37] The Lord can use the heartbreaking evils in this fallen world as tools for good, to save his lost and wandering sheep.[38] No matter how sinful we are, our sins can be washed away by the blood of Christ. "Though your sins are as scarlet, they will be as white as snow; though they are red like crimson, they will be like wool."[39] If Jeffrey Dahmer can be forgiven, who among us cannot be forgiven?

33. https://medium.com/belover/jeffrey-dahmer-was-an-evangelical-christian-390c6394d864

34. https://people.com/archive/cover-story-the-final-victim-vol-42-no-24/

35. https://curbarchive.journalism.wisc.edu/2009/12/01/are-you-there-god-its-me-jeffrey/index.html

36. Luke 23:42-43

37. 2 Cor 5:19

38. Luke 15:3-7

39. Isa 1:18

For believers, the evils they experienced can be used as tools by God to make them more Christlike,[40] as in the case of Job.

However, citing "the vast array of horrendous evils," pains, and sufferings in the world, Dr. Trakakis argued for God's non-existence.

> *It borders on the absurd to believe that good states of affairs are so related to the vast array of horrendous evils that an infinitely powerful and infinitely loving being is unable to prevent any of these evils without (a) forfeiting a greater good 1, (b) forfeiting a greater good 2 if he enables the sufferer to understand good 1, (c) forfeiting a greater good 3 if he is consciously present to those who suffer for a good 1 they cannot understand, and (d) forfeiting a greater good 4 if he enables the sufferers to understand good 3. Such a view strains our credibility to such an extent that we would require strong evidence for the existence of God before we could reasonably accept it.*[41]

In other words, according to Dr. Trakakis, it is "absurd" to believe in "an infinitely powerful and infinitely loving being" who cannot prevent evils without forfeiting some greater goods (e.g., greater goods 1, 2, 3, and 4). Also, one cannot "reasonably accept" the existence of a god who is not "consciously present" to explain the reasons for a sufferer's calamity.

In response, using the story of Job as an example, we understand that God can use evils (Job's losses of his children, property, and health)[42] as tools to bring greater good 1 (Job's *edification*, Job 42:5).

Also, sufferers can forfeit a greater good 2 if they are enabled to understand greater good 1 (Job did not understand why he needed to suffer evils for his edification. Yet, he freely chose to remain loyal and *earned God's praise*, greater good 2, Job 2:3).

Sufferers can forfeit a greater good 3 if God is consciously present to them (God did not appear to Job until the very end so Job could *freely strengthen his faith*, greater good 3, Job 19:25–26).

Sufferers can forfeit a greater good 4 if they are enabled to understand greater good 3 (Job did not understand why he needed to strengthen his faith. He eventually *learned the lesson*, greater good 4, Job 42:5–6, that his faith in God was not as strong as he thought since he demanded answers from his Creator, Job 23:4–5).

---

40. Rom 8:29
41. Nick Trakakis, *The God Beyond Belief*, 196-97.
42. Job's calamities were caused by Satan (Job 1:12, Job 2:6-7).

Thus, it is reasonable to believe that God can use the evils in this world as tools to edify and strengthen his beloved children (with greater goods 1, 2, 3, and 4).

Yet, whether the trial achieves its good intent or not depends on the sufferer's response[43] (e.g., Job was free to follow his wife's advice to "curse God and die!").[44] If they (believers and non-believers) decide to repent and turn back to God, the evils they encounter will not be gratuitous and all things (good and evil) will work together for good to those who love God (e.g., a renewed relationship with their Creator). However, if they insist on their ill-considered ways, the evils they endure may well be gratuitous and their excruciating pains may be utterly "wasted." The choice is theirs, for God does not coerce anyone into a love relationship with him.

While Job's trials were for his growth and maturity, why did God let evils (deaths) fall on Job's ten children?[45] What possible good *to them*[46] could come from that? A possible good might be, "The righteous perish, and no one takes it to heart; the devout are taken away, and no one understands that the righteous are taken away to be spared from evil."[47] Job's children were spared from seeing their livelihood destroyed, experiencing their abject poverty, mourning their ruined social standing, watching the bitter conflict between their parents, witnessing the pains and sufferings of their father, and enduring the public shame of God's (supposed) wrath and punishment.[48]

By not clearly revealing the reasons for sufferings (e.g., the deaths of Job's children), God may be shielding his people from further griefs and sorrows as he did with Corrie ten Boom in the Scheveningen prison.

---

43. God intended the trial for Job's edification. However, Job was free to "curse God and die." "Nothing hinders one act from having two effects, only one of which is intended, while the other is beside the intention." Thomas Aquinas, *Summa Theologica*, 2.2.64. "According to the principle of double effect, sometimes it is permissible to cause a harm as an unintended and merely foreseen side effect (or "double effect") of bringing about a good result." Alison McIntyre, "Doctrine of Double Effect."

44. Job 2:9

45. Job 1:19

46. A "successful theodicy requires attention to how evils affect the particular people who suffer them." Dustin Crummett, "Sufferer-Centered Requirements on Theodicy," 71. Marilyn McCord Adams, *Horrendous Evils and the Goodness of God*. Eleonore Stump, *Wandering in Darkness*.

47. Isa 57:1 NIV.

48. Job 16:11-12

> *The hardest thing for him (the Nazi interrogator) seemed to be that Christians should suffer. "How can you believe in God now?" he'd ask. "What kind of a God would have let that old man (Corrie's eighty-four-year-old father) die here in Scheveningen?" I got up from the chair and held my hands out to the squat little stove. I did not understand either why Father had died in such a place. I did not understand a great deal. And suddenly I was thinking of Father's own answer to hard questions: "Some knowledge is too heavy . . . you cannot bear it . . . your Father will carry it until you are able."*[49]

Even amidst our tribulations and unanswered questions, we can trust our heavenly father to care for his children. "If you then, being evil, know how to give good gifts to your children, how much more will your Father who is in heaven give what is good to those who ask Him!"[50] No true evil can hurt faithful believers, as they are protected by the power of God. "The righteous person may have many troubles, but the Lord delivers him from them all."[51] God can use the existing evils in this world (without condoning them) as tools for his purpose, the growth and maturity of his followers![52]

## God Restrains Evil in This Realm

In his mercy, the omnipotent Lord also restrains sins and evil in the world lest people destroy themselves and their environment. "For the mystery of lawlessness is already at work; only he (the Holy Spirit) who now restrains will do so until he is taken out of the way."[53]

Humans, left to their own expedient, have devised increasingly destructive ways to exterminate people. The spear was invented ca. 400,000 BC. The atlatl (a spear-thrower) was contrived ca. 40,000 BC. Arrowheads turned up ca. 20,000 BC. Bronze daggers were forged ca. 5000 BC. The Chinese trebuchet (a device with a swinging arm to throw projectiles) and the Greek ballista (a heavy bolt-thrower) were both conceived ca. 500 BC. Gunpowder was formulated in China ca. 800 AD. Hand cannons and firearms were developed by Egypt ca. 1200 AD. The

---

49. Corrie Ten Boom, *The Hiding Place*, 159.
50. Matt 7:11
51. Ps 34:19 NIV.
52. Jas 1:2-4
53. 2 Thess 2:7

first submarine used in battle was designed in 1775 by the American David Bushnell. Samuel Colt patented the revolver in 1836. In 1914, the British brought tanks into battle.[54] Zyklon B (cyclone B), a cyanide-based pesticide was synthesized in Germany in 1920 and used to murder millions of Holocaust victims. In 1945, nuclear bombs were dropped on Hiroshima and Nagasaki resulting in 199,000 casualties. There are now enough nuclear weapons to destroy the entire world many times over. "FAS (Federation of American Scientists) currently estimates that the U.S. has 1,800 nuclear weapons at the ready, compared to Russia's 1,950 . . . It is an enormous overkill and vastly in excess of what we need for national security and international commitments."[55] Will God's call for people to live at peace with one another be heeded? "Blessed are the peacemakers, for they shall be called sons of God."[56]

Humans have despoiled their soil with toxic wastes; they have poisoned their water with sewage and chemicals; they have released enormous amounts of pollutants into the air. "There is a 'catastrophic' gap between what needs to be done on climate change and what governments and companies are actually doing, the UN has warned."[57] Pope "Francis described man's destruction of the environment as a sin and accused mankind of turning the planet into a 'polluted wasteland full of debris, desolation and filth.'"[58] Will humans respond in time to the dire warnings they have been given?

Thankfully, much evil has been restrained by the Holy Spirit and believers who function as "salt and light" in their society (Mother Teresa, Billy Graham . . .). US faith-based non-government organizations (NGO) "are known to contribute substantial resources—financial, technical, human, and in-kind—to poverty alleviation, health care provision, and relief of suffering through international development activities and humanitarian

54. https://www.newscientist.com/article/dn17423-timeline-weapons-technology/

55. Chelsea Bailey, "How Many Nuclear Weapons Exist?" https://www.nbcnews.com/news/us-news/how-many-nuclear-weapons-exist-united-nations-calls-total-elimination-n804721

56. Matt 5:9

57. Andrew Griffin, "UN Releases Warning About 'Catastrophic' Lack of Action on Climate Change." http://www.independent.co.uk/environment/un-climate-change-global-warming-paris-agreement-warning-heat-rising-melting-a8028961.html

58. Josephine McKenna, "Pope Francis Says Destroying the Environment Is a Sin." https://www.theguardian.com/world/2016/sep/01/pope-francis-calls-on-christians-to-embrace-green-agenda

assistance."⁵⁹ In 2015, the top 20 US faith-based NGO reported almost 6 billion dollars raised for international aid, with the money going toward helping children (e.g., Compassion International), relieving famines and poverty (e.g., Food for the Hungry), health care (e.g., Catholic Medical Mission Board), and various international projects (e.g., Samaritan's Purse). Religious people are more generous to churches and often give substantial gifts to charitable causes. Thus, God endeavors to restrain evil through his followers, by putting their time, talents, and resources into effective use to relieve the world's sufferings.

The virtuous God also intervened through his people to curtail some vicious evils on this earth (e.g., the Holocaust). The German theologian Niemöller courageously challenged Hitler in "a heated exchange: 'Neither you nor any power on earth can remove the responsibility placed on us by God to care for our people.'"⁶⁰ Niemöller organized a movement to oppose Nazi interference in German protestant churches, resulting in his imprisonment in a concentration camp from 1938 to 1945.

Besides Protestants, God also used Catholics in the struggle against the evils of genocides.

> *In a great sea of suffering, as the Pope undoubtedly saw it, there was indeed the possibility that things could be worse. This was the possibility that Pius XII reflected upon in his famous address to the College of Cardinals in 1943: "Every word directed by us in this regard to the competent authorities [to ease suffering], and every public allusion, should be seriously considered and weighed in the very interest of those who suffer."*⁶¹

Golda Meir, foreign minister of Israel (and later prime minister) eulogized Pope Pius XII in 1958: "When fearful martyrdom came to our people in the decade of Nazi terror, the voice of the Pope was raised for the victims. The life of our times was enriched by a voice speaking out on the great moral truths above the tumult of daily conflict."⁶²

In 1944, during the Nazi occupation of Greece, the Germans ordered the mayor of Zakynthos to hand over the Jews living on the island. The Greek Orthodox Bishop Chrysostomos gave the Nazis a list with

---

59. The Center for Faith & The Common Good. http://www.faithforcommongood.org/uploads/4/8/4/9/48493789/updated_sources_of_revenue_and_international_expenditures_of_us_faith-based_ngos_fy2011-15.pdf

60. John Conway, "The Political Theology of Martin Niemöller," 527.

61. Michael Marrus, "Pius XII and the Holocaust," 49.

62. David Dalin, *The Myth of Hitler's Pope*, 102.

only two names, his and the mayor's. The clergyman bravely announced: "Here are your Jews. If you choose to deport the Jews of Zakynthos, you must also take me, and I will share their fate."[63] The Germans relented, and the 275 Jews on the island survived the Holocaust.

Evils in this world could be much worse without God's restraining activity through the Holy Spirit and the Church (Catholic, Protestant, and Greek Orthodox branches).

Besides restraining evil, God also bestows blessings on all his creatures. "He causes his sun to rise on the evil and the good and sends rain on the righteous and the unrighteous."[64] "He himself is kind to ungrateful and evil men."[65] God loves all people and "desires all men to be saved and to come to the knowledge of the truth."[66] With compassion and great concern, God keeps evil in check, while he endeavors to call his wayward people back into a close relationship with him.

## Summary

In answer to our second question, while God does not need evil or cause people to commit sins for the "greater good," he does use the existing evils in this world (murders, wars with countless refugees . . .) as tools to bring people to himself, without condoning the perpetrated wrongs. Also, he cloaks his actions in "divine hiddenness" to give humans the freedom to acknowledge him or not. In love, he restrains evil to keep his creatures from destroying themselves and their environment in a quest to satisfy their ravenous desires.

In his wisdom, God lets non-theists choose their own paths and live with the results. Meanwhile, the offer of salvation and reconciliation is available to anyone who would be willing to turn back and acknowledge God's existence. He "is patient toward you, not wishing for any to perish but for all to come to repentance."[67]

Concerning believers, God promises to cause "all things to work together for good to those who love God" (e.g., Job's edification). Nothing

63. United States Holocaust Memorial Museum. "Zakynthos." https://www.ushmm.org/information/exhibitions/online-exhibitions/special-focus/holocaust-in-greece/zakynthos
64. Matt 5:45
65. Luke 6:35
66. 1 Tim 2:4
67. 2 Pet 3:9

truly harmful can happen to loyal followers (e.g., Corrie ten Boom). "He will not be afraid of the terror by night, or of the arrow that flies by day; of the pestilence that stalks in darkness, or of the destruction that lays waste at noon. A thousand may fall at your side, and ten thousand at your right hand, but it shall not approach you."[68] Faithful believers are shielded by God from experiencing gratuitous evils for "greater is he who is in you than he who is in the world."[69]

In this fallen realm, we are prone to temptations and sin, "for all have sinned and fall short of the glory of God."[70] Would the creation of humans who cannot sin (i.e., impeccable) not be better for humanity who would not have to endure the Fall and suffer in this world of evil? Why doesn't God create people with free will who never commit evil, like sinless humans in heaven (our third question)?

68. Ps 91:4-7
69. 1 John 4:4
70. Rom 3:23

# 3

# Why Doesn't God Create Humans with Free Will Who Never Commit Evil?

*There was open to him the obviously better possibility of making beings who would act freely but always go right. Clearly, his failure to avail himself of this possibility is inconsistent with his being both omnipotent and wholly good.*

—J. L. MACKIE[1]

SUN WAS BORN IN 1920 in North Korea to poor farmers with eight children. When he was ten years old, his family converted from Confucianism to Christianity and joined the Presbyterian Church. On Easter Sunday 1936, he claimed that Jesus appeared to him in person and that he recognized Christ from a vision he had when he was three years old.

> He spoke with Jesus in Korean. "We carried conversation with mind-to-mind, heart-to-heart" . . . during that conversation, Jesus made a startling revelation. "I did not come to die. I came to find my perfect bride, and we would create this thing called the true family, and we would encourage all of humanity to graft onto that true family through this thing called holy blessing." Since Jesus' plan was thwarted by the Crucifixion, he told the 16-year-old to complete his mission. Moon began that in earnest in 1954, when he started his church. James Beverley, a professor at Tyndale Seminary in Toronto and an expert on Moon, says

---

1. J. L. Mackie, "Evil and Omnipotence," 209.

> Moon believed he was the Messiah, that he was sinless and that he was the true father of mankind.[2]

Can God create a sinless human being (e.g., Rev. Sun Myung Moon)? The French philosopher René Descartes asserted: "There is no doubt that God could have created me such as that I should never be deceived."[3] Dr. Hick opined: "It appears to me that a perfectly good being, although formally free to sin, would in fact never do so."[4] An impeccable Adam would not have fallen, and we, his descendants, would still be in Eden instead of this world full of evil, pain, and suffering.[5]

Using the concepts of God's impeccability and simplicity, we will address the question "Why doesn't God create an impeccable human being?"

## God's Impeccability

The South African theologian Vincent Brümmer affirmed: "In the Christian tradition, God's perfect goodness has generally been held to entail that he has the attribute not only of *impeccantia* (freedom from sin), but also of *impeccabilitas* (inability to sin)."[6] Impeccability requires more than just an inability to commit evil, it also emphasizes the attribute of moral virtue.[7] The Westminster Confession of Faith declares: "God, who, being most holy and righteous, neither is nor can be the author or approver

---

2. https://www.npr.org/2012/09/02/159032325/rev-moon-a-savior-to-some-lived-a-big-dream

3. René Descartes, *Meditations on First Philosophy*, IV.5

4. John Hick, "Soul-Making Theodicy," 268.

5. "If for any world X that requires or permits evil, there is some world Y that models pure goodness in God such that God has no good reason to create X rather than Y, then God has no good reason to permit evil in the world." J. L. Schellenberg, "A New Logical Problem of Evil," 42. Adam chose to sin and had to depart from world Y (Eden with "pure goodness") and go to world X (our world with evil).

6. Vincent Brümmer, *Brümmer on Meaning and the Christian Faith*, 271.

7. "Under this conception of impeccability, the agent not only will be unable to perform acts of sin or evil, the agent's character will be so virtuous that he or she will be unable to form the desire, motivation, and intention to perform acts of sin or evil." Luke Henderson, "Heaven," 180.

of sin."[8] The morally virtuous God does not sin, cannot sin,[9] is not evil[10] (contrary to Buddha's thought),[11] cannot be tempted by evil, and does not tempt anyone to sin.[12]

## God's Simplicity

Besides impeccability, there are many more attributes of God (omnipotence, love, justice . . .). The attributes of God are not a collection of characteristics added together, nor are they additions to his being. Aquinas asserted: "It is clear that God is nowise composite but is altogether simple."[13] Augustine explained: "What is meant by 'simple' is that its (God's) being is identical with its attributes."[14] Anselm concurred: "That he is simple in such a way that all the things that can be said of his essence are one and the same thing in him."[15] "God's whole being includes all of his attributes . . . *every attribute of God also qualifies every other attribute.*"[16]

As an analogy, a diamond has four characteristics, the four Cs: carat, cut, color, and clarity. The cut affects the carat (weight) of the final product. The clarity of the gem (the presence of inclusions) may change its color. The color of the raw specimen may influence the way it is cut. Likewise, the attributes of God are not divisible and separate. They are all one and the same with God. "From the simplicity of God, it follows that God and his attributes are one."[17]

God is omnipotence/omniscience/love/justice/impeccability . . . The attributes of God are like the facets of a precious stone. Each attribute/

---

8. *Westminster Confession of Faith*, Chapter V, section IV. http://www.reformed.org/documents/wcf_with_proofs/index.html?body=/documents/wcf_with_proofs/ch_V.html

9. Matt 5:48, Hab 1:13

10. 1 John 1:5

11. "If the pleasure and pain that beings feel are caused by the creative act of a Supreme God, then the Niganṭhas (monks following Jainism, a religion from India) surely must have been created by an evil Supreme God, since they now feel such painful, racking, piercing feelings." Buddha, *The Middle Length Discourses of the Buddha*, 832–33.

12. Jas 1:13

13. Thomas Aquinas, *Summa Theologica*, 1.3.7.

14. Augustine, *Concerning the City of God*, XI. 10

15. Anselm, *Basic Writings*, 24.

16. Wayne Grudem, *Systematic Theology*, 212.

17. Louis Berkhof, *Systematic Theology*, 44.

facet describes the same gem, although with a slightly *different emphasis from a human point of view* (e.g., God's just love versus God's loving justice).

A diamond's attribute cannot be transmitted piecemeal to a different material. For example, a diamond's color cannot be given to iron. The four Cs of a diamond, if transmitted, must be given as a whole. Likewise, God's attributes (or better, "attribute," singular), if given, must be conveyed in toto. If so, can God create a human being with the attribute of impeccability?

## The Creation of Humans

"God created man in his own image, in the image of God he created him; male and female he created them."[18] After the creation of Adam, "God saw all that he had made, and it was very good."[19] Hence, Adam was made "very good." He was created "in the image of God," but he was obviously not the same as God. "You have made him a little lower than God."[20] God has free will[21] and is impeccable.[22] Adam also has *some* free will, but he is peccable in nature (able to sin).[23] Adam does not have more free will than God because he can sin, and God cannot.[24] He can sin because he is

18. Gen 1:27

19. Gen 1:31

20. Ps 8:5. The Hebrew text of Psalm 8:5 has "Elohim" translated as "God" in NASB and "angels" in NIV. Calvin commented: "The Septuagint renders . . . Elohim, by angels . . . but as the other translation (lower than God) seems more natural, and as it is almost universally adopted by the Jewish interpreters, I have preferred following it." John Calvin, *Commentary on Psalms*, Ps 8:5. "The Hebrew text is probably best construed as 'you made him [man] lower than God', while the Septuagint conveys the meaning 'you made him [man] lower than the angels.'" Radu Gheorghita, *The Role of the Septuagint in Hebrews*, 46. Also see Albert Pietersma, "Text–Production and Text–Reception: Psalm 8 in Greek," 487–501.

21. Ps 115:3

22. 1 John 1:5, Jas 1:13

23. "Man's original capacities included both the power not to sin and the power to sin (posse non peccare et posse peccare). In Adam's original sin, man lost the posse non peccare (the power not to sin) and retained the posse peccare (the power to sin)—which he continues to exercise. In the fulfillment of grace, man will have the posse peccare taken away and receive the highest of all, the power not to be able to sin, non posse peccare." Augustine, *Enchiridion*, Chapter 28, note 229.

24. God "seems constitutionally incapable of choosing (or even wanting) to do what is wrong. According to Plantinga's description of morally significant free will, it does not seem that God would be significantly free." James Beebe, "Logical Problem of Evil."

lower than God and does not share God's attribute of impeccability. His free will is much more restricted than God's as he can only control a few of his circumstances. For example, even the greatest control freaks among us cannot prevent accidents or diseases!

Why didn't God create Adam with the attribute of impeccability in Eden? Would it not be better that Adam had free will but was unable to sin?

Unfortunately, impeccability cannot be given apart from the other attributes of God (due to God's simplicity). For example, impeccability cannot be transmitted separately from omnipotence. For Adam to have impeccability/omnipotence, God would have to create God. Can there be more than one God? "Is there any God besides Me, or is there any other Rock? I know of none."[25] "I am the Lord, and there is no other; besides me there is no God."[26] God did not create another God as there can only be one God.

Furthermore, a "created" god is not God since God is not "created" but always existed.[27] All things are created by the uncreated God,[28] and exist through him.[29] Irenaeus affirmed: "Created things must be inferior to Him who created them, from the very fact of their later origin; for it was not possible for things recently created to have been uncreated . . . For this very reason do they come short of the perfect."[30] Thus, a created human is an inferior being and not God.

The answer to our question, "Why doesn't God create humans with free will who never commit evil (i.e., impeccable beings)?" is that the uncreated God cannot create uncreated Gods.[31]

Adam was created "lower than God," with limited free will and the ability to sin.[32] According to Aquinas, humans lived in a "state of

---

In the Tough Love Theodicy, even though God has complete free will (Eph 1:11), God's impeccability prevents him from doing evil.

25. Isa 44:8
26. Isa 45:5
27. Ps 90:2
28. John 1:1-3
29. Col 1:16
30. Irenaeus, *Against Heresies*, IV.38.
31. Lee Thai and Jerry Pillay, "Can God Create Humans with Free Will Who Never Commit Evil?" 1-7.
32. Humans' inability to sin in heaven (impeccability) will be discussed later in the book.

innocence,"[33] in a close relationship with God, and without the knowledge of good and evil. He was tasked by God to rule over the animals and care for his environment (Eden).

## The Fall of Adam and the Origin of Evil on Earth

How did Adam who was created sinless, innocent, and "very good," fall into evil? God did not put a kernel of evil, a malicious desire in his heart that would later blossom into unbelief. Nor did the "very good" somehow spontaneously deteriorate and corrupt itself into evil.[34]

As explained in my previous book, *Boundaries of Freedom*,[35] the sovereign Lord gave Adam two choices:[36] the path of obedience/life (where he can continue to live in a close fellowship with God without the knowledge of evil) and the path of disobedience/death, a separation from the living Creator. In love, God forbade Adam (and Eve) from selecting the disobedient option.[37] Dr. van Inwagen observed: "They were not children and were at least as intelligent as we; they fully understood the warning and the wisdom and authority of its Source."[38] Adam and Eve were free to choose their path, without God's interference. The omnipresent God was intentionally "absent," as he appears to be absent now in this fallen world.

After a season of obedience in the garden of Eden, Adam chose to disobey God and lost his state of innocence.[39] He committed evil and

---

33. "Many authorities of the Saints declare that man possessed grace in the state of innocence." Thomas Aquinas, *Summa Theologica*. 1.95.1

34. "The first sin does not originate from one good thing corrupting another but from a good thing corrupting itself." Phillip Cary, "A Classic View," 22. "The answer to the question why God made corruptible things cannot be that it belongs essentially to creatures to be corruptible, unless one gives up the view that in the new creation, we will be unable to sin and to get sick and die." William Lane Craig, "The Molinist Response," 144.

35. Lee Thai, *Boundaries of Freedom*. This book addresses the problem of God's sovereignty and human free will. The problem of evil is intertwined with the problem of God's sovereignty and human free will.

36. "If we had thought that we had a serious choice, but did not, we would have been deceived, and God cannot deceive us." Atle Søvik, *The Problem of Evil and the Power of God*, 28.

37. Gen 3:11

38. Peter van Inwagen, "The Magnitude, Duration, and Distribution of Evil: A Theodicy," 373.

39. "The basic criticism, then, is that a flawless creation would never go wrong and that if the creation does in fact go wrong, the ultimate responsibility for this must be

was no longer holy and sinless. His "iniquities have made a separation between" him and his holy God,[40] for "without holiness, no one will see the Lord."[41] The holy God and the unholy Adam could *no longer* live together in close communion. Adam had to depart and live far away from his Creator (Paradise lost).

The path/world chosen by Adam was not the "best of all possible worlds."[42] It was the forbidden way, the "world of death," the path of evil that condemned (sinful, unholy) Adam and all his descendants to untold miseries. Adam gratified his desire for the knowledge of good and evil and, consequently, his descendants fully experienced the heartbreaks of horrendous moral (e.g., genocides) and natural calamities (e.g., earthquakes). "For we know that the whole creation groans and suffers the pains of childbirth together until now."[43]

The obedient path would have been a better choice as Adam could continue to fellowship with God in the total absence of evil. Regrettably, Adam forfeited this option when he disobeyed God's command.[44]

## Summary

In answer to our third question, "Why doesn't God create humans with free will who never commit evil?" contrary to J. L. Mackie's and Reverend Moon's claims, the uncreated God cannot create uncreated Gods. Creatures are made lower than God, peccable, and fallible.

The origin of moral and natural evils in this world stems from Adam's poor choice of disobedience. As he willfully trespassed God's command, he had to shoulder full responsibility for his action. Since he wished to know evil, he and his descendants experienced evil in full measure in this fallen realm.

Humans are now separated from God and alienated from him. Despite his repeated appeals to reconsider, they steadfastly disavow his existence and sovereignty over them. Insisting on their independence,

---

with its creator." John Hick, *Philosophy of Religion*, 43. In the Tough Love Theodicy, God is not to blame for Adam's disobedient choice, made against God's command and warning.

40. Isa 59:2
41. Heb 12:14
42. Gottfried Leibniz, *Leibniz Selections*, 345-55.
43. Rom 8:22
44. Gen 3:17

they leave God no other choice but to let them go, like he did with the Prodigal Son.[45] Romans 1:28 states, "just as they did not see fit to acknowledge God any longer, God gave them over to a depraved mind, to do those things which are not proper," untold horrendous and heartbreaking evils. Where do these unwelcome calamities come from (the fourth question of our project)?

---

45. Luke 15:11-23

# 4

# Where Do the Evils in Our Lives Come From?

*We are each our own devil, and we make this world our hell.*

—Oscar Wilde[1]

Believers, as well as non-believers, greatly suffer from various evils in this fallen realm. Let us first define what we mean by evil (moral, natural)[2] and suffering.

## Evil

"Evil is not an easy term to define in a precise and comprehensive manner."[3] Some people even claimed that evil does not exist.[4] The Scottish Enlightenment philosopher David Hume depicted some instances of evil: "Were a stranger to drop, on a sudden, into this world, I would show him, as a specimen of its ills, a hospital full of diseases, a prison

---

1. Oscar Wilde, *The Duchess of Padua*, Act 5.
2. We will not address social evil or systemic evil. Ted Poston, "Social Evil." "The entire biological system on which nature is based is fundamentally evil. Hence, I call it the 'problem of systemic evil.'" Yujin Nagasawa, "The Problem of Evil for Atheists," 154.
3. Meister and Dew, eds. *God and the Problem of Evil*, 2.
4. "There is, at the bottom, no design, no purpose, no evil and no good." Richard Dawkins, *River Out of Eden*, 133. "There is no evil, there's no bad; there's no good. These are human ideas." Frederick Lenz. https://www.azquotes.com/author/44029-Frederick_Lenz/tag/creation

crowded with malefactors and debtors, a field of battle strewed with carcasses, a fleet foundering in the ocean, a nation languishing under tyranny, famine or pestilence."[5]

Combining the definitions of various leading scholars, evil can be construed as follows:

Evil is a privation of the good, a lesser good, a deviation from moral law, a hindrance from possessing anything that is good, a wrong choice, and an action that fails to meet a standard of goodness. Evil is the occurrence of anything less than good and involves serious harm that causes fatal or lasting physical and non-physical injury.

## Moral Evil

Moral evils are evils resulting from the actions or inactions of a person or persons. Moral evils include genocides, child abuses, robberies . . . They may not be actual deeds (murders) as an intent to commit evil (soliciting a murder-for-hire) is still considered a crime. Evils can be intentional (assault with a baseball bat) or unintentional (foul ball injuries). They can be caused by one's own action (car accident while texting) or someone else's action (killed by a drunk driver). They can be individual (theft) or corporate (insider trading). They can be categorized by quantity (number of homicides) or severity (injury levels). They can be deemed gratuitous (no redeeming greater good) or non-gratuitous (with a greater good).

Dr. Wykstra recounted: "Philosophers, I once heard Nicholas Wolsterstorff say, should tell more stories."[6] Here is one from Uganda, Africa. Under the military rule of General Idi Amin, 300,000 to 500,000 people were murdered for ethnic, political, or financial reasons. Amin's soldiers casually grabbed and killed innocent people in broad daylight. Witnesses dared not intervene for fear of losing their own lives. Pastor Kefa Sempangi recounted his dreadful experience:

> *The soldiers were kicking him from every side, and I could hear their heavy boots crunching against his flesh. They laughed and cursed as the man groaned, rolling from side to side. He was barely conscious . . . The soldiers were only machines. They were nothing to me and I was nothing to them . . . In that moment I learned a new truth. I learned that just as there is a boundary*

---

5. David Hume, *The Philosophical Works of David Hume*, 76.
6. Stephen Wykstra, "A Skeptical Theist View," 99.

> *beyond which human beings cannot comprehend the glory of God, so there is a boundary beyond which they cannot comprehend the evil in the world. There is a boundary beyond which everything is a senseless chasm. It is here in the nightmare of utter chaos that human feeling dies. It is here, where death and terror seem to have full dominion, that even the deepest of human sorrows becomes but a distant grief.*[7]

Sadly, moral evils are not the only curses we encounter in this wretched world! Nature also seems to conspire against us, unleashing devastating earthquakes and tsunamis.

## Natural Evil

"Natural evil is evil that results from the operation of natural processes, in which case no human being can be held morally accountable for the resultant evil."[8] Examples of natural evils include hurricanes, earthquakes, droughts, diseases (e.g., COVID-19). However, hurricanes that appear in the middle of the ocean with no sentient beings around to be harmed cannot be considered natural evils. Earthquakes in the middle of uninhabited Antarctica are not natural evils. "These events are not in themselves evil but take on the label of being evil when they cause human or animal suffering."[9]

Natural evils can be further subdivided into natural evils connected to acts of moral evil ("attached" natural evils) and those not linked to moral evil ("unattached" natural evils).[10] Deaths from a not-up-to-code building's collapse in an earthquake are "attached" natural evils as they are "attached" to acts of moral evil (e.g., greed in skimping on construction costs). Deaths from arson-caused forest fires are "attached" natural evils as they are the results of callous criminal actions. Deaths from lightning-caused fires are "unattached" natural evils.

Andre, a survivor of Hurricane Katrina, detailed his experience of horrific natural evils:

> *Nothing to do, no food, no water, no blankets, but I figured somebody would come directly. They wouldn't just leave us there, no*

---

7. F. Kefa Sempangi, *A Distant Grief*, 112-14.
8. Nick Trakakis, "The Evidential Problem of Evil."
9. Jeremy Evans, *The Problem of Evil*, 4.
10. John Feinberg, *The Many Faces of Evil*, 181.

> sir. But they did, they left us. Then they up and forgot us, and that's when things started to get bad. Really bad . . . Some kid, maybe eight years old, climbed up on the overpass railing, and as soon as he got to the top, he just slips and falls right over. Down maybe 50ft and into the water. Everybody rush [sic] to that side and look [sic] for him, but he don't come up. And nobody goes down to try and get him . . . So, we just saw that baby die and nobody did a thing . . . Not a thing.[11]

Do we have a responsibility to help one another in a natural disaster? Or is "survival of the fittest" the rule of the game? These many evils (natural and moral) bring us unwanted and unwelcome pain and suffering on this earth.

## Suffering

Suffering is broadly defined as "(physical, mental, or emotional) pain that is caused by injury, illness, loss . . ."[12] "The distinction between evil and suffering is an important one, for these terms are not coextensive."[13] Evil may happen without any suffering (daydreaming about robbing banks) and suffering may occur without any evil (a successful vaccination). Suffering can be the result of moral (e.g., murders), or natural (e.g., earthquakes) evils.

Dr. Ngor, an obstetrician hiding his training and identity under the genocidal rule of the Khmer Rouge, related the sufferings of his starving wife as she tried to give birth without food or medicine.

> She was wet from perspiration and from clenching. Even when she didn't have labor pains, she was crying. The unthinkable was happening. Seng Orn (the midwife) pulled me aside for a conference. 'Caesarean?' she whispered. "Cannot!" I hissed. "The chhlop (Khmer Rouge spy) is outside! Do you want to die too? We will all die!" . . . We ran to the Khmer Rouge headquarters in Phum Phnom. To the center of enemy operations. And the cadre laughed at me. I was barefoot, in torn clothes, and they could not comprehend why I was so upset . . . They could not understand why I insisted my wife has a Caesarean section. They did not

---

11. Jim Gabour, "A Katrina Survivor's Tale.'" https://www.theguardian.com/us-news/2015/aug/27/katrina-survivors-tale-they-up-and-forgot-us

12. https://www.britannica.com/dictionary/suffering

13. Jeremy Evans, *The Problem of Evil*, 4.

*know what it was. By the time I came back to the house, it was midmorning . . . "I need food. I need medicine. Sweet, save my life. Please save my life. I'm too tired. I just need a spoonful of rice." Before she died, she asked me to cradle her. I swung her onto my lap, held her in my arms. She asked me to let her kiss me. I kissed her, and she kissed me. She looked up at me with her great round eyes, and they were full of sorrow. She didn't want to leave. "Take care of yourself, sweet."*[14]

Why is there so much evil, pain, and suffering in this world? Where do all those evils come from?

## Evil Coming from One's Own Action

Moral evil from one's own action.

We can bring evil on ourselves by choosing a path that is forbidden by God. Johnny was only fourteen when he joined the Ku Klux Klan at the behest of David Duke, the Grand Wizard. Johnny eventually moved up the ranks and became the Imperial Wizard of the KKK (the Klan's top position). In that role, he debated with the African American pastor Wade Watts.

At the radio station, Johnny

> *withdrew his hand after accidentally shaking the hand of Watts, recalling the Klan rule that "physical touch of a non-white is pollution." Instead of being insulted, the Reverend laughed and consoled him saying "he need not worry as his black wouldn't come off." The debate was filled with slurs and insults heaped upon Wade . . . And through it all, Wade smiled and said, "Jesus loves you . . . God bless you . . . You can't do enough to me to make me hate you. I'm gonna love you and I will pray for you whether you like it or not."*[15]

In response, Johnny sent death threats to Pastor Watts, and burned down his McAlester church. He "felt like gloating, so he called Wade, using a disguised voice. Watts greeted him cordially, saying, 'Well, hello . . . A man like you takes the time to call me. Let me do something for you.'

---

14. Haing Ngor, *Survival in the Killing Fields*, 355-57.
15. http://www.godyears.net/2017/08/the-redemption-of-ku-klux-klan-leader.html

He begins to pray, 'Dear Lord, please, forgive Johnny for being so stupid.' Then he invited all of them to dinner at Pete's Place in Krebs."[16]

The FBI got involved and "Johnny decided his only shot of staying out of prison was to step down as Imperial Wizard. But when he did, the Klan turned on him, fearing that he was an FBI informant . . . 'Now, they all hated me. I became a person without any friends.'"[17]

Johnny chose his path and had to live with the bitter consequences. He was threatened with imprisonment; he feared death from his ex-partners. He could not find a job due to the earlier association with the KKK, was totally broke and without a friend in the world (his father committed suicide with a gun and his mother disowned him). As he chose to preach the gospel of hate toward others, he now faced the same intolerance toward him. "For in the way you judge, you will be judged; and by your standard of measure, it will be measured to you."[18]

Sadly, we can bring much evil on ourselves by disregarding God's admonition to do what is right. We can make a royal mess of our lives, wake up one morning, and wonder how we end up in this bottomless and inescapable pit!

> *I thought of my daddy, and I thought that daddy had the right idea. I sat down and was looking at the gun and there was a Bible sitting there. I thought that there is no possible way that the good Lord can forgive somebody like me, because I had been so full of hate. I had all the violence and lived such a bad life, but I looked at that Bible and it fell open to Luke 15, the story of the prodigal son . . . I finally got on my knees and said, "God, my life is screwed up. God, I'm in a mess. I need your help."*[19]

Was it too late for God to forgive and take back his prodigal son Johnny? What could God do at this late stage? How could all the disasters be reversed?

> *The next morning, he claims, his phone rang. It was a man he knew who ran a car dealership asking if Clary would be interested in coming to work for him . . . "By the time I left that day I had made $700 in commission." Keeping a promise to God to go to church, Clary said he picked Tulsa's Victory Christian Center out of the newspaper and went there. He said he almost turned*

---

16. http://thislandpress.com/2013/08/29/watts-and-clary/
17. http://www1.cbn.com/700club/johnny-lee-clary-christ-and-ku-klux-klan
18. Matt 7:2
19. http://www1.cbn.com/700club/johnny-lee-clary-christ-and-ku-klux-klan

> *around when he saw its integrated congregation. "You don't say one prayer after being hateful and prejudiced all your life and then get up and say, 'I love black people,' and call up Michael Jackson and sing 'We are the World with him,'" Clary said, "I still had all the prejudice. The same way I was taught to hate, I had to learn to love other people."*[20]

Two years later, Johnny returned to McAlester, "but found no one ready to accept him . . . So, Johnny turned to the only person in his surroundings capable of helping him—Reverend Wade Watts. The Reverend welcomed his old nemesis with open arms and so it came to be that Johnny Lee Clary gave his first sermon in the very same church (now rebuilt) that he had burned down years ago, a lone white man now standing in front of a crowd of annoyed black men and women,"[21] with half of the church boycotting the service.

On November 28, 2009, Johnny Lee Clary was ordained a minister in the six-million-member Church of God in Christ, the first Caucasian elder in the predominantly African American denomination.

> *Not only has He (God) given me a good wife to stand by my side, but He's given me good friends. He's given me a good life here on earth. He's given me hope, gave me the gift of love. Taught me what love's all about. Isn't that what God is? God is love. I'm not that mixed up kid looking for a family anymore. I've got a family. I've got a relationship with my Lord and Savior Jesus Christ.*[22]

In love, God does not wish "for any to perish but for all to come to repentance."[23] It is never too late to recognize one's mistake and helplessness and turn to God who can bring good out of evil. "Behold, I am the Lord, the God of all flesh, is anything too difficult for Me?"[24]

The evils Johnny committed and the sufferings he endured were redeemed at the cross, resulting in peace and reconciliation between former adversaries. All things may yet work together for good if we are willing to take God's escape path.[25]

---

20. http://www.joplinglobe.com/johnny-lee-clary-and-his-road-to-damascus/article_d11edc01-b32a-553a-8468-a0c941c63c11.html

21. http://www.godyears.net/2017/08/the-redemption-of-ku-klux-klan-leader.html

22. Ibid.

23. 2 Pet 3:9

24. Jer 32:27

25. 1 Cor 10:13

However, these self-caused moral evils (whether by believers or non-believers), if not followed by repentance, may not lead to any greater good and may cause great harm to the wrongdoers (e.g., King Saul).[26]

## Natural evil from one's own action.

Natural evils can come into the lives of people because of their unwise and ill-considered actions or inactions.

What is the world's biggest killer? It is not war, genocides, famines, epidemics, or accidents. It is what we call "lifestyle diseases," illnesses resulting from the abuse of alcohol, tobacco, drugs, junk foods, and the lack of exercise. "Lifestyle diseases are responsible for 63 per cent of global deaths based on WHO's (World Health Organization's) estimates for 2008."[27] "By 2030, the proportion of total global deaths due to chronic diseases is expected to increase to 70 per cent."[28]

In the United States, "chronic diseases and conditions... are among the most common, costly, and preventable of all health problems. As of 2012, about half of all adults—117 million people—had one or more chronic health conditions... Seven of the top 10 causes of death in 2014 were chronic diseases."[29]

Natural evils are often brought on by our own actions as we ignore ominous biological warnings and dire scientific predictions concerning our inappropriate relationship with our environment (e.g., cancers from air and water pollutions, lifestyle chronic diseases).

Besides the natural evils of rampant diseases in this fallen world, what can we say about the natural calamities of earthquakes or hurricanes?

The 2010 Haiti earthquake caused 160,000 deaths. The Lithuanian philosopher Dranseika commented on the glaring discrepancy between the death tolls of comparable earthquakes in Haiti and New Zealand.

> One widely discussed example was a comparison of the Haiti and New Zealand earthquakes of 2010. These two events share significant similarities in terms of the power of the earthquake and their

---

26. 1 Sam 31

27. Alison Caldwell, "'Lifestyle' diseases the world's biggest killer." http://www.abc.net.au/news/2011-04-28/lifestyle-diseases-the-worlds-biggest-killer/2695712

28. Fatma Al-Maskari, "Lifestyle Diseases." https://unchronicle.un.org/article/lifestyle-diseases-economic-burden-health-services

29. http://medbox.iiab.me/modules/en-cdc/www.cdc.gov/chronicdisease/overview/index.htm

> epicentres being in the vicinity of major population centres but had very different outcomes in terms of deaths: at least 100,000 people died in Haiti, and nobody died in New Zealand. At least part of the explanation for this difference is attributed to different levels of disaster preparedness and resilience.[30]

Humans should use their God-given common sense to mitigate natural evils (e.g., earthquake preparedness). They should learn from their previous experiences with the environment and avoid obviously dangerous situations (e.g., sea travel in hurricane season).

The apostle Paul and other prisoners were taken to Rome to face Caesar's judgment. After stops in Sidon, Cyprus, and Myra, the centurion Julius found an Alexandrian ship heading for Italy. They "sailed slowly for a good many days and with difficulty" arrived at Fair Havens in Crete.[31]

> Fair Havens would have been the westernmost harbor Paul's ship could reach while staying under the lee of Crete. Beyond the cape (Matala) west of Fair Havens, the shore turns north dramatically, exposing the ship to the winds they were trying to avoid. The fact that the harbor was 'unsuitable to winter in' was confirmed in 1853 by an explorer named Captain T. A. B. Spratt, who observed that winter winds from the east and southeast blow right into the harbor. But the decision to make a run for Phoenix was not wise. Vegetius (4th century AD) records that sailing in the Mediterranean after September 15th was dangerous, and after November 11th was impossible.[32]

"Since even the fast (i.e., the Day of Atonement on October 5, AD 59)[33] was already over,"[34] Paul urged his fellow travelers to desist from their perilous plan to sail to the Cretan harbor of Phoenix, a forty-mile journey on open sea around Cape Matala, exposing the ship to violent winds (i.e., the Euraquilo) sweeping down from the 8056 feet high Mount Ida. "But the centurion was more persuaded by the pilot and the captain of the ship, than what was being said by Paul."[35] So, "they weighed anchor

---

30. Vilius Dranseika, "Moral Responsibility for Natural Disasters," 73-79.
31. Acts 27
32. https://www.bibleplaces.com/fair-havens/
33. *Expositor's Greek Testament.* https://biblehub.com/commentaries/acts/27-9.htm
34. Acts 27:9
35. Acts 27:11

and began sailing along Crete, close inshore,"[36] past Cape Matala and the protection of the lee of Crete.

The result was to be expected. They were caught by the Euraquilo, driven westward into the open sea toward the island of Malta (more than 500 miles), lost their cargo, their ship, and only saved their lives by the grace of God.

We (believers and non-believers) can bring disastrous moral and natural evils on ourselves by our poor decisions made against God's commands and God-given common sense. Besides self-inflicted calamities, we may suffer horrendous evils at the hands of others.

### Evil Coming from Other People's Action

Moral evil from other people's action.

People's misdeeds may bring much moral evil into our lives. We can be maimed by a drunk driver. We can be targets for criminals.[37] Non-theists who do not believe in God's existence can rely only on themselves to ward off the dangers inherent in a precarious life on earth.

In contrast, Christians are able to rest on God's promises of help and protection. "God is our refuge and strength, a very present help in trouble."[38] "The Lord is faithful, and He will strengthen and protect you from the evil one."[39]

Michael was born in Brooklyn and adopted as an infant. Dropping out of college, he asked to join the "family's business." "But first, there was an important matter to clear up . . . 'If you had to kill somebody, do you think you could do it?' Michael thought for a moment. 'If the circumstances were right,' he said. 'For the right reasons, I'd do it. Yeah.'"[40]

His father then cleared his way to join the Mafia. Michael moved up the ranks and became the "caporegime" of the Colombo crime family. Six years later, he was caught by the police, resulting in a 10-year prison sentence and a 15 million dollars fine.

---

36. Acts 27:13
37. We can also be assailed by the flaming arrows of the evil one (Eph 6:16).
38. Ps 46:1
39. 2 Thess 3:3
40. https://www.vanityfair.com/news/1991/02/john-gotti-joe-columbo-fbi-investigation-witness

When Michael was in jail, "a prison guard pushed a Bible through a slot in his cell door . . . 'It was the only night in my life I experienced hopelessness,' he recalled. As he began to examine the character and the claims of Christ, he was born again. 'That Bible, and reading about Jesus, really brought me through some very tough times.'"[41] "It's almost as if God was with me in that 6 by 8 cell . . . I had nothing but enemies that night. The government was against me. My father betrayed me. The boss of my [mob] family had a contract against me. I'm sitting in that cell and I'm alone. It's almost as if the Lord said, I know you have enemies, but you come with me, and I can take care of that."[42]

Despite the threats of murder from the Mafia, Michael Franzese decided to quit the mob and start a foundation for helping youth. "'That's what I live for,' he said. 'I'm in the ministry now and I am sharing the Gospel at any opportunity I can get.'"[43] What about the contract on Michael's life?

> *For years, the government tried to get him to turn on his former colleagues and join the witness protection program. Michael refused and for years was forced to move his family when the threats became too real . . . He didn't return to New York for 12 years and only then with security . . . Asked if he lives in fear of retribution from the mob, Franzese said: "I really don't worry about dying. But you know what? Who knows what's gonna happen tomorrow? I don't know."*[44]

No one knows the future and God's ultimate plans. However, we can say with Michael Franzese and the prophet Samuel, "Thus far the Lord has helped us."[45] "Because he has loved Me, therefore I will deliver him; I will set him securely on high, because he has known My name. He will call upon Me, and I will answer him; I will be with him in trouble; I will rescue him and honor him. With a long life, I will satisfy him and let him see My salvation."[46]

---

41. Ibid.

42. https://www.christianpost.com/news/former-prince-of-the-mafia-michael-franzese-headlines-evangelist-greg-lauries-socal-harvest-124859/

43. http://blog.godreports.com/2014/08/former-new-york-mobster-captain-of-the-colombo-crime-family-found-christ-in-prison/

44. http://www.nytimes.com/2001/07/12/sports/baseball-from-captain-to-coach-ex-goodfella-s-new-life.html?src=pm

45. 1 Sam 7:12

46. Ps 91:14-16

Moral evils can come to us from other people's actions (e.g., death threats and murder contracts). Non-theists can only count on themselves for their own protection. But to those who love him, God provides security and causes "all things to work together for" their good. He encourages his people to persevere amid trials as they must dwell for a brief time in this fallen world. "In the world you have tribulation but take courage; I have overcome the world."[47] He assures them of his concern and continuous presence. "Never will I leave you; never will I forsake you. So, we can say with confidence, 'The Lord is my helper; I will not be afraid. What can mere mortals do to me?'"[48] With the faithful children who obey him, God expresses his tender love and blesses them with many good things.[49]

## Natural evil from other people's action.

Natural evils can come in the lives of believers and non-believers from other people's actions or inactions.[50]

Hurricane Harvey, the second-costliest in US history, inflicted 152 billion dollars in damage to metropolitan Houston and caused 91 fatalities in 2017. Sadly, Houston builders did not give up building new developments in floodplains.

> *In the months following Hurricane Harvey, Houstonians face an important decision: respect the floodplain and stop building homes wherever or continue to ignore the lessons taught by countless flood events and build more homes in the most vulnerable areas of town. The latest example of the city attempting to do the latter is in western Houston, where plans have been drawn up to build single-family homes on the site of the Pine Crest Golf Club . . . Harris County Flood Control District maps show the entire 151-acre plot of land is located in a floodplain.*[51]

Hurricane Katrina in 2005 caused 191 billion dollars in damage and 1833 fatalities. Breaches in the New Orleans levees were responsible for

---

47. John 16:33
48. Heb 13:5-6 NIV.
49. Matt 6:33
50. Natural evils can also come from the evil one (Eph 6:11-16).
51. Sean Breslin, "Houston Might Continue Building Homes on Floodplains." https://weather.com/news/news/2017-11-01-houston-hurricane-harvey-rebuilding-floodplains

most of the deaths and destruction in the city. However, the levees' failures were not unexpected.

> For years, Louisiana officials have been warning of the tragedy that could result if the levees surrounding New Orleans were breached. Every year, they begged for more money to strengthen the walls that kept the waters of Lake Pontchartrain and the Mississippi River from overwhelming the Big Easy—and almost every single year for the last decade, they were turned down.[52]

Can such natural evils be blamed on God when people blithely do whatever they want to others for convenience or money (e.g., decrepit levees, houses built in floodplains)?

We have all heard of Herpes infections transmitted from mother to infant (1 out of every 3,500 babies born in the US contracts neonatal herpes).[53] However, there is a more prevalent newborn illness. It is the Neonatal Abstinence Syndrome (NAS), babies born addicted to opioids or other drugs (e.g., "crack baby"). "Nationally, the rate of American children born with neonatal abstinence syndrome . . . has quadrupled over the past 15 years."[54] In 2020, 43 newborns out of every 1000 hospital deliveries were diagnosed with NAS in West Virginia.[55] "Infants with NAS experienced serious medical complications, with 97.1% being admitted to an intensive care unit, and had prolonged hospital stays, with a mean duration of 26.1 days,"[56] at an astronomical cost. Crippling health issues can plague innocent babies for the rest of their lives due to the unwise actions of their mothers.

In this world, evils (moral and natural) befalling us can be the results of other people's twisted wills and misdeeds. We are given a choice by our Creator, either proceed alone at our own risk or ask for the protection, guidance, and help which he solemnly promises to his followers.[57] In God's sovereignty, we are given the freedom to decide.

---

52. ABC News. "New Orleans Levee Warnings Went Unheeded." http://abcnews.go.com/Primetime/HurricaneKatrina/story?id=1089398

53. https://www.childrenshospital.org/conditions/neonatal-herpes-simplex#:~:text=The%20virus%20is%20inactive%20at,baby's%20first%20month%20of%20life.

54. https://www.nbcnews.com/storyline/americas-heroin-epidemic/born-addicted-number-opioid-addicted-babies-soaring-n806346

55. https://www.cdc.gov/pregnancy/opioids/data.html

56. Jennifer Lind et al., "Infant and Maternal Characteristics in Neonatal Abstinence Syndrome," 213-16.

57. Isa 41:10

Do we genuinely believe that God has our best interests at heart? If so, does evil ever come from him?

**Evil Used by God**

God may use the moral and natural evils in this world as tools to accomplish his purposes. For non-believers, the calamities can be a call to repent (e.g., Nebuchadnezzar's mental illness),[58] or the outcome of God's justice (e.g., Sodom and Gomorrah's fire and brimstone).[59] For believers, suffering (e.g., Job's trial) is meant for good with the goal of Rehabilitation, Edification, Shielding, or Training (REST). Of course, a trial meant for good by God is *not* evil. If we love God, all things (good or bad) will turn out for our good.[60]

Moral evil for the rehabilitation of believers.

God can use moral evil to rehabilitate his children. Believers who are going astray can expect corrective measures to bring them back to usefulness in the kingdom.

During the Last Supper, "there arose also a dispute among them (Jesus' disciples) as to which one of them was regarded to be greatest." After a rebuke and an admonition for them to be servants (rather than lords), Jesus revealed that "Satan has demanded permission to sift you (plural, meaning all the disciples) like wheat." And who was the "weakest link" among the disciples? Who needed Jesus' prayer and protection the most? "I have prayed for you (singular, meaning Peter) that your faith may not fail."

Nevertheless, Peter boastfully claimed, "Lord, with You I am ready to go both to prison and to death!" (therefore deserving the title "the greatest of all the disciples"?). To disabuse him of that notion and remediate his character flaw, Jesus pronounced, "Peter, the rooster will not crow today until you have denied three times that you know Me."[61] Was Peter convinced that Jesus was correct in his assessment of Peter's character?

58. Dan 4
59. Gen 19
60. Rom 8:28
61. Luke 22:24-34, also John 13:36-38

After the Last Supper, Jesus and his disciples went to the Mount of Olives. "And Jesus said to them, 'You will all fall away.'" What was Peter's response? "Even though all may fall away, yet I will not." Jesus revealed a second set of three denials (a stronger remedial measure), "Truly I say to you, that this very night, before a rooster crows twice, you yourself will deny Me three times." "But Peter kept saying insistently, 'Even if I have to die with You, I will not deny you!'"[62]

Can we find six denials in the Scriptures?[63] At Annas's house,[64] Peter was questioned by a doorkeeper and denied Christ (denial #1). *Standing* by a charcoal fire, Peter was challenged by some "slaves and officers" and denied Christ (denial #2). Peter was then confronted by a relative of Malchus (Peter cut off Malchus's ear during a fight in the Garden of Gethsemane)[65] and denied Christ (denial #3), "and immediately a rooster crowed."[66]

Later, in Caiaphas's courtyard,[67] Peter was *sitting* by a fire when he was accosted by a servant-girl and denied Christ (denial #4). He was then approached by another servant-girl at the gateway and denied Christ (denial #5). Finally, he was called out by some bystanders and denied Christ (denial # 6). "And immediately, a rooster crowed *a second time.*"[68]

The remedial measures succeeded for "the Lord turned and looked at Peter. And Peter remembered the word of the Lord, how He had told him, 'Before a rooster crows today, you will deny Me three times.' And he went out and wept bitterly."[69] The moral evils (Peter's lies)[70] used by God as tools to restore Peter were meant for good. The rehabilitation was successful as Peter was later given the special privilege of being God's under shepherd.[71]

---

62. Mark 14:27-31
63. Johnston Cheney, *The Life of Christ in Stereo*, 218–20.
64. John 18:13
65. John 18:10
66. John 18:17-27
67. Matt 26:57-58
68. Matt 26:70-74, Mark 14:67-72, Luke 22:56-60
69. Luke 22:61-62
70. Luke 22:31, Satan "sifted Peter like wheat."
71. John 21:16

Natural evil for the rehabilitation of believers.

Erwin Lutzer, the longtime pastor of Moody Bible Church, declared: "Natural disasters are a megaphone from God, and they teach us various lessons. First of all, natural disasters show us the uncertainty of life . . . We can't get away from the reality that life is very, very short and it's possible for us to delude ourselves."[72] Natural evils can serve as a wake-up call for Christians, reminding them of the necessity to grow in Christlikeness[73] and prepare for the afterlife in heaven.[74]

Unloving Jonah refused to obey God's call to go and warn Nineveh of its upcoming disaster. Instead, he fled from the Lord on a ship to Tarshish. Following the painful experiences of a "great storm" and a "great fish" that swallowed him, Jonah finally came to his senses and repented. "Jonah prayed to the Lord his God from the stomach of the fish . . . Then the Lord commanded the fish, and it vomited Jonah up onto the dry land."[75] Jonah was rehabilitated and went on to proclaim the Lord's message in Nineveh.

Michael was born in New York and attended a parochial grammar school. "I give thanks to the Catholic training because, of course, they brought me to the heart of Jesus."[76] He started a musical career at the age of fifteen with the Five Gents (Doo Wop rhythm and blues). His first successes came at the age of sixteen with the hit songs, "Bless You" and "Hallway to Paradise." He recorded more albums and worked his way up to become a vice president of CBS music.

However, his personal life fell apart. "I wanted to be that tough, bad boy, at least for just a little period of time. And the bad boy point of view got me into trouble, and I began to self-destruct like probably half the performers of the 70s, if not more."[77]

In 1977, Michael's close friend Freddie Prinze, star of the show *Chico and the Man*, depressed and despondent after a divorce, shot himself in the head at the age of twenty-two. Michael wistfully reminisced: "When Freddie Prinze passed, that had an impact on me, because I loved him. I

---

72. Erwin Lutzer, "Where Is God in Natural Disasters?" https://billygraham.org/story/where-is-god-in-natural-disasters-2/

73. Eph 4:13

74. 1 Tim 6:19

75. Jonah 2:1,10

76. http://www1.cbn.com/music/tony-orlando%27s-brush-with-death

77. Ibid.

still love him, to this day."⁷⁸ Soon after, the evil tide struck again. "Then, I lost my sister that same year, same period of time. My sister Rhonda was 20 years old. She had cerebral palsy . . . There was all this passing away going on, and I was 32 then, hitting this stride in my career. I had this national television show. I had the hits. I had everything going, and it just seemed like everything was coming apart."⁷⁹

Michael Anthony Orlando (of *Tony Orlando and Dawn*) had a mental breakdown and retired from singing. However, God did not abandon him.

> *Fortunately, I was brought up with the Lord as my Savior . . . I began to pay attention to Scripture and meet people who walked the walk, and little by little, I guess you could call me a born-again Christian. 1978 is when I found my walk with the Lord. I hopefully do the best I can, in walking that walk, and maybe have inspired others to follow in it, and am very proud of my Christian faith.*⁸⁰

He later returned to television and continued his musical career with his own show "Saturday Nights with Tony Orlando." Concerning his abiding faith in Jesus, he reflected: "[People asked] What's the whole Jesus thing? What's going on with you? What's that? And I just say, 'It's my heart. It's what I feel.' And they see my actions, and they see my lifestyle, and they see how I treat people and how I treat them, and they get it. Those who know it need no explanation."⁸¹

In his wisdom, the omnibenevolent God can use the natural evil in this realm (e.g., a mental breakdown) as a wake-up call to rehabilitate his children to a fruitful ministry. In true compassion, he strengthens "the hands that are weak and the knees that are feeble, and make straight paths for your feet, so that the limb which is lame may not be put out of joint, but rather be healed."⁸²

Besides rehabilitation, God can also use evils as tools to edify his children.

---

78. Ibid.
79. Ibid.
80. Ibid.
81. Ibid.
82. Heb 12:12-13

Moral evil for the edification of believers.

Obviously, God's goal is not to destroy the believers, but to edify them. Christians who respond correctly to their evil experiences will become stronger.

Job was "blameless, upright, fearing God, and turning away from evil."[83] Yet, God let evil fall on Job[84] as he lost his servants, his possessions, his children, and even his own health.

At the end of his tribulation, "Job answered the Lord, and said, 'I know that You can do all things, and that no purpose of yours can be thwarted.'"[85] Job acknowledged that "I have declared that which I did not understand, things too wonderful for me, which I did not know."[86] His former assumption that evil should not happen to believers was badly mistaken.

Job also affirmed, "I have heard of you by the hearing of the ear; but now my eye sees you,"[87] with a fuller appreciation of God's wisdom and perfection.

Finally, Job learned that "his attitude towards God (is) one unbefitting a creature."[88] Demanding answers and questioning the Creator's fairness are not the ways of a faithful believer. "Therefore, I retract, and I repent in dust and ashes."[89]

To dispel any doubt that Job's troubles were meant for good, "the Lord restored the fortunes of Job . . . and the Lord increased all that Job had twofold."[90] In Job's case, God's goal of edification was accomplished as the blameless, upright, God-fearing Job was edified and blessed by a deeper knowledge of God and a more intimate relationship with him.

However, whether we respond quickly (Job), slowly (Samson),[91] or not at all (King Saul)[92] to the evils in our lives is up to us, for God does not force anyone to repent and have a love relationship with him.

83. Job 1:1
84. Job's evils came from Satan (Job 1:12, Job 2:6-7).
85. Job 42:2
86. Job 42:3
87. Job 42:5
88. *Pulpit Commentary*. http://biblehub.com/commentaries/job/42-6.htm
89. Job 42:6
90. Job 42:10
91. Judg 14-16
92. 1 Sam 31

When I was in the last year of my anesthesia residency, I heard rumors that some attendings overseeing the residents had decided that I should not be allowed to graduate. Puzzled, I made some discreet inquiries, but could not determine the reasons behind their animosity. I took care of the patients, I stayed out of trouble, never complained, and did well on my exams. Why were they upset with me?

So, I cried out to God for help and protection! After much prayer, I decided to ask for support from a friendly professor (a native of India) who counseled me to transfer to an outlying clinic and stay out of the way of my antagonists. Eagerly taking his advice, I laid low for the few remaining months of my residency. I reasoned that I was such a small fish that they would not waste their time frying me. Being out of sight, I would soon be out of mind.

But that was not to be! I heard through the grapevine that they did not forget and were just biding their time, waiting for the customary departmental meeting convened just before graduation to evaluate each resident's performance. This was usually a formality as any truly important matter had to be addressed long before this time. For example, unsatisfactory residents had to be officially warned about their deficiencies early in the year and given opportunities to make corrective actions. Nevertheless, my adversaries planned to use this meeting to derail my graduation.

My department was composed of equal numbers of Caucasian and foreign attending physicians (mostly from India). The relationship between these two groups was tenuous. As you can guess, my detractors were exclusively from one group, but they held most of the power. Sadly, I had no chance to survive this challenge as residents were not allowed to be present at the performance evaluation to defend themselves. God would have to be there to protect me. Desperately, I implored him to vanquish my foes. Would God save me from my enemies? What means did he have to change the foreordained outcome?

My friendly Indian professor later told me what had happened at the departmental meeting. When my name came up for discussion, my foes fiercely blocked my graduation, citing many reasons. As the discussion dragged on, my benevolent attending physician finally stood up and said: "There is only one question to settle here. Do you think that he can safely provide anesthesia?" With that, he sat down. The room was quiet. A vote was taken and wonder of wonders, I passed!

God said to his children: "Call upon me in the day of trouble; I shall rescue you, and you will honor me."[93] From that painful experience, I learned that no one could challenge the preeminent Lord and win. "Many are the plans in a man's heart, but the counsel of the Lord, it will stand."[94] God is omnipotent, he "is in the heavens; he does whatever he pleases."[95] Consequently, "the king's heart is like channels of water in the hand of the Lord; he turns it wherever he wishes."[96] Moral evils in this world (e.g., human bigotry) can be used by the benevolent Lord to edify his followers and strengthen their trust in him. Praise be to God!

## Natural evil for the edification of believers.

After the Hurricane Katrina disaster in New Orleans, a survey was conducted among 680 randomly selected adult evacuees to Houston shelters by the *Washington Post*. When asked "How important a role has religion played in helping you get through these past two weeks?" 92 percent said that religion's role was important. In answer to the subsequent question, "Has this experience strengthened your religious faith, weakened your faith, or has it made no difference to your religious faith?" 81 percent claimed that the event had strengthened their religious faith.[97]

In 2012, a study was done "to explore the role of spirituality in the lives of earthquake survivors in Haiti." 108 subjects were interviewed, all of whom had "experienced some degree of loss (e.g., loss of family members, health, job, home, school, vocation)." The survey concluded that the sufferers' "trauma can be an impetus for spiritual growth ... despite the nature and severity of their losses."[98] Hence, God can use natural evils to strengthen and edify his people.

Born in Belfast, Ireland, Clive came to England to study and teach. Though raised in a Christian family, he adopted atheism at the age of fifteen. Thanks to the help of a colleague, Clive returned to Christianity at the age of thirty-one. Being a bachelor, he focused on writing fiction

---

93. Ps. 50:15
94. Prov 19:21
95. Ps 115:3
96. Prov 21:1
97. "Survey of Hurricane Katrina Evacuees." https://www.washingtonpost.com/wp-srv/politics/polls/katrina_poll091605.pdf
98. Kari O'Grady et al., "Earthquake in Haiti: Relationship with the Sacred in Times of Trauma," 289-301.

and non-fiction books for adults and children, an endeavor which brought him much acclaim.

In 1950, a female fan in America, a writer and poet, corresponded with him for two years before they finally met in person in London. She was a child prodigy, having earned her master's degree in English literature at the age of nineteen. During that visit, Clive learned that she was married to an alcoholic and abusive husband. After her divorce, she moved to England with her two sons.

Clive considered her an intellectual companion and a close friend. In 1956, her visa was not renewed, jeopardizing any further stay in England. Clive offered to marry her in a civil union so that she could legally remain in the country. "Neither of them regarded a civil marriage as of any validity in the eyes of God, and they would both continue to live as before, she in her house and he in his."[99]

A few months later, she was diagnosed with terminal breast cancer with metastases to the bone. By this time, Clive had fallen in love with her, and they decided to be married by a friend, an Anglican priest,[100] at her hospital bed. Miraculously, she went into remission, and they enjoyed three years together before she died in 1960 at the age of forty-five.

C. S. Lewis (Clive Staples Lewis) was heartbroken and wrote *A Grief Observed*, a raw, emotional book, relating the agony of his bereavement and the dreadful stages of his journey "through the valley of the shadow of death."[101] From his cry "Where is God?" to "Is it rational to believe in a bad God?" he came to question his faith. "I thought I trusted in the rope until it mattered to me whether it would bear me. Now it matters, and I find I didn't."[102]

Yet, like Julian of Norwich and Horatio Spafford, the writer of the famous hymn *It Is Well with My Soul*, C. S. Lewis came to the realization that "all shall be well, and all manner of thing shall be well . . . I

---

99. https://www.narniaweb.com/2022/03/why-c-s-lewis-married-the-same-woman-twice/

100. The Church of England did not sanction the marriage due to the previous divorce. The Anglican priest, Peter Bide, explained his reason for performing the ceremony: "After long cogitations—and it took me the best part of an hour—I said to myself, 'What would He [Jesus] have done?' and then there wasn't any further answer at all. Of course, He would have married them, wouldn't He?" https://mereinkling.net/2016/07/06/c-s-lewis-wedding/#:~:text=Since%20the%20church%20could%20not,His%20name%20was%20Peter%20Bide.

101. Ps 23:4

102. C. S. Lewis, *A Grief Observed*, 37.

need Christ not something that resembles Him . . . I must stretch out the arms and hands of love—its eyes cannot here be used—to the reality, through—across—all the changeful phantasmagoria of my thoughts, passions, and imaginings . . . not my idea of God, but God."[103]

That was the same conclusion I came to in my trial with my son Daniel's heart problems. By God's grace and wisdom, I needed to experience, not my idea of God, but the reality of God himself, the faithful, sustaining presence of the benevolent Father who carries us and comforts us in our times of trials. "Even to your old age and gray hairs I am he, I am he who will sustain you. I have made you and I will carry you; I will sustain you and I will rescue you."[104] Therefore, we shall proclaim, "Great is the Lord and most worthy of praise; his greatness no one can fathom."[105]

Natural evils in this realm (e.g., heart defects, death of a loved one from cancer) can strengthen our faith despite the great pain and suffering. All things, including natural evils, can "work together for good" and be used by God for the edification of his children.

Besides rehabilitation and edification, God can also use evils as tools to shield believers from disasters.

## Moral evil for the shielding of believers.

According to the National Institute of Justice, "the *certainty* of being caught is a vastly more powerful deterrent than the punishment."[106] If so, God's omniscience and justice (guaranteeing the apprehension and punishment of wrongdoers) should serve as a powerful deterrence among believers, shielding them from committing evils. Of course, non-theists who do not believe in the existence of God cannot be deterred by such a notion.

Following the example of Barnabas, Ananias and Sapphira decided to sell some property and give the proceeds to the church. However, they agreed together not to donate the full amount while pretending otherwise. Somehow, Peter found out about the deceitful scheme. "Ananias, why has Satan filled your heart to lie to the Holy Spirit, and to keep back some of

---

103. Ibid., 65-67.
104. Is 46:4 NIV.
105. Ps 145:3 NIV.
106. National Institute of Justice. "Five Things about Deterrence." https://nij.gov/five-things/pages/deterrence.aspx

the price of the land?"[107] God's judgment was swift as "Ananias fell down and breathed his last." Three hours later, Sapphira "came in, not knowing what had happened." Questioned by Peter, and allowed an opportunity to "come clean," she lied and replied, "Yes, that was the price." For that, she also "breathed her last." "And great fear came upon the whole church, and upon all who heard of these things."[108] From this experience, the Church learned that lying to the Holy Spirit is a capital offense. God can use moral evils (e.g., deaths) as tools to shield/deter his followers from falling into the trap of greed and covetousness.

Likewise, "pride goes before destruction."[109] According to Josephus, King Herod Agrippa "put on a garment made wholly of silver, of a truly wonderful texture, and came into the theater early in the morning . . . Presently his flatterers cried out, one from one place, and another from another, (though not for his good) that he was a god."[110] "The people kept crying out, 'The voice of a god and not of a man!' And immediately an angel of the Lord struck him because he did not give God the glory, and he was eaten by worms and died."[111] This serves as a deterrence for anyone who is so prideful as to usurp God's unique position as the Creator of the universe!

In this world, affairs between doctors and nurses are commonplace. One day, I noticed that an anesthesiologist was spending a lot of time with a particular nurse, bantering and flirting, even though they were both married with children.[112] Soon, he requested her to be in his operating room, displacing another nurse who previously held that role. Suffice it to say that the competition between the two nurses was fierce. One won and one lost. The one who lost overdosed and died (suicide?). The anesthesiologist and the winning nurse subsequently married after divorcing their spouses.

Watching that sad spectacle, I was reminded of the dangers inherent in the long hours spent with the nurses at work,[113] often under great stress, yet with a sense of comradeship and a common purpose. Physicians often joke about their "wives at work" with whom they spend much more time

107. Acts 5:3
108. Acts 5:11
109. Prov 16:18
110. Flavius Josephus, *Antiquities of the Jews*, 19.8.2
111. Acts 12:22-23
112. Details have been changed to preserve privacy.
113. Ex 20:14

than with their "wives at home." In this taxing situation where people are thrown together under intense physical and mental pressures, boundaries are easily crossed, leading to much marital turmoil and suffering!

In his wisdom, God can use moral evils (e.g., affairs) as object lessons to shield believers from committing sins and succumbing to the many temptations in this world.[114]

### Natural evil for the shielding of believers.

God used "fire and brimstone" (a cosmic airburst)[115] to destroy Sodom and Gomorrah on account of their wickedness. "He condemned the cities of Sodom and Gomorrah to destruction by reducing them to ashes, having made them an example to those who would live ungodly lives thereafter."[116] The destroyed cities served as a deterrence to other towns from the folly of indulging in wrongdoing. "Whoever does not receive you, nor heed your words, as you go out of that house or that city, shake the dust off your feet. Truly I say to you, it will be more tolerable for the land of Sodom and Gomorrah in the day of judgment than for that city."[117]

The sufferings befalling some can prevent others from making the same mistakes. Of course, it is a lot cheaper (and a lot less painful) to learn from someone else's trials and tribulations!

God allowed a "thorn in the flesh" (a physical illness?) in Paul's life, "a messenger of Satan to torment me—to keep me from exalting myself!"[118] "Even the holiest Christians . . . are not out of danger of pride, or of being too much exalted."[119] Paul's "thorn" shielded him from the destructive sin of spiritual pride as he had been given "surpassingly great revelations" and, in paradise, had "heard inexpressible words, which a man is not permitted to speak."[120]

Like Paul, God gave me a "thorn in the flesh" to protect me from the danger of drinking (to excess). I had my first taste of alcohol when

---

114. 1 John 2:15-16

115. Ted Bunch et al., "A Tunguska Sized Airburst Destroyed Tall El-Hammam a Middle Bronze Age City in the Jordan Valley near the Dead Sea."

116. 2 Pet 2:6

117. Matt 10:14-15

118. 2 Cor 12:7

119. *Benson Commentary.* http://biblehub.com/commentaries/2_corinthians/12-7.htm

120. 2 Cor 12:4

I attended an exclusive party at a palatial home. After a sumptuous dinner, expensive champagne was served for a toast. Who could turn down such a gracious and considerate offer from a generous host? So, I politely enjoyed a glass of this divine nectar!

Almost immediately, I turned beet red, and the room started spinning! Although I was wide awake, I could not walk straight and had to stumble to the bathroom. Fortunately, no one noticed my awkward departure as they were all busy with the celebration. After traversing some dark bedrooms, I finally found the lair of the porcelain god, proceeded to hug him in a death-grip embrace, and quickly offered him the remains of my libation. When I finally came out of my private conference with the divine, I foreswore any future meetings with Bacchus, a promise I even kept at my son's wedding reception!

In his grace, God may use natural evils (e.g., a lack of alcohol metabolizing enzyme, Paul's "thorn") to shield his followers from some inherent perils in this fallen world.

Besides rehabilitation, edification, and shielding of his followers, God can also use evils as tools to train his children.

## Moral evil for the training of believers.

Believers cannot commit wrongdoing with impunity. God, as a father, is responsible for correcting and training his children. "God deals with you as with sons; for what son is there whom his father does not discipline?"[121] "All Scripture is inspired by God and profitable for teaching, for reproof, for correction, for training in righteousness."[122] The purpose of training is not to destroy but to teach with the goal of growth and maturity.[123] "He disciplines us for our good, so that we may share his holiness."[124]

However, training and discipline do not always fulfill their desired goal of bringing people to repentance and Christlikeness. God, in his sovereignty, gives humans the freedom to take or spurn his advice. No one is coerced to love and obey God. The faithful believer "is made a better man

---

121. Heb 12:7
122. 2 Tim 3:16
123. 1 Cor 13:11
124. Heb 12:10

by receiving afflictions as they should be received . . . the sinner is made more hardened by resisting them."[125]

Ignoring his duty, King David stayed home, ordering Joab to go to battle in his stead. This chain of events led to the encounter with Bathsheba, her subsequent pregnancy, and the murder of her husband Uriah to cover the crime. God's discipline was swift! "Now therefore, the sword shall never depart from your house, because you have despised Me and have taken the wife of Uriah the Hittite to be your wife. Thus says the Lord, 'Behold, I will raise up evil against you from your own household; I will even take your wives before your eyes and give them to your companion, and he will lie with your wives in broad daylight.'"[126] David's son with Bathsheba died. His oldest son Amnon raped Tamar (Amnon's half-sister) and was murdered by her brother Absalom. Absalom rebelled against David and slept with his father's wives "in broad daylight." Absalom was later killed in the civil war.[127]

In David's case, the Lord's discipline fulfilled its desired goal of bringing him back to God. David repented and confessed his sins.[128] "Then he died in a ripe old age, full of days, riches and honor."[129] Through God's wise discipline, David succeeded in his "training in righteousness" and earned the much-coveted title of a man after God's own heart.[130]

King Jehoshaphat of Judah was blessed by the Lord for "he followed the example of his father David's earlier days."[131] However, when he "had great riches and honor" from God's blessings, he allied himself with Ahab, the wicked king of Israel. Spurning the Lord's warning, he unwisely agreed to join Ahab in a war against Ramoth-Gilead. God's discipline came swiftly upon him! Ahab was killed in battle, the coalition army was defeated, and Jehoshaphat barely escaped by the Lord's mercy.[132] When Jehoshaphat returned to Jerusalem, he was rebuked by God's prophet and told not to help the wicked or love those who

---

125. Albert Barnes, *Notes, Explanatory and Practical, on the Epistle to the Romans*, 179.
126. 2 Sam 12:10-11
127. 2 Samuel 11-18.
128. 2 Samuel 12:13
129. 1 Chr 29:28
130. Acts 13:22
131. 2 Chr 17:3
132. 2 Chr 18:1-31

hate the Lord for that would bring further chastisement.[133] Aiming for a change in behavior, God explained the reason for the discipline and mapped out a positive way forward.

Did Jehoshaphat learn his lesson and progress in his training in righteousness and holiness? Hardly! He decided to partner with Ahaziah, Ahab's wicked son, in building ships for the gold trade of Ophir.[134] The Lord disciplined Jehoshaphat again by wrecking the ships! "Because you have allied yourself with Ahaziah, the Lord has destroyed your works."[135] Did this second training session bring the desired change in behavior and progress in holiness?

Later, Jehoshaphat was asked by the evil king Jehoram, another son of Ahab, to join him in his campaign against Moab. Did Jehoshaphat finally learn not to help the wicked in their ungodly ways? Unfortunately not! He went with Jehoram and almost perished with his army in the wilderness due to the lack of water. The Lord was merciful to his stubborn king, and miraculously provided sustenance through the prophet Elisha.[136] However, the campaign was not successful as Moab continued to be a thorn to Judah for another 300 years!

As with Jehoshaphat, I experienced the Lord's needful training in my own life. The university where I served as an adjunct provided employees with a nearby parking garage. However, when a ball game was scheduled to be held on campus, we were told to park at a more remote facility to accommodate the guests of the special event. That would add significant commuting time from garage to classroom, something I would rather avoid. So, I told my wife of my plan to park at a nearby strip mall. As she did not think that was a very good idea, I had to explain that the mall was half-deserted, and the parking lot was huge.

On the special event day, I left my white sedan in the strip mall and went to my classes. When I finished, I walked back to the parking lot to find my car missing! Talking to the passersby, I learned that my auto was towed, necessitating an unwelcome trip to the impound lot to pay a large fine!

We need to remember that the gracious and merciful Lord provides ways of escape for his people (e.g., do not park where you are not allowed, do not join the wicked in their wickedness). However, if we insist on our

---

133. 2 Chr 19:2
134. 1 Kgs 22:48
135. 2 Chr 20:37
136. 2 Kgs 3:13-18

ill-considered ways, discipline is sure to come since "whom the Lord loves, He disciplines, and He scourges every son whom He receives"[137] with the aim of training them in Christlikeness and holiness.[138]

## Natural evil for the training of believers.

The Bible recorded many instances of natural evils as God's training sessions for believers. For example, King Uzziah was struck by God with leprosy for usurping the priests' prerogative to offer incense.[139] God punished King Ahab with a drought for worshiping other gods.[140] God decreed a plague on David's kingdom for ordering a census.[141]

Did the disciplinary actions accomplish their desired goals of bringing the kings to repentance? "King Uzziah was a leper to the day of his death; and he lived in a separate house, being a leper."[142] It isn't clear whether Uzziah repented. King Ahab persisted in his evil ways, instigating the murder of Naboth to seize his vineyard.[143] In contrast, King David was contrite and obtained a reprieve from the Lord who spared Jerusalem from the plague.[144]

As with the kings of old, the Lord had to bring some natural evil in my life for my "training in righteousness." Hoping to stay healthy, I had bought a set of weights and a bench for my improvised "home gym." Having set an ambitious goal in weightlifting, I eagerly and doggedly pursued that dream. After more than a year, I was finally able to lift that desired weight, a notable achievement for someone my age and my size. Unfortunately, "Pride goes before destruction, a haughty spirit before a fall."[145] The too-heavy weights injured my left shoulder, preventing me from lifting my arm over my head for months. From this episode, I belatedly learned my lesson that pride can be detrimental to one's spiritual life!

137. Heb 12:6
138. Rom 8:29
139. 2 Chr 26:16-21
140. 1 Kgs 17:1
141. 2 Sam 24:13-15
142. 2 Chr 26:21
143. 1 Kgs 21
144. 1 Chr 21
145. Prov 16:18

Natural evils (e.g., shoulder problems) can be used by God for the training of believers with the goal of bringing them to maturity. However, as Christians (like non-Christians) are free to make their own decisions, they may choose to ignore God's discipline and persist in their chosen paths.

Since God is gracious and merciful, a belated contrition may yet bring a measure of respite from evil. For example, the Prodigal Son had a late change of heart. As a result of his repentance, he was saved from starvation and destitution.[146] Believers would do well to respond quickly to God's discipline. "Do not be as the horse or as the mule which have no understanding, whose trappings include bit and bridle to hold them in check, otherwise they will not come near to you."[147]

## Summary

In answer to our fourth question, we have shown that, for non-believers, evils can come from their own actions and from other people's misdeeds. Afflictions can also be used by the Lord as tools to bring his creatures back to him (e.g., Paul's blindness on the Damascus Road).[148]

For believers, moral and natural evils can come from their own choices and from other people's transgressions. God may also use adversities for the purpose of rehabilitation, edification, shielding, and training (REST). Christians can take comfort in God's promise that he "causes all things to work together for good to those who love God,"[149] if not immediately, then definitely in the future. Thus, will our pains and sufferings be redeemed in heaven (our fifth question)?

---

146. Luke 15:22-23
147. Ps 32:9
148. Acts 9
149. Rom 8:28

# 5

# Will the Evils and Sufferings Be Redeemed in Heaven?

> *At the end of all things, when the sun rises here and the twilight turns to blackness down there, the Blessed will say, "We have never lived anywhere except in heaven," and the Lost, "We were always in hell." And both will speak truly.*
>
> —C. S. Lewis[1]

THE BELIEVERS' SUFFERINGS ON earth will be redeemed by their rewards in heaven.[2] The non-believers' trials and tribulations in this world may not have a positive result, an outcome a loving God earnestly seeks to prevent, ceaselessly calling his beloved creatures to return, being patient, "not wanting anyone to perish, but everyone to come to repentance."[3]

## Hell

According to Dr. Kvanvig's "Self-Determination"[4] model, hell, as separation from God,[5] is the natural outcome of humans' decision to acknowledge or

1. C. S. Lewis, *The Great Divorce*, 69.
2. Matt 5:12, Jas 1:12
3. 2 Pet 3:9
4. "Those in hell are there because of their determination to avoid the company of the redeemed and the God who redeems." Jonathan Kvanvig, *The Problem of Hell*, 158.
5. "As a state of eternal separation from God, hell would frustrate this central

not acknowledge their Creator, to reside or not reside with God. This is in contrast with the views of various scholars (e.g., Marilyn McCord Adams,[6] John Hick,[7] and John Bishop[8]) who advocated universal salvation/no hell. "The history of the doctrine of universal salvation (or *apokastastasis*) is a remarkable one. Until the nineteenth century almost all Christian theologians taught the reality of eternal torment in hell."[9]

Besides Christianity, the concept of hell is also found in Judaism,[10] Islam,[11] Buddhism,[12] Hinduism,[13] Shintoism,[14] and Zoroastrianism.[15] Hell is a belief deeply ingrained in the human psyche and widely accepted by human cultures.

Concerning the finality of hell, C. S. Lewis stated: "There are only two kinds of people in the end: those who say to God, 'Thy will be done,' and those to whom God says, in the end, 'Thy will be done.'"[16] Likewise, Pope John Paul II affirmed: "It (hell) is the state of those who definitely reject the Father's mercy, even at the last moment of their life."[17] On our death bed, as we live in a world of universal death, the choice we make concerning our eternal destiny is final and irrevocable.[18] Therefore, we need to weigh the facts carefully and make a well-thought-out decision concerning our future.[19]

---

human desire (eternal union with God)." C. P. Ragland, "Hell."

6. "My brand of universalism offers all the advantages of Augustine's and Calvin's sola gratia approaches." Marilyn McCord Adams, "The Problem of Hell," 325.

7. "God will eventually succeed in His purpose of winning all men to Himself." John Hick, *Evil and the God of Love*, 342.

8. "If God *is* a supreme personal agent, there would be a defect in either his power or goodness if he could not provide for universal salvation." John Bishop, "On Identifying the Problem of Evil," 51.

9. Richard Bauckham, "Universalism," 47.

10. Dan Cohn-Sherbok, "The Jewish Doctrine of Hell."

11. Christian Lange (ed.), *Locating Hell in Islamic Traditions*.

12. Eileen Gardiner (ed.), *Buddhist Hell*.

13. Knut Jacobsen, "Three Functions of Hell in the Hindu Traditions."

14. Ō no Yasumaro, *The Kojiki: An Account of Ancient Matters*, 14.

15. Michael Stausberg, "Hell in Zoroastrian History."

16. C. S. Lewis, *The Great Divorce*, 75.

17. John Paul II, "General Audience," quoted by Thomas Rausch, *Systematic Theology*, 212.

18. Heb 9:27, Matt 25:46

19. Andrei Buckareff and Allen Plug, "Hell and the Problem of Evil," 128-43. "The traditional conception of hell is committed to arbitrary cutoffs between the unsaved and the saved . . . incompatible with God's perfect justice." This problem of "vagueness"

He was born in the prohibition era to a conservative Methodist family, descendants of Plymouth governor William Bradford. His devout mother wanted him to be a missionary. Instead, he joined the Army and later went to college, graduating with a degree in psychology and a minor in creative writing. He first worked as a copywriter for Esquire but then decided to start his own magazine with money from various sources, including a thousand dollars from his mother, "not because she believed in the venture . . . but because she believed in her son."[20] His biggest asset at the time was a nude photograph of Marilyn Monroe which he had bought the rights for five hundred dollars. "When Playboy reached newsstands in December 1953, its press run of 51,000 sold out. The publisher, instantly famous, would soon become a millionaire; after five years, the magazine's annual profit was $4 million, and its rabbit-head logo was recognized around the world."[21]

Hugh Hefner left his childhood sweetheart wife and indulged in his physical appetites, living in the Playboy Mansion, and claiming that he had slept with more than a thousand women. He famously said, "If a man has a right to find God in his own way, he has a right to go to the Devil in his own way also."[22] He died in 2017 at the age of ninety-one.

Francis was raised on a small farm and homeschooled until the sixth grade. He studied at the University of Virginia and received a PhD in Physical Chemistry from Yale. After going to medical school at the University of North Carolina, he returned to Yale as a fellow in human genetics. He subsequently oversaw the International Human Genome Sequencing Consortium tasked with the Human Genome Project which

---

("arbitrary cutoffs") is addressed in 2 Timothy 2:19. "The Lord knows those who are his." Since God is omniscient, he knows who is saved and who is lost. As such, there are no *arbitrary* cutoffs for God since he perceives "the motives of men's hearts" (1 Cor 4:5). The problem of "diminished capacities" ("agents do not have it in their power to fully appreciate the gravity of their circumstances") is answered in Romans 1:20. "For since the creation of the world His invisible attributes, His eternal power and divine nature, have been clearly seen, being understood through what has been made, so that they are without excuse." Despite their "diminished capacities," humans can *clearly* see God's creation and are therefore held responsible for rejecting God. The "problem of morally culpable procreation" (parents are morally culpable for bringing children who "may wind up in hell") is resolved by Ezekiel 18:20. "The person who sins will die. The son will not bear the punishment for the father's iniquity, nor will the father bear the punishment for the son's iniquity."

20. https://www.bbc.com/news/world-us-canada-11642188

21. https://www.nytimes.com/2017/09/27/obituaries/hugh-hefner-dead.html

22. https://www.ajc.com/news/national/funny-iconic-hugh-hefner-quotes-remember-the-playboy-legend/cNJNtMu3cdZhAsOca1y9xH/

was successfully completed in 2003. In 2009, Dr. Francis Collins was appointed director of the National Institutes of Health. He was an atheist but became a Christian in 1977. He said concerning his conversion:

> *I was an atheist, finding no reason to postulate the existence of any truths outside of mathematics, physics, and chemistry. But then I went to medical school, and encountered life and death issues at the bedsides of my patients . . . I had always assumed that faith was based on purely emotional and irrational arguments, and was astounded to discover, initially in the writings of the Oxford scholar C. S. Lewis and subsequently from many other sources, that one could build a very strong case for the plausibility of the existence of God on purely rational grounds. My earlier atheist's assertion that 'I know there is no God' emerged as the least defensible.*[23]

Like Hugh Hefner and Francis Collins, we can decide our paths without any coercion. Hell is a free will choice given to all humans by their sovereign Creator. After a lifetime of denying God's existence and refusing God's gift of eternal life from the Savior Jesus Christ, non-believers may continue to do so in the afterlife. The Danish theologian Kierkegaard asserted: "And as for seeking help from any other—no, that he will not do for all the world; rather than seek help he would prefer to be himself—with all the tortures of hell . . . Even if at this point God in heaven and all his angels were to offer to help him out of it—no, now he doesn't want it."[24] "Hell is God's great compliment to the reality of human freedom and the dignity of human choice."[25] Seeking true love and freely given acceptance from his creatures, the omnibenevolent Father respects humans' decisions, not willing to coerce anyone to believe, but longing to bring all to repentance and the knowledge of the truth.[26]

In his acclaimed drama *No Exit*, the French philosopher Jean Paul Sartre (who declined the 1964 Nobel Prize in Literature) described hell as a place where people were trapped, yet of their own will.[27] They chose to live in the company of kindred souls, far away from their Creator.

---

23. http://www.cnn.com/2007/US/04/03/collins.commentary/index.html
24. Søren Kierkegaard, *The Sickness unto Death (Sygdommen til Døden)*, 114-15.
25. G. K. Chesterton, quoted by Lee Strobel, "The Case for Faith," 169.
26. 2 Pet 3:9, 1 Tim 2:4
27. Jean Paul Sartre, *No Exit (Huis Clos)*.

God's ceaseless efforts[28] to call self-declared independent people to return may be rejected as humans desire to control their own destiny.

Also, they may reason that the loving and just God will not condemn[29] wrongdoers eternally to hell for some finite sins on earth. Dr. Kershnar declared:

> *I specifically argue that human beings do not deserve hell because they either cannot cause an infinite amount of harm or are not responsible for doing so. Also, since humans don't have infinitely bad characters, hell can't be deserved on the basis of character. Since humans don't deserve hell, God may not (or perhaps cannot) impose unjust punishments and hence may not (or cannot) send or allow persons to go to hell.*[30]

However, rejection and denial of an infinite being's existence may call for an infinite punishment. In answer to the question of proportionality between the penalty and the offense, Augustine affirmed: "Eternal punishment appears harsh and unjust . . . [but] the more intimate the first man's enjoyment of God, the greater his impiety in abandoning God. By so doing he merited eternal evil, in that he destroyed in himself a good that might have been eternal."[31] Anselm explained: "Sin is nothing else than not to render to God his due . . . everyone who sins ought to pay back the honor of which he has robbed God,"[32] and "satisfaction should be proportionate to guilt."[33] Aquinas stated:

> *The magnitude of the punishment matches the magnitude of the sin; according to the measure of the sin, shall the measure of the stripes also be. Now a sin that is against God is infinite; the higher the person against whom it is committed, the graver the sin—it is more criminal to strike a head of state than a private citizen—and God is of infinite greatness. Therefore, an infinite punishment is deserved for a sin committed against him.*[34]

---

28. through the tireless and costly work of the Church and the Holy Spirit.
29. "Hell is both the creature's choice and divine punishment." Heath White, *Fate and Free Will*, 319.
30. Stephen Kershnar, "The Injustice of Hell," 103.
31. Augustine, *Concerning the City of God*, XXI. 12.
32. Anselm, *Cur Deus Homo*, Chapter XI.
33. Ibid., Chapter XX.
34. Thomas Aquinas, *Summa Theologica*, 1.2.87.

# WILL THE EVILS AND SUFFERINGS BE REDEEMED IN HEAVEN?

The Early Church ("triple-A team of Augustine, Anselm, and Aquinas")[35] was unanimous concerning an eternal reckoning for abandoning an eternal God. This has not changed in the contemporary religious landscape.

Dr. Craig declared: "To reject Christ is to reject God himself. And in light of God's status, this is a sin of infinite gravity and proportion and therefore plausibly deserves infinite punishment."[36] Dr. Sproul asserted: "Sin, the church has argued, must be punished infinitely because we sin against an infinitely holy God."[37] Dr. Ryrie concurred: "All sin is ultimately against an infinite God and deserves infinite punishment."[38] The *Catechism of the Catholic Church* states: "Hell's principal punishment consists of eternal separation from God."[39] Throughout the history of the Church, the belief of an everlasting punishment for rejecting an everlasting God is strongly affirmed.[40]

Seeking reconciliation, the benevolent Creator proclaims: "I have no pleasure in the death of anyone . . . so turn, and live."[41] "'Return to Me, and I will return to you,' says the Lord of hosts."[42] In long-suffering, God earnestly beseeches his wayward people to come back to him.

Whether we heed the call or reject it, "as people are destined to die once, and after that to face judgment,"[43] we will eventually have to meet our maker and "give an account of ourselves to God."[44] The Lord is neither cruel nor indifferent to our sins. He is a God of justice and "will repay each person according to what they have done."[45]

---

35. Stephen Wykstra, "The Skeptical Theist Response," 173.
36. William Lane Craig, "Diversity, Evil, and Hell," 233.
37. R. C. Sproul Jr., "How Can an Infinite Hell Be Just When Our Sins Are Finite?" https://www.ligonier.org/blog/how-can-infinite-hell-be-just-when-our-sins-are-finite/
38. Charles Ryrie, *Basic Theology*, 521.
39. The Catholic Church, *Catechism of the Catholic Church*, 275.
40. Blanchette and Walls disagreed. "The claim that any offense against an infinite God merits infinite punishment pushes this principle far beyond the realm of plausibility." Kyle Blanchette and Jerry Walls. "God and Hell Reconciled," 255.
41. Eze 18:32
42. Mal 3:7
43. Heb 9:27 NIV.
44. Rom 14:12 NIV.
45. Rom 2:6

## Heaven

In the garden of Eden, God gave Adam two choices/paths: life or death.[46] Against God's command, Adam chose the path of disobedience and death, this world with its many evils. The Fall and evil in this realm are the consequences of Adam's ill-fated decision.

In his grace and mercy, God provided a substitute/savior for humans in this forbidden path. "When the fullness of the time came, God sent forth His Son, born of a woman, born under the law, so that He might redeem those who were under the Law, that we might receive the adoption as sons."[47] Nevertheless, God's plan of salvation is not forced on anyone. People are free to accept or reject the Savior's offer.

"But as many as received Him (Jesus Christ the Savior), to them He gave the right to become children of God, even to those who believe in His name, who were born, not of blood nor of the will of the flesh nor of the will of man, but of God."[48] After his death (as a substitute for humans), resurrection, and ascension, Christ is preparing a place for believers/children of God in heaven. "The place of the final abode of the righteous is sometimes called a house as when the Savior said,"[49] "In My Father's house are many dwelling places; if it were not so, I would have told you; for I go to prepare a place for you. If I go and prepare a place for you, I will come again and receive you to Myself, that where I am, there you may be also."[50]

At the right time,[51] "the Lord Himself will descend from heaven with a shout, with the voice of the archangel and with the trumpet of God, and the dead in Christ will rise first. Then we who are alive and remain will be caught up together with them in the clouds to meet the Lord in the air, and so we shall always be with the Lord."[52] Christ "is at the right hand of God, having gone into heaven, after angels and authorities and powers had been subjected to Him."[53] Thus, believers will always be in heaven with God.

---

46. Lee Thai, *Boundaries of Freedom*.
47. Gal 4:4-5
48. John 1:12-13
49. Charles Hodge, *Systematic Theology*, Vol. 3, 744.
50. John 14:2-3
51. Gal 4:4, Mark 13:32
52. 1 Thess 4:16-17
53. 1 Pet 3:22

In the Final State (The New Heaven and the New Earth),[54] Satan will be banished forever from the presence of the Lord. "And the devil who deceived them was thrown into the lake of fire and brimstone, where the beast and the false prophet are also; and they will be tormented day and night forever and ever."[55] With Satan banished and his power of death[56] destroyed,[57] "death is swallowed up in victory."[58] There will be no death, sin, or evil before the holy God and the spotless Lamb/Christ in heaven. "Nothing unclean, and no one who practices abomination and lying, shall ever come into it, but only those whose names are written in the Lamb's book of life."[59]

In heaven, believers will have a glorified body for the Lord "will transform the body of our humble state into conformity with the body of His glory, by the exertion of the power that He has even to subject all things to Himself."[60] This glorified body will not grow old, weak, sick, or die. "He will wipe away every tear from their eyes; and there will no longer be any death; there will no longer be any mourning, or crying, or pain; the first things have passed away."[61]

Since there is no death in heaven, there is no need for procreation.[62] Also, "there will be no night there,"[63] and "there is no longer any sea."[64] Our new minds will be able to understand things fully. "For now, we see in a mirror dimly, but then face to face; now I know in part, but then I will know fully just as I also have been fully known."[65] "We know that when He appears, we will be like Him, because we will see Him just as He is."[66] We will partake of the "marriage supper of the lamb."[67] We will

---

54. Rev 21:1
55. Rev 20:10
56. Heb 2:14
57. 1 Cor 15:26
58. 1 Cor 15:54
59. Rev 21:27
60. Phil 3:21
61. Rev 21:4
62. Matt 22:30
63. Rev 21:25
64. Rev 21:1
65. 1 Cor 13:12
66. 1 John 3:2
67. Rev 19:9

receive our inheritance as children of God,[68] and a reward for our work on earth.[69] We will enjoy "a sabbath rest,"[70] worship God face to face,[71] and "reign forever and ever."[72]

Dr. Erickson affirmed: "The nature of the future states is far more intense than anything known in this life. The images used to depict them are quite inadequate to fully convey what lies ahead."[73] Whatever pains, sufferings, and evils believers encounter in their brief time on this earth will be redeemed by the goods/rewards[74] God has prepared for us, his children, in heaven.

In that eternal state, "how can Christians be free from committing evil (i.e., receive impeccability)?"

## Some Questions and Speculations

### How can peccable believers receive impeccability?

At this time in the present world, believers are betrothed to Christ. "I (Paul) betrothed[75] you to one husband, so that to Christ I might present you as a pure virgin."[76] The Church is now Christ's future bride,[77] eagerly awaiting his prophesied return. The betrothal period will end with a future marriage of Christ and the Church in heaven.

Believers will attend the ceremony as the bride, with Christ as the groom.[78] God's desire to have his "finished image" expressed in union

---

68. Rom 8:17, 1 Pet 1:4
69. 1 Cor 3:13-14
70. Heb 4:9
71. Rev 22:3-4
72. Rev 22:5
73. Millard Erickson, *Christian Theology*, 1139.
74. While it is true that believers will receive rewards for what they have done on earth, their motivation should be serving the Lord for the sake of love rather than with the expectation of rewards. "So, you too, when you do all the things which are commanded you, say, 'We are unworthy slaves; we have done only that which we ought to have done'" (Luke 17:10).
75. The Greek "Harmozo" means "to betroth, to give one in marriage to anyone." *Thayer's Greek Lexicon*. https://biblehub.com/greek/718.htm
76. 2 Cor 11:2
77. Eph 5:25-32
78. Rev 19:7-9

with humanity[79] will be accomplished when believers become part of the body with Christ as the head,[80] for "the two shall become one flesh. This mystery is great; but I am speaking with reference to Christ and the church."[81]

Concerning this union, Tatian declared: "Just as incorruptibility belongs to God, in the same way man might share God's lot and have immortality also."[82] Through "union with Christ" in marriage, as partakers of the divine nature,[83] we will share his immortality,[84] impeccability,[85] and incorruptibility,[86] being one with him and forever delivered from the presence of evil (moral, natural . . .).[87] "That impeccability belongs to the orthodox Christian concept of heaven is . . . beyond any doubt."[88] "Just as Jesus is free from all sin, so those who are in him . . . have no further power to sin left in them."[89] "The redeemed in heaven will be impeccable forever."[90] We will be free[91] from sins,[92] pains, and sufferings,[93] and enjoy our sabbath rest from the toils of this world.[94]

79. Herman Bavinck, *Reformed Dogmatics, Vol. 2*, 577.
80. Eph 5:23
81. Eph 5:31-32
82. Tatian, *Oratio ad Graecos and Fragments*, 12.
83. 2 Pet 1:4
84. Rev 21:4
85. Rev 21:27, Isa 35:8-9
86. 1 Cor 15:52 KJV
87. Rev 21:27
88. Simon Francis Gaine, *Will there Be Free Will in Heaven? Freedom, Impeccability and Beatitude*, 11.
89. Edward Malatesta, *Interiority and Covenant*, 247.
90. Luke Henderson, "Heaven," 179.
91. "If the redeemed (in heaven) are kept from sinning, their wills must be reined in, at least in some way. And, if their wills are reined in, it doesn't seem right to say that they are free. We will refer to this as the 'Problem of Heavenly Freedom.'" Timothy Pawl and Kevin Timpe, "Incompatibility, Sin, and Free Will in Heaven," 399. The redeemed in heaven are *impeccable* and, like God, can no longer sin. Yet, they are free like their Lord. "If the Son makes you free, you will be free indeed" (John 8:36). "The heavenly world . . . lacks . . . the good of being able to reject the good . . . there was some kind of reduction of freedom." Simon Gaine, *Will There Be Free Will in Heaven?* 108. The ability to reject the good and commit evil is not a good. Doing evil is to become a slave to evil, not having freedom. "Everyone who commits sin is the slave of sin" (John 8:34). In heaven, believers enjoy complete freedom from sin.
92. Rev 1:5 NIV.
93. Rev 21:4
94. Heb 4:9-10

However, we will not become Gods since the uncreated God cannot create uncreated Gods. Theologians over the centuries were careful to point out the difference between unity of love/fellowship and unity of essence/substance. "For Irenaeus . . . this is an exchange of properties, but it does not produce an identity of substance."[95] Dr. Fairbairn further elaborated on the concept:

> Like Athanasius,[96] but with much more precision, Cyril[97] distinguishes two kinds of unity between the Father and the Son. The first is a unity of substance, and the Father and the Son do not share this kind of unity with us in any way whatsoever. The second, though, is a unity of love or fellowship that the Father and the Son have enjoyed from all eternity precisely because of their unity of substance. Cyril argues that God does share this kind of unity with us.[98]

"We are said to be partakers of the Divine nature, not by any communication of the Divine essence to us, but by God's impressing upon us, and infusing into us, those divine qualities and dispositions (knowledge, righteousness, and true holiness) which do express and resemble the perfections of God."[99] By the marriage of Christ and the Church, we become partakers of the divine nature *without* sharing the divine essence/substance.[100] We will not experience God's uncreated self-existence/essence for we are created beings. Nevertheless, we will be like him "because we will see him just as he is."[101]

---

95. Paul Collins, *Partaking in Divine Nature*, 55.

96. "For he (Christ) was made man that we might be made God." Athanasius, *On the Incarnation*, 93.

97. "We are also made one with God    partakers of His Divine Nature." Cyril of Alexandria, *Commentary on John*. XI.12.

98. Donald Fairbairn, *Life in the Trinity*, 35-36.

99. Matthew Poole, *Annotations upon the Holy Bible*, Vol 3, 918.

100. "He has called men gods, that are deified of His Grace, not born of His Substance." Augustine, *Exposition on the Psalms*, 50:2. "They (God's promises) make us partakers of the divine nature . . . nature here is not essence but quality." John Calvin, *Commentaries on the Catholic Epistles*, 370–71. The doctrine of theosis (union with God, becoming like God) can be found in both eastern and western branches of Christianity. Daniel Clendenin, "Partakers of Divinity: The Orthodox Doctrine of Theosis." Kyle Strobel, "Jonathan Edwards's Reformed Doctrine of Theosis." Robert Rakestraw, "Becoming Like God: An Evangelical Doctrine of Theosis."

101. 1 John 3:2

"Union with Christ is the central truth of the whole doctrine of salvation."[102] Following our permanent and unbreakable union, we will be ushered into the eternal state. "We shall always be with the Lord,"[103] in an eternal love relationship with him.[104]

For Christians, the non-recommended path (our world of death, Adam's unwise choice) will eventually lead to the same eternal state as the original Eden/paradise, through holiness and impeccability in a marriage union with Christ,[105] albeit after a long and horribly painful detour, the loss of billions of souls to evil, and the required atoning death of Christ for humanity's sins.

Thus, God's recommended option (e.g., the path of life commanded to Adam) is *always* the better alternative.

## Why did God not immediately create impeccable creatures through marriage?

God's reasons are not explained in the Scriptures. Irenaeus decried: "For we cast blame upon Him (God), because we have not been made gods from the beginning."[106] We could speculate that God was waiting for Adam and Eve to procreate, as they were commanded *before* the Fall. "God blessed them; and God said to them, 'Be fruitful and multiply, and fill the earth, and subdue it.'"[107] The marriage to Christ could proceed once the full number of people (Adam, Eve, and their descendants, all alive as there is no death in Eden) was reached after a certain amount of time.

As the result of their union with Christ, all humans in heaven will share God's divine nature, including holiness and impeccability.[108]

Furthermore, it makes sense that, for a successful marriage, God wants Adam and Eve (and their descendants) to love him freely and

---

102. John Murray, *Redemption Accomplished and Applied*, 170.
103. 1 Thess 4:17
104. Rom 8:37-39
105. Eph 5:31-32
106. Irenaeus, *Against Heresies*, IV.38.
107. Gen 1:28
108. "Knowing God, he will be made like God." Clement of Alexandria, 167. "With regard to the full participation of the Divinity, which is the true bliss of man and end of human life; and this is bestowed upon us by Christ's humanity." Thomas Aquinas, *Summa Theologica*, 3.1.2.

willingly.[109] "A person's freely coming to love another being is intrinsically more valuable than a person's being made to love another being."[110] Prior to the start of the blessed eternal state, a testing period of love and obedience is necessary, since a no-choice love, or robotic love is no love at all! As "God is love,"[111] he does not coerce anyone to have a relationship with him. Jean Paul Sartre asserted:

> *The man who wants to be loved does not desire the enslavement of the beloved. He is not bent on becoming the object of passion which flows forth mechanically. He does not want to possess an automaton . . . The total enslavement of the beloved kills the love of the lover . . . the lover does not desire to possess the beloved as one possesses a thing; he demands a special type of appropriation. He wants to possess a freedom as freedom.*[112]

Origen observed: "If you take away the spontaneity of virtue, you destroy its essence."[113] A free will to choose to love God (the spontaneity of virtue) requires the *possibility* of denying him (evil). "He can't give these creatures the freedom to perform evil and at the same time prevent them from doing so,"[114] a "logical straitjacket to which even God is subject."[115] As God desires freely given love from his creatures, he must *logically* accept freely given rejection.

Adam's descendants who choose to follow God will enter heaven and be able to love the Lord for eternity. Those who decide otherwise will be ushered into an eternal state away from God, fulfilling their desire to assert their independence.

---

109. "Love . . . must be freely given and freely received." John Peckham, *Theodicy of Love*, 11. "It is clear that a relationship of love can only be maintained as long as the personal integrity and free autonomy of *both* partners is upheld." Vincent Brümmer, *The Model of Love*, 161.

110. William Rowe, "Paradox and Promise," 114.

111. 1 John 4:8

112. Jean Paul Sartre, *Being and Nothingness (L'Etre et le Néant)*, 343.

113. Origen, *Contra Celsum*, 4.3

114. Alvin Plantinga, *God, Freedom, and Evil*, 30.

115. Richard Swinburne, *Providence and the Problem of Evil*, 127.

## What would have happened had Adam chosen the path of obedience as commanded by God?

The Scriptures did not address the issue, except to say that Adam would have lived (rather than died).[116] We could speculate that, after a time of continued love and obedience, Adam, Eve (and their progeny) would be granted permanent righteousness and everlasting life. Dr. Horton opined: "Had Adam fulfilled the probation in the garden, God would have confirmed him and his descendants in righteousness and everlasting life forever."[117] Dr. Ashby disagreed: "My response is that this must be *read into* the text; it certainly is not something that a reader naturally gets from the text by normal exegetical methodology."[118] Following the historical-grammatical system of hermeneutics,[119] we agree and call Adam's "probation period" a speculation.

## What happened to Adam and Eve (and their descendants) when they disobeyed God?

Adam and Eve were created peccable, but in a state of innocence, without any actual sin. After the serpent's temptation, they fell and became slaves to sin. "Truly, truly, I say to you, everyone who commits sin is the slave of sin."[120] They were "held captive by him (the devil) to do his will,"[121] and became "by nature, children of wrath."[122]

However, in his great mercy, God provided Adam, Eve, and their descendants with a Savior (Eve's seed) who will "bruise you (the serpent) on the head."[123] People can be set free from their slavery to sin and Satan by Jesus the Messiah. "It was for freedom that Christ set us free; therefore, keep standing firm and do not be subject again to a yoke

---

116. Gen 2:17
117. Michael Horton, "A Classical Calvinist View," 32.
118. Stephen Ashby, "A Reformed Arminian Response," 51.
119. The "Chicago Statement on Biblical Inerrancy" signed by noted evangelicals stated: "We affirm that the text of Scripture is to be interpreted by grammatico-historical exegesis, taking account of its literary forms and devices, and that Scripture is to interpret Scripture." Norman Geisler, ed., *Inerrancy*, 497.
120. John 8:34
121. 2 Tim 2:26
122. Eph 2:3
123. Gen 3:15

of slavery."¹²⁴ "Live as free people, but do not use your freedom as a cover-up for evil."¹²⁵

Like our primordial ancestors, in God's sovereignty, we are given the freedom to choose good or evil, to follow God or reject him.

Antony was the youngest of three brothers. His father was a banker and his mother a farmer's daughter. As a schoolboy, he "went to chapel every day and twice on Sundays, but he didn't feel very 'religious.'"¹²⁶

After a stint in the Royal Aircraft Establishment during WWII, Antony resumed his studies and earned a PhD from Cambridge. "He successfully convinced the administration of Cambridge University to allocate £20,000 to the creation of Interplanetary Scintillation Array . . . this radio telescope was one of the pioneering projects of its type at that time. The high-quality data of this radio telescope allowed Antony Hewish and his student Jocelyn Bell to discover the first pulsar."¹²⁷ For his contribution to science, Dr. Hewish received the 1974 Nobel Prize in Physics.

Concerning God, Sir Antony Hewish said: "While I have been a doubter all my life and still am, I do believe in God and believe in supporting the local parish church; having thought a lot about it, I can't account for the world without God; to take the atheist view of Richard Dawkins seems to me to be total nonsense; I have read his book carefully and his arguments fall flat as far as I am concerned."¹²⁸ "It makes no sense to me to assume that the universe and our existence is [sic] just a cosmic accident, that life emerged due to random physical processes in an environment which simply happened to have the right properties."¹²⁹

Everyone is free to use his/her intellect to decide about the existence of God. The scholars Richard Dawkins and Antony Hewish considered the same facts and came to different conclusions.¹³⁰ No one is coerced

---

124. Gal 5:1

125. 1 Pet 2:16 NIV.

126. https://scienceandbelief.org/2013/02/07/antony-hewish-a-life-in-science-and-religion/

127. http://www.countercurrents.org/ziabari171012.htm

128. Antony Hewish, 2008. "Interview of Sir Antony Hewish." https://www.repository.cam.ac.uk/handle/1810/197579

129. Antony Hewish, "Science and God," 173.

130. Many scientists are theists. Isaac Newton developed the principles of Newtonian physics. Gregor Mendel was the father of modern genetics. Louis Pasteur was the proponent of the germ theory. Florence Nightingale was the founder of modern nursing. Samuel Morse developed the Morse code. George Lemaître formulated the Big Bang theory. Werner Heisenberg was a founder of quantum mechanics. 51% of scientists

by God to believe or disbelieve. Like Adam and Eve, sentient beings are endowed by their Creator with the unalienable right[131] to choose freely, follow their own paths, and live with the consequences.

## Why did God let animals suffer and die?

Several answers have been advanced. For example, animals are not fully conscious of their pains.[132] God loves animal species as a group, not as individuals, resulting in some animal suffering.[133] "God is not an animal as men are, and if he does not change his designs to avoid pain and suffering in animals, he is not violating any natural sympathies."[134] For various reasons, these suggestions have not garnered wide acceptance among philosophers and theologians.

We propose a different approach to answer the question. Before the Fall, Adam was created innocent in the Garden of Eden and enjoyed the benefit of living with God.[135] We could speculate that there were no sufferings and deaths of animals since creation was declared to be "very good."[136] The idyllic path of life was enjoyed by Adam and Eve for a time until the appearance of the serpent-tempter.[137]

In Eden, the sovereign Lord gave Adam the freedom[138] to choose between two options: remain in the path of life or depart to the path of death.[139] In love, God commanded Adam to choose the path of life. However, Adam was free to make up his mind, without God's interference.

---

who are members of the American Association for the Advancement of Science believe in God or a higher power. https://www.pewresearch.org/religion/2009/11/05/an-overview-of-religion-and-science-in-the-united-states/#:~:text=A%20poll%20of%20scientists%20who,God%20or%20a%20higher%20power.

131. "We hold these truths to be self-evident, that all men are created equal, that they are endowed by their Creator with certain unalienable Rights, that among these are Life, Liberty and the pursuit of Happiness." US Declaration of Independence, 1776. https://www.archives.gov/founding-docs/declaration-transcript

132. Peter Harrison, "Theodicy and Animal Pain."

133. Mark Maller, "Animals and the Problem of Evil in Recent Theodicies."

134. Peter Geach, *Providence and Evil*, 80.

135. Gen 1:28

136. Gen 1:31

137. Gen 3:1

138. Lee Thai, *Boundaries of Freedom*.

139. Gen 2:17

Sadly, in disobedience, Adam willfully made his ill-fated choice, was driven out of the world of life and condemned to live in the world of death. Observing this realm where death prevails, Dr. Dawkins bemoaned: "Natural selection is out there, and it is a very unpleasant process. Nature is red in tooth and claw. But I don't want to live in that kind of a world. I want to change the world in which I live in such a way that natural selection no longer applies."[140]

The path of death (our fallen world) entails the affliction and demise of animals and humans ("nature red in tooth and claw"). Obviously, this is neither the ideal world nor God's recommended option. The horrendous pains and atrocious sufferings in this fallen realm are not part of God's best plan for his creatures. "The whole creation groans and suffers the pains of childbirth together until now."[141]

Recognizing this universal principle of death and suffering, Buddha "proclaimed that suffering is an unavoidable reality of ordinary human existence (the First Noble Truth)."[142]

However, if we are unhappy with this world of death, we can choose a different path. We can decide to take the "way of escape,"[143] acknowledge God's existence, and receive the gift of eternal life (in the heavenly world) from the Savior Jesus Christ. "I am the way, and the truth, and the life; no one comes to the Father but through Me."[144] "The last Adam (Christ) became a life-giving spirit."[145] God provides everyone with a "safe exit" through the Messiah. "I am the door; if anyone enters through Me, he will be saved."[146] We can decide to accept this generous offer or reject it!

## Summary

As a result of the Fall, we now live in a world of death with its horrendous evils (e.g., the 9/11 terrorist attack, COVID-19). However, we are free to escape and accept the Messiah's offer of substitution or persist and perish in this "vale of suffering." The final destiny of hell (living without

---

140. Frank Miele, "Darwin's Dangerous Disciple: An Interview with Richard Dawkins," 84.
141. Rom 8:22
142. Phillip Moffitt, *Dancing with Life: Buddhist Insights*, 28.
143. 1 Cor 10:13
144. John 14:6
145. 1 Cor 15:45
146. John 10:9

God) or heaven (living with God) is determined by humans endowed with free will by their omnibenevolent Creator. The Christians' pains and sufferings on this earth will be redeemed by the goods (rewards) they will receive in heaven (the answer to our fifth question).

Concerning the believers' "union with Christ and impeccability," we advocate that union is accomplished through the marriage of Christ (the second person of the Trinity) and the Church (the body of believers). Believers will be *one with Christ* in an everlasting bond of matrimony and will share the divine attributes (e.g., impeccability, immortality).

So far, we have provided compelling answers to five difficult problems raised at the beginning of our journey. Let us now consider our sixth question, "What are some practical means to manage the evils in our lives and help others in their sufferings?"

# 6

# What Are Some Practical Means to Manage the Evils in Our Lives and Help Others in Their Suffering?

> *We bereaved are not alone. We belong to the largest company in all the world—the company of those who have known suffering. When it seems that our sorrow is too great to be borne, let us think of the great family of the heavy-hearted into which our grief has given us entrance, and, inevitably, we will feel about us their arms, their sympathy, their understanding.*
>
> —Helen Keller[1]

PASTORAL LOVE AND CARE for people are no less important than a theological and philosophical defense of the coexistence of God and evil. "The *religious problem of evil* is not primarily about justifying God's ways to man but about how one can live with this God, how can we help people through this difficult time in their life."[2] The question can be addressed on a personal level and a pastoral care level. We will offer some practical means to manage the evils in our lives and some concrete steps to relieve the sufferings of our fellow human beings.

---

1. Helen Keller, *We Bereaved*, Preface.
2. John Feinberg, *The Many Faces of Evil*, 321.

## How to Manage Personal Evils

Evils may come into our lives as trials or temptations. How should we cope with these unwelcome predicaments that plague our existence? In these trying circumstances, we can adopt five practical measures to manage our personal adversity: Refocus, Escape, Change, Accept, and Praise (RECAP). Let us first address the problem of temptations.

### Temptations.

A temptation is "the desire to have or do something, especially something wrong, or something that causes this desire."[3] Temptations may be the results of our own doing (e.g., cheating on our taxes) or may come from the twisted actions of others (e.g., enticement to commit adultery). Temptations *never* come from God for he "does not tempt anyone."[4]

### Temptations of our own doing (Refocus).

"Each one is tempted when he is carried away and enticed by his own lust. Then when lust has conceived, it gives birth to sin; and when sin is accomplished, it brings forth death."[5] The German theologian Rudolf Bultmann asserted: "Men are often carried away by their passions and are no longer master of themselves, with the result that inconceivable wickedness breaks forth from them."[6]

As human beings, we are tempted by the desire for power, prestige/pride, pleasures, and possessions (the four Ps of temptation). Lord Acton asserted: "Power tends to corrupt, and absolute power corrupts absolutely."[7] Pope Gregory affirmed: "Pride is the root of all evil."[8] Hugh Hefner declared: "The major civilizing force in the world is not religion, it is sex."[9] Christopher Hitchens acknowledged: "Of course, I

---

3. https://dictionary.cambridge.org/us/dictionary/english/temptation
4. Jas 1:13
5. Jas 1:14-15
6. Rudolf Bultmann, *Rudolf Bultmann: Interpreting Faith*, 294.
7. Lord Acton, quoted by David Sorensen, "Power Tends to Corrupt," 83.
8. Pope Gregory, quoted by Michael Dyson, *Pride: The Seven Deadly Sins*, 10.
9. Hugh Hefner, quoted by John Helpern, "To the Mansion Born." https://www.vanityfair.com/culture/2010/08/playboy-hugh-hefer-201008

do everything for money."[10] "For all that is in the world, the lust of the flesh and the lust of the eyes and the boastful pride of life, is not from the Father, but is from the world."[11]

The road to success for many people starts with the accumulation of wealth (*possessions*). Of the four Ps, this is usually the easiest to attain. The next item on the agenda (for men) is the acquisition of a "trophy wife/mistress" for *pleasure*. Extravagant wealth and the company of beautiful women bring more *prestige* in the eyes of the world, feeding one's pride. Finally, as the crowning achievement of one's life, one seeks the ultimate prize of *power* (e.g., president of the US).

The path of the four Ps can lead to utter disaster. In the eyes of God, "many who are first will be last; and the last, first."[12] "If anyone wants to be first, he shall be last of all and servant of all."[13] Being first in the world (climbing up the ladder of success) is being last in heaven (sliding down the ladder of rewards). Up is down and down is up in the kingdom of God!

King Solomon had everything, total *power* over his subjects, enormous *prestige* as the ruler of a major empire, untold *pleasures* (700 wives and 300 concubines),[14] and vast *possessions*.[15] Despite the successful acquisition of the four Ps, how did his life end? "The Lord was angry with Solomon because his heart was turned away from the Lord . . . I will surely tear the kingdom from you and will give it to your servant."[16] What must we do then to counter the four Ps of evil and temptation?

Instead of lusting after the four Ps, one should follow King David's example and pursue one goal alone. "One thing I have asked from the Lord, that I shall seek: that I may dwell in the house of the Lord all the days of my life, to behold the beauty of the Lord and to meditate in His temple."[17] In the New Testament, we observe the same principle. "But only one thing is necessary, for Mary has chosen the good part, which

---

10. Christopher Hitchens, quoted by Deborah Solomon. "Questions for Christopher Hitchens: The Contrarian." https://www.nytimes.com/2010/06/06/magazine/06fob-q4-t.html?ref=magazine

11. 1 John 2:16

12. Matt 19:30

13. Mark 9:35

14. 1 Kgs 11:3

15. 1 Kgs 10:11-29

16. 1 Kgs 11:9,11

17. Ps 27:4

shall not be taken away from her."[18] What is the good part chosen by Mary and David? It is summarized in the "Great and Foremost" commandment: "You shall love the Lord your God with all your heart, and with all your soul, and with all your mind."[19]

Richard was born in California, the son of a Baptist minister and a high school librarian. He felt the call to full time ministry when he was a 19-year-old college student. After seminary, he started a small church of 200 people in a high school theater. He subsequently pioneered some novel church growth methods and expanded his ministry to encompass 80 different facilities, reaching 20,000 people a week. He authored works on church growth and Christian development. His blockbuster devotional book, *The Purpose Driven Life*, sold over 20 million copies and was on the New York Times Bestseller list for 96 weeks. His net worth was said to be 25 million dollars.

What did Rick (Richard Duane) Warren do with all this wealth? "Kay and I had to make a decision about what we would do with those resources. We decided to start reverse-tithing. We started giving away 90% of the income we were receiving and living off the other 10%, and I stopped taking a salary. I'm Saddleback's busiest volunteer!"[20] "I drive a 12-year-old Ford, have lived in the same house for the last 22 years, bought my watch at Wal-Mart, and I don't own a boat or a jet."[21]

The French friar Brother Lawrence counseled: "We ought to give ourselves up to God, with regard both to things temporal and spiritual, and seek our satisfaction only in the fulfillment of His will, whether He leads us by suffering or by consolation, for all would be equal to a soul truly resigned."[22] If we *refocus* single-mindedly on the Lord, we will overcome the four Ps of temptations and live worthy of our calling as children of God.[23]

---

18. Luke 10:42

19. Matt 22:37

20. Rick Warren. "Rick Warren on the 3 Privileges & Temptations of Leadership." https://www.visionroom.com/rick-warren-3-privileges-temptations-leadership/

21. Megan Schmidt, "8 Richest Pastors in America." http://www.beliefnet.com/faiths/christianity/8-richest-pastors-in-america.aspx?p=8

22. Brother Lawrence, *The Practice of the Presence of God*, 2.

23. Col 1:10

*Temptations from other people (Escape).*

In this fallen world, we often face many temptations coming from people around us.[24] For example, Michael Franzese was tempted by the Mafia to sell illegal gasoline. 14-year-old Johnny Lee Clary was persuaded by David Duke, the KKK Grand Wizard to join the secret organization.

In times of temptations,[25] God always provides a way of escape. No one is "doomed" to sin and commit evil. "But with the temptation, (God) will provide the way of escape also, so that you will be able to endure it."[26] Temptations from others can (and must) be resisted.[27]

William was the eldest of four children, the son of a Scotch-Irish dairy farmer. When he was fifteen, with the end of Prohibition in 1933, his teetotaler father force-fed him and his sister beer, and made him "so sick that he developed a lifelong distaste for drinking alcohol."[28] After college, he launched a radio program called *Songs in the Night* with George Beverly Shea. William subsequently became the first full-time evangelist of Youth for Christ and traveled extensively throughout the US and Europe.

In 1949, Billy (William Franklin) Graham started his trademark crusade in Los Angeles and eventually preached at 417 evangelistic campaigns in 185 countries. He became a spiritual adviser to presidents, being particularly close to Richard Nixon. "Billy Graham loved and trusted Richard Nixon and saw the best in him." This close relationship led to "the now-famous 1973 Nixon White House tape recording in which Graham makes disparaging comments about the Jews (for which he apologized in 2002) . . . He said, 'I think it was like locker room talk. I was just trying to go along and ingratiate myself.'"[29]

When I was a young Christian, an older believer asked me to partner with him in a novel evangelistic venture to share the good news of Christ with some "unreached people." He proposed a scheme to go as a team to *strip clubs*, meet some patrons and workers there, have some

---

24. and from spiritual powers (1 Thess 3:5).

25. Gen 39:11-12

26. 1 Cor 10:13

27. Jas 4:7

28. Seth Dunn. "Billy Graham, America's Pastor." http://pulpitandpen.org/2018/02/21/billy-graham-americas-pastor-dead-age-99/

29. Timothy Morgan. "Billy in the Oval Office." https://www.christianitytoday.com/ct/2018/billy-graham/billy-graham-presidents-oval-office-confidante.html

drinks, and explain God's plan of salvation. Being young and single, I was tempted by the suggestion, especially with its spiritual justification. Thankfully, remembering my "thorn in the flesh," the lack of alcohol metabolizing enzyme, I declined the offer. He then proceeded to ask for my financial support in this innovative "ministry," request which I refused as I had no significant source of income.

Hence, we need to be vigilant and watchful for temptations from others (e.g., to ingratiate ourselves with presidents, to evangelize in strip clubs) when we rub shoulders with people in the halls of power, the circles of prestige, the houses of pleasure, and the temples of wealth and possessions. "Be of sober spirit, be on the alert. Your adversary, the devil, prowls around like a roaring lion, seeking someone to devour."[30] Amid temptations, we must be mindful of the Lord's admonition and take the *escape* path that God provides (e.g., avoid locker room talk and strip clubs). "Your ears will hear a word behind you, saying, 'This is the way, walk in it.'"[31]

Besides temptations, we also faced many trials in this fallen world. Where do trials come from and how do we manage them?

## Trials.

A trial is "an annoying or frustrating or catastrophic event."[32] Trials and difficulties can be of our own doing, often come from other people's actions, and may be brought in our lives by God.

### *Trials of our own making (Change).*

He was born in a poor family surviving on government aid and charity from neighbors. His identical twin, delivered 35 minutes before him, died at childbirth. His father was jailed for check fraud.[33]

Being an average student in school, he found his special calling in music. Success followed success as he cut records, performed on radio and television shows, starred in 31 films, won 3 Grammy awards for his

---

30. 1 Pet 5:8
31. Isa 30:21
32. https://www.vocabulary.com/dictionary/trial
33. https://elvisdaily.com/2020/02/07/february-6-1939-elvis-presleys-father-vernon-was-released-from-the-parchman-farm/

gospel music, went on concert tours packed with adulating crowds, and even met President Nixon at the White House.

From his early upbringing, he loved breakfast of eggs, sausage, bacon, and fried biscuits, dinner of meatloaf, and "party meatballs" (meatballs wrapped in bacon), snacks of the famous fried "peanut butter, banana, and bacon" sandwich.

On this diet of 12,000 calories per day, he ballooned to 350 pounds.[34] Elvis Presley, the king of Rock and Roll, died at the youthful age of forty-two from a heart attack, leaving behind a great legacy, sadly cut short. In 2018, he was honored with a posthumous Presidential Medal of Freedom, the highest civilian award of the United States, for his contribution to American culture.

Cognizant of diet-related health problems, "Americans spend north of $60 billion annually to try to lose pounds, on everything from paying for gym memberships and joining weight-loss programs to drinking diet soda."[35] Unfortunately, it is difficult to keep up the motivation to diet and workout. "The number of active dieters is estimated to have fallen 10% since 2015, to 97 million, due to a growing size acceptance movement and dieter fatigue."[36]

Even though I weighed only 130 pounds, I could eat quantities of food that would put sumo wrestlers to shame! On a trip to an all-you-can-eat restaurant that served my favorite fare, crab legs, I went back to the buffet so many times that the attendant started to give me the evil eye! Not to be deprived, I decided to delegate the refill chores to my "better half." That lasted for a while until "honeybunny" retreated into her rabbit hole and refused to come out, despite my earnest pleadings. What was there to do? How about my mother-in-law? "Mom, can you get me some more crab legs?" Mom obligingly took over the catering duties. "Let the boy eat, he is still hungry!" At the end of the feast, mom contemplated the piles of shells, napkins, and plates filling the table to overflowing and sweetly commented in awe (and hopefully admiration): "I have never seen anything like this my whole life!"

---

34. https://www.thestatesman.com/entertainment/kings-bizarre-diet-1502440622.html

35. Geoff Williams, "The Heavy Price of Losing Weight." https://money.usnews.com/money/personal-finance/articles/2013/01/02/the-heavy-price-of-losing-weight

36. Market Research. https://www.prnewswire.com/news-releases/us-weight-loss-market-worth-66-billion-300573968.html

Unfortunately, all this culinary excess in my early days dropped a monkey wrench in my digestive system, ushering in the unholy trifecta of high cholesterol, high blood pressure, and high glucose, forcing me to make some drastic changes. The standard meal for me now is "Buddha's Delight," a dish doubly healthy for the body as well as for the soul, but dreadfully unappetizing for my taste buds!

When trials come (e.g., health issues, financial difficulties, marital problems), we need to be proactive in formulating an appropriate response. For example, an illness due to smoking calls for a personal change in lifestyle. Money problems require asking for help in establishing a budget. Marital discord may necessitate sessions with a counselor. Charles Spurgeon observed: "Trials teach us what we are; they dig up the soil and let us see what we are made of."[37]

If we need wisdom in managing our trials, we can come to "God's throne of grace with confidence, so that we may receive mercy and find grace to help us in our time of need."[38] "If any of you lacks wisdom, let him ask of God, who gives to all generously and without reproach, and it will be given to him."[39] With God's help, we can *change*, overcome our trials, and grow in Christ's likeness.[40]

While some trials are of our own making, others can come from people and God.

### Trials from other people and from God (Accept).

One day, as I came home from the hospital, my wife met me at the door with the disturbing news that we had been sued for medical malpractice. My wife was also named in the lawsuit as we lived in a community property state. I promptly reported the incident to my malpractice carrier and was assigned an attorney for my defense. After reviewing the facts of the case, the lawyer concluded that the patient was suing everyone connected to the surgery, not just me. Meetings with legal professionals, depositions for the plaintiff's counsel, and sleepless nights followed. This went on for two years before my wife and I were finally

---

37. Charles Spurgeon, *The Complete Sermons of C.H. Spurgeon, Book 1*, 208.
38. Heb 4:16 NIV.
39. Jas 1:5
40. 2 Cor 3:18

dropped from the lawsuit. Even so, I had to report the occurrence to all the hospitals where I was on staff.

Trials may come from other people's actions (lawsuits, drunk drivers . . .). We can take some measures to minimize these occurrences (e.g., not driving late at night). However, unexpected afflictions are just part of living in this fallen world. The Lord forewarned: "In the world you have tribulation but take courage; I have overcome the world."[41] As children of God, we are exhorted, "Never pay back evil for evil to anyone,"[42] and "Love your enemies, do good to those who hate you, bless those who curse you, pray for those who mistreat you."[43] We need to *accept* our adversities, forgive others,[44] and "live at peace with everyone,"[45] for we are "called to peace."[46]

Besides trials from others, we may also experience trials from God. It hardly ever rained in Phoenix. However, the monsoon season (June to September), when it arrived, could be brutal. One summer, hail, torrential rains, and violent winds lashed my neighborhood. My water damage was extensive. This necessitated a call to the insurance company to help with the repairs. From that experience, I learned that I needed to better control my temper and frustration in dealing with the insurance company, the contractor, the mounds of paperwork, and the haggling about the insurance money. I thought that I was a "pretty good Christian," but I was quickly disabused of that notion! This trial taught me to better control my emotions (edification), prevented me from embarking into any house remodeling (deterrence/shielding), and made me a little more mature and useful to the Lord (rehabilitation). Trials from God's hands are necessary for my personal growth (training), and I am thankful that he brings them without asking for my consent (which I would have probably refused)!

"In this you greatly rejoice, even though now for *a little while, if necessary*, you have been distressed by various trials."[47] How long is "a little while"? Even if the trial lasts our whole life, we can still consider the eighty or ninety years a "short while" in the light of eternity. Fanny Crosby was blind almost from birth (six weeks old) and yet persevered in

41. John 16:33
42. Rom 12:17
43. Luke 6:27-28
44. Mark 11:25
45. Rom 12:18
46. Col 3:15 NIV.
47. 1 Pet 1:6

the faith until her death at the age of ninety-four. She penned more than eight thousand hymns including the beloved "Blessed Assurance,"[48] and "To God Be the Glory."

"Consider it *all joy*, my brethren, when you encounter various trials, knowing that the testing of your faith produces endurance."[49] I must confess that I do not meet the standard of the apostle's exhortation. Nevertheless, like the rest of my fellow pilgrims, I have not given up and will continue to fight "the good fight" and grow in Christlikeness. In humility[50] and trust, we need to *accept* trials, whether from people or God, as they are meant for our edification.

Sadly, no one is immune from tribulations. In our short stay on this earth, facing the evils in our lives, we are free to decide how to respond to God amid our pain and suffering.

## How Should We Respond to God Who Does Not Prevent the Evils in Our Lives?

### Rejection of God.

"We find that anywhere between one third and two thirds of people we've surveyed in the United States admit they sometimes feel angry at God in response to some current thing they are suffering with, such as a cancer diagnosis."[51] Rejections of God for perceived injustices (e.g., deaths of innocent children) or undeserved pains and sufferings (e.g., excruciating illnesses) are common occurrences.

Robert was the son of a billboard mogul who raised him to be a self-made man by beating him with a coat hanger and charging him rent in the summer. He "really was a deeply religious boy, despite his father's emotional abuse. He intended at one point to become a missionary."[52] His only sibling, Mary Jean, a bright and pretty girl two years younger,

---

48. co-written with Phoebe Knapp.

49. Jas 1:2-3

50. "Humility involves the full knowledge of our status as creatures, a clear consciousness as having received everything we have from God." Dietrich von Hildebrand, *Transformation in Christ (Die Umgestaltung in Christus)*, 157.

51. Lee Dye, "Are You Angry at God?" https://abcnews.go.com/Technology/angry-god-thirds-americans-blame-god-problems-survey/story?id=12540557

52. Rod Dreher, "God Bless Ted Turner." https://www.nationalreview.com/2003/02/god-bless-ted-turner-rod-dreher/

developed a rare form of lupus at the age of twelve. She was treated by many doctors, unfortunately without much success, and subsequently developed severe encephalitis that left her brain damaged. She was continually in pain and begged God to let her die.

Robert prayed to God an hour a day for the recovery of his beloved sister. However, all his desperate entreaties were for naught. She suffered for five long years before she finally passed away.

This disastrous event shattered Robert's world. "My family broke apart. I thought, 'How could God let my sister suffer so much?'"[53]

> "It shook my faith," he said, "particularly since I prayed a lot and she had not done anything wrong at all and she suffered so badly. We were taught that God was all powerful and all-loving, that God was love. It was hard for me to rationalize how he could let her suffer, because she'd lost her mind, too." She used to say, "God, I'm in so much pain; please let me die." It took five years, and finally he let her die. I was not happy about it. I didn't feel like it was warranted.[54]

"What had she done wrong? And I couldn't get any answers. Christianity couldn't give me any answers to that."[55]

"These events happened nearly half a century ago, but he speaks of them as if they had occurred last week."[56] This agonizing experience led Ted Turner (Robert Edward Turner III), the founder of CNN and head of Time Warner, to declare that "Christianity is a religion for losers."[57]

Withdrawals from God are often the results of traumatic events like the death of a child, the birth of a special needs offspring, divorces, or atrocities in the world (e.g., murders). While such a response is understandable in this realm replete with heartbreaking evils, is there a better alternative?

---

53. Ibid.

54. Steve Fennessy, "Ted Turner." https://www.atlantamagazine.com/great-reads/ted-turner-may2011/

55. Ann O'Neill. "The Reinvention of Ted Turner." https://www.cnn.com/2013/11/17/us/ted-turner-profile/index.html

56. Rod Dreher, "God Bless Ted Turner." https://www.nationalreview.com/2003/02/god-bless-ted-turner-rod-dreher/

57. Ann O'Neill. "The Reinvention of Ted Turner." https://www.cnn.com/2013/11/17/us/ted-turner-profile/index.html. Ted Turner later said: "I regret anything I said about religion that was negative." https://www2.cbn.com/article/judging-others/enlightenment-ted-turner

## Submission to God (Praise).

Christians can choose to submit to God and accept their pains and sufferings, remembering the promise of their Lord, "After you have suffered for a little while, the God of all grace, who called you to His eternal glory in Christ, will Himself perfect, confirm, strengthen and establish you."[58] Whatever happens, happens only by the will of a loving Father *for the good of his children*.[59] "For the Lord God is a sun and shield; The Lord gives grace and glory; no good thing does He withhold from those who walk uprightly."[60] Thus, we can confidently say, "The Lord is my helper, I will not be afraid. What will man do to me?"[61] No matter what circumstances we are in, we can trust and obey our benevolent Creator.

She was the youngest child of a Dutch Calvinist watchmaker who taught her the intricate craft. She became the first licensed woman watchmaker in the Netherlands. She never married and collaborated with her father Casper in their small sales and repair shop. "The family members were devout Christians, active members of the Dutch Reformed church, and . . . participated in several charitable aid projects in Haarlem."[62]

In 1940, Germany invaded the Netherlands and herded Jews to concentration camps. Her family started hiding Jews and Dutch resistance members in a specially built secret room in their house. Unfortunately, on February 28, 1944, they were betrayed by an informer, arrested, and sent to prison. 84-year-old Casper died ten days later and was buried in a pauper's grave. Corrie ten Boom and her sister Betsie were sent to Ravensbrück concentration camp "where they lived under conditions of near-starvation, backbreaking manual labor, and vermin infestation."[63] Betsie's health deteriorated, and she died in Ravensbrück on December 16, 1944. Corrie was released on Christmas day, 1944, probably due to a "clerical error."

Corrie ten Boom recounted:

---

58. 1 Pet 5:10

59. unless we choose to disobey his commands and do whatever we want. "God causes all things to work together for good *to those who love God*" (Rom 8:28).

60. Ps 84:11

61. Heb 13:6

62. https://www.encyclopedia.com/history/encyclopedias-almanacs-transcripts-and-maps/ten-boom-corrie

63. Ibid.

> "Often I have heard people say, 'How good God is! We prayed that it would not rain for our church picnic and look at the lovely weather!' Yes, God is good when He sends good weather. But God was also good when He allowed my sister, Betsie, to starve to death before my eyes in a German concentration camp. I remember one occasion when I was very discouraged there. Everything around us was dark, and there was darkness in my heart. I remember telling Betsie that I thought God had forgotten us. 'No, Corrie,' said Betsie, 'He has not forgotten us. Remember His Word: For as the heavens are high above the earth, so great is His steadfast love toward those who fear Him.'"[64]

"God has plans—not problems—for our lives. Before she died in the concentration camp in Ravensbrück, my sister Betsie said to me, 'Corrie, your whole life has been a training for the work you are doing here in prison—and for the work you will do afterward.'"[65] "[We] must tell people what we have learned here. We must tell them that there is no pit so deep that He (God) is not deeper still. They will listen to us, Corrie, because we have been here."[66]

After the war, Corrie spoke about her experience, and endeavored to redress the evils perpetrated during the Nazi reign of terror.

> [She] became a popular speaker around the world. Thousands attended her meetings as she talked about how she had learned to forgive her captors just as Christ had forgiven her sins. After each meeting, people surrounded her and heaped accolades on her for her godly qualities and thanked her for encouraging them in their walk with the Lord. Corrie said she would then return to her hotel room, get down on her knees, and present those compliments in thanks to God. She called it giving God "a bouquet of praise."[67]

Amid our pain and suffering (e.g., Ted Turner, Corrie ten Boom), we are free to choose between the two paths offered in the ancient book of Job. We can "curse God and die,"[68] or we can *praise* God in full submission and obedience, "The Lord gave, and the Lord has taken away.

---

64. Corrie ten Boom, quoted by Emerson Eggerichs, *The 4 Wills of God*, 108.
65. Corrie ten Boom, *Tramp for the Lord*, 11.
66. Corrie ten Boom, *The Hiding Place*, 211.
67. Anne Cetas, "A Bouquet of Praise." https://odb.org/US/2011/02/27/a-bouquet-of-praise
68. Job 2:9

Blessed be the name of the Lord."[69] Whatever decision we make, we will have to live with the consequences.

In times of trials and temptations, we need to *refocus* our priorities away from the four Ps to God, take the way of *escape* provided by our loving Lord, *change* when he reveals our weaknesses, *accept* and love others, and *praise* God for his goodness and help (RECAP).

Once we have learned that "God causes all things to work together for good to those who love God," we can draw strength from his comfort and in turn comfort others. "Blessed be the God and Father of our Lord Jesus Christ, the Father of mercies and God of all comfort, who comforts us in all our affliction so that we will be able to comfort those who are in any affliction with the comfort with which we ourselves are comforted by God."[70] How can we help others with God's comfort?

## How to Help People Suffering from Evil

People in the throes of pain and suffering may not be open to a theological or philosophical discussion about the problem of evil. Dr. Ekstrom cautioned: "Alleged divine justifications . . . are often the last thing a suffering person needs to hear."[71] How can we best help sufferers in their difficulties? We will first discuss what we should avoid doing. We will then explain what is more helpful in these demanding situations.

### What to avoid.

There are five main things we need to avoid: Downplay, Advise, Rebuke, Evaporate, and Sermonize (DARES).

### Downplay.

We can inadvertently downplay other people's feelings. The top spot in this category goes to the widely used "I know how you feel." 100 percent of the respondents surveyed[72] disliked this expression of sympathy. Dr.

---

69. Job 1:21
70. 2 Cor 1:3-4
71. Laura Ekstrom, "A Christian Theodicy," 267.
72. Northwest Infant Survival & SIDS Alliance. https://www.nwsids.org/Dos%20 and%20Donts.pdf

Krauss, a professor of counseling, acknowledged: "I can only imagine how another feels, and sometimes the reach of my experience is so short as to only approximate what another feels."[73]

> Shortly after my loss, I was filling out a form at the bank. One of the questions was what my status was. In the past, the answer was always 'married,' but now, I was being forced to check the 'widowed' box. I could not bring myself to check the 'single' box because in my heart I was still married. So, I did what any normal griever would do in that situation, I started to cry. The teller asked me if I was okay. Did I need anything? The response in my head was, "Yes, I wish that I was still able to check the 'married' box!" I told her that I lost my spouse and she said, "I am so sorry. I know how you feel." So, I asked her if she also lost her spouse and she said no, that he was alive and well. I know that she was feeling sorry for me, and maybe even trying to help, but could she possibly know how I felt if she had never lost a spouse?[74]

Since our feelings and emotions are uniquely our own, *no one* can know how we feel. And even if others do know (e.g., they had the same situation in their lives), they do not *presently* feel the gut-wrenching pain we do. Observing their calm demeanor amid the agony of our inner turmoil, our feelings seem unvalidated and devalued. Many sufferers "said that the comment ("I know how you feel") caused them to feel robbed of the dignity of their particular and unique relationship with the person who died."[75]

Equating the sufferer's situation with our own is counterproductive. Harvey Fierstein related a stormy scene between a recent widow and her child who had experienced a painful break-up.

> Wait, wait, wait. Are you trying to compare my marriage with you and Alan? Your father and I were married for thirty-five years, had two children and a wonderful life together. You have the nerve to compare yourself to that? . . . How could you possibly know what that felt like? It took me two months until I could sleep in our bed alone, a year to say 'I' instead of 'we' . . . How dare you?[76]

---

73. Kurt Krauss, quoted by John Sommers-Flanagan and Rita Sommers-Flanagan, *Counseling and Psychotherapy Theories*, 110.

74. Gary Sturgis, *Grief: Hope in the Aftermath*, 64.

75. Russell Friedman, "Why You Should Never Say 'I Know How You Feel!'" https://www.griefrecoverymethod.com/blog/2013/08/why-you-should-never-say-i-know-how-you-feel-0

76. Harvey Fierstein, *Torch Song Trilogy*, 154.

Well-meaning friends and relatives also try to comfort sufferers by comparing their pains with other people's travails, unwittingly minimizing the felt torments. "My neighbor's pains are much worse than yours." "It's not that bad, there is someone worse off." "It's no big deal, my friend had it many times." "It could be worse; it could be cancer like your sister's leukemia." All these statements, while true, do not alleviate the suffering and ease the pain. If anything, the grief-stricken feel the harsh sting of "crybaby!" as their afflictions are discredited. Psychological downplaying of the sufferers' emotions can be exceedingly detrimental to their well-being.

Good-hearted individuals may also attempt to cheer the wounded by pointing out the positive side of the situation. "At least, you still have one child left." As we all know, this does nothing to ease the torment of the loss of the other child. "At least, it was quick." However, was it not too quick as we desperately want to spend a little more time with our loved one? "At least he died happy" or "She would have wanted it this way." Maybe so. However, the mourner whom we are trying to comfort is not happy and does not want it to happen this way! "At least he had a long life." Obviously, that is not long enough for the bereft widow! All these attempts at comforting the broken-hearted, while well-intentioned, fall far short of the mark as they *downplay* the sufferers' feelings.

Dr. Parkes, a psychiatrist, suggested instead: "We can often reassure them (the sufferers) of the normality of grief . . . and show by our own behavior and attitudes that it is permissible to express grief. If we feel moved to tears at such times, there is no harm in showing it."[77] "In everything, therefore, treat people the same way you want them to treat you, for this is the Law and the Prophets."[78]

*Advise.*

Suffering people do not appreciate the barrage of prying questions coming from relatives, friends, acquaintances, and even strangers. What happened? What are you going to do? Did she have surgery? How much did that operation cost? Meddlers intrude in matters that do not concern them. Presumptuous inquiries cause much embarrassment and hard feelings as privacy is not respected. "The bereaved indicate that (a) they

---

77. Colin Parkes, "Coping with Loss," 859.
78. Matt 7:12

conceptualize information surrounding the death and their grief as private, (b) they create rules to govern their private information, and (c) violations of those rules result in turbulence."[79] It is best to respect these boundaries in our attempt to support those who grieve.

Furthermore, after some nosy scrutiny, people often feel entitled to give unsolicited advice. "Have you tried this new medicine?" "Here is what you should do." "This is what worked for me." "You can always have more children." "You can get remarried." Nobody wants to hear unsolicited advice. "At all ages, unasked-for support was regarded as more unpleasant than pleasant, primarily because it implied incompetence."[80]

Being a physician, I am sometimes asked to call sick church members to offer "medical advice." I always make it a rule to have them contact me rather than me contacting them. Often, I hear nothing more, meaning that my advice is not needed or even welcome. "Make it your ambition to lead a quiet life and attend to your own business."[81] Prayers (rather than *advice*) are sometimes the best things we can do for our brothers and sisters during their trials. "Pray for one another so that you may be healed. The effective prayer of a righteous man can accomplish much."[82]

*Rebuke.*

People often process their own griefs by rebuking the sufferers. What did you do (causing that death)? Why did you do that? What did you learn from that? Obviously, this is not helping the situation since the guilt-ridden person is already well-aware of his/her shortcomings and does not need to be reminded and rebuked.

Furthermore, "grieving men are at a disadvantage compared to women because their grieving is compared against their female counterparts, which puts them in a double bind. On one hand, they feel expected to be strong and not express their sadness, and on the other hand, they are criticized for not expressing their feelings."[83]

---

79. Erin Basinger et al., "Grief Communication and Privacy Rules."

80. Jacqui Smith and Jacqueline Goodnow, "Unasked-for Support and Unsolicited Advice."

81. 1 Thess 4:11

82. Jas 5:16.

83. Jeanne Rothaupt and Kent Becker, "A Literature Review of Western Bereavement Theory," 10.

After my mother's suicide over my dad's adultery, my maternal grandmother, who was living with us, packed her bags to go live with my aunt. However, before leaving, she caused a scene right in front of our house, in clear view of the assembled neighbors and curious passersby, loudly berating my grieving (yet stoic) dad over his affair, the wretched betrayal that "killed my daughter!"

While I understood the reason for her anger-laden outburst, the rebuke neither changed the heartbreaking plight (three little kids without a mother and now without a grandmother) nor caused my guilt-ridden dad to apologize for his trespass. If anything, the harsh reprimand only aggravated the problem and prolonged the healing process necessary for any future reconciliation.[84] "Forgive, and you will be forgiven."[85]

Accusations directed at the grieving parties by relatives are often meant to deflect blame or take revenge for past slights. "It's your fault!" "These are the natural consequences of your actions!" This situation is not uncommon even among Christians. "'Living with the saints above may be glory but living with the saints below is quite another story.' When people stumble, they need help, not criticism from the 50-yard line. Maybe you've heard the quip: 'Only Christians shoot their wounded.'"[86]

The criticisms may also be aimed at the sufferers' spiritual states, calling into question the genuineness of their faith. "A good Christian should not be depressed." "Healing (from grief and depression) is available if you truly believe," "if you have enough faith," "if you pray harder." The suffering person is now doubly burdened by the adversity and the supposed "lack of faith."

Grief must not be criticized. Instead of *rebuking* the sufferer, we should offer encouraging words that may bring "grace to those who hear."[87]

*Evaporate.*

We have all heard the promise: "I will pray for you." While that is fine, is that all the sufferers need in their grief and sorrow? "One of you says

---

84. Sadly, as far as I know, my grandmother and my dad never reconciled.
85. Luke 6:37
86. Bonnie Sala. "Be an Encourager!" https://www.guidelines.org/devotional/be-an-encourager/
87. Eph 4:29

to them, 'Go in peace, be warmed, and be filled,' and yet you do not give them what is necessary for their body, what use is that?"[88] Besides material help (meals, money, transportation . . .), people in the throes of suffering also need our physical presence and comfort (e.g., a hug).

People who come to visit are often afraid to touch the grieving parties as they embody the callers' greatest fears (cancer, Alzheimer, AIDS . . .). Acquaintances may offer the vague, non-committal, "If you need something, give me a call." Relatives may change the conversation if it comes too close to the issue at hand (e.g., an impending death). Friends may slowly distance themselves (emotionally and physically) and then disappear altogether.

The counselor Ossefort-Russell recounted her grief experience:

> *My husband, Marty, died of a sudden illness at age 39 . . . Five months after Marty died, my friend Sadie phoned me . . . She asked how I was doing. Haltingly, I told her that I was still struggling. "Still?" she sighed. We sat in awkward silence . . . She said, "It's uncomfortable for me to be around you because you're still in so much pain. Marty's death makes me realize that what happened to you could happen to me and I can't stand to think about it." Somehow, I extricated myself from the excruciating conversation and hung up. I slumped in speechless disbelief as her words seeped into my pores. Sadie was honest. But at what cost? In the midst of my traumatic loss, she abandoned me . . . Because she was uncomfortable. Anguished and forsaken, I screamed at the silent phone, "YOU'RE uncomfortable?! Try waking up in my empty bed every morning!"*[89]

"We are not patient with moral indifference in others."[90] To be abandoned in a time of need can be discouraging and disheartening. "We who grieve are exiled in our society. Exiled by the turning away of a face so that they do not witness my agony. Exiled by the silence left as friends and family drift away. Exiled by the lack of recognition of this universal experience. Soon enough, we sit in solitary confinement feeling as if no one else has ever felt what we feel."[91] As children of God,

---

88. Jas 2:16

89. Candyce Ossefort-Russell. "Want to Support Your Grieving Friend?" https://medium.com/the-mission/want-to-support-your-grieving-friend-5-truths-about-what-really-helps-f478a04f611a

90. Norman Care, *Decent People*, 142.

91. Stephanie Ericsson, quoted by Candyce Ossefort-Russell. "Want to Support Your Grieving Friend?" https://medium.com/the-mission/want-to-support-your-

we are exhorted to act worthy of our calling and support those who are grieving and hurting. "There is a friend who sticks closer than a brother,"[92] rather than *evaporates* into thin air!

*Sermonize.*

100 percent of the respondents to a survey[93] disliked the comment, "It's for the best." How can the death of an innocent child be "for the best"? How can the murder of a beloved wife and devoted mother be "for the best"?

Also, 93 percent of the people interviewed disapproved of the statement, "It's God's will." Was everything that happened "God's will" and the "best" possible outcome? God never did and does not want child abuses, gang rapes, mass shootings, or the other vicious evils humans do to one another. These calamities are strictly people's ill-considered actions, as they insist on doing whatever they want. Dr. Hasker affirmed: "The Bible . . . makes it abundantly clear on many different occasions that God is *not at all* pleased with some of the things that happen."[94]

Furthermore, 88 percent of the survey's participants deplored the remark that "God doesn't give you more than you can manage." "In 2021, suicide was the second leading cause of death for Americans ages 10 to 24," surpassing homicide.[95] It is obvious that not everyone responds well to pains and sufferings, as many people resort to suicide to escape their "more-than-they-can-manage" situations.

The comments invoking God or his will, though well-meant, are not helpful as generalizations about God are often mistaken. Dr. Ekstrom put it bluntly: "[Rather than] barraging them (sufferers) with alleged divine justifications for permitting such things—they ought simply to shut up."[96]

> *After the unexpected death of our son, Turner, everything I knew and felt about my faith and God was shattered . . . As a grieving Christian mother, and from one Christian to another, I ask you to really take a look at just a few of these platitudes and*

---

grieving-friend-5-truths-about-what-really-helps-f478a04f611a

92. Prov 18:24

93. Northwest Infant Survival & SIDS Alliance. https://www.nwsids.org/Dos%20and%20Donts.pdf

94. William Hasker, "The Open Theist Response," 154.

95. https://www.cbsnews.com/news/suicide-homicide-rates-young-americans-increased-sharply-cdc-report/

96. Laura Ekstrom, "A Christian Theodicy," 266.

> comments. God only takes the best/God needed another angel. First, I don't believe in a God that "takes" people or "needs angels." And he certainly doesn't need children and babies as those angels. Second, being told that your child was so "good" that God "took them from you" and caused their death, this heartbreak, and gut-wrenching pain you feel every day, only makes it hurt worse. How would you feel if one of your children died and my explanation and words of comfort were that your child was so good that they needed to pass away?[97]

Sermonizing platitudes uttered as consolations for people in grief are often not helpful. "Everyone dies eventually," while true, is not much solace for the mother of a two-year-old who drowned in the family's swimming pool. "Life is not fair," though correct, does nothing to comfort parents who lost their children in a drunk driving accident. "Time heals all wounds," albeit commonsensical, does not cure the present gnawing pain from the loss of a loved one. Trite sayings and *sermons* are best left unspoken rather than shared with the wounded people we want to help. "Let no unwholesome word proceed from your mouth, but only such a word as is good for edification according to the need of the moment."[98]

Rather than downplaying, advising, rebuking, evaporating, or sermonizing (DARES), what should we do instead to help the wounded?

## What to do.

The five practical things we can do to assist sufferers are: Help, Empathy, Legitimation, Presence, and Strengthening (HELPS).

### Help.

When I was in school, being poor and a foreigner without parents or country, I was resigned to be alone. That was fine most of the time, except during certain occasions when my classmates paired up on dates (e.g., Valentine's Day) or when they went home to visit their families (e.g., Christmas). Since I had nowhere to go, I would stay in the deserted dorm and cry out to God for comfort and help.

---

97. Desiree Crocker, "Christian-Ese and Grief." https://stillstandingmag.com/2018/05/07/common-christian-platitudes-said-to-grieving-parents/

98. Eph 4:29

One Valentine's Day, I trudged over to the mailroom to get the customary "chocolate kiss" candy left by the college in everyone's mailbox (a very nice thought). Surprisingly, I also found an envelope with some cash as a valentine. Someone does love me! To this day, I do not know who gave me that gift. Yet, more than forty years later, I still remember the comfort I received in my time of grief from that one act of kindness!

Actions speak louder than words. Can we bring a meal? Can we babysit the kids? Can we run errands? Can we help with the funeral arrangements? Can we fill out the insurance forms? Can we send money or gift cards? Practical things, while small, show hurting people that we care, and that we are willing to help them with their difficulties. Give little but often is much better than a one-time larger gift.

In a major study, Joanne Cacciatore and her colleagues reported that sufferers mentioned these practical assistance measures as being especially helpful: "People checking on me, inviting me to places, being available week after week to walk and chat, mowing the lawn, watching the kids, doing the dishes, helping with household chores, cards months and months even after, written notes, buying gift cards for our family, money for the expenses, gifts from neighbors of homemade cakes, bringing meals."[99]

Yet, the help provided can be better as only "just over one-third of the sample rated the level of social support they received post-loss as excellent or good, with 38% rating it as poor or very poor."[100] Furthermore, the respondents were dissatisfied or extremely dissatisfied with the support from their faith leaders (41%), their family (41%), or their friends (25%). A particularly interesting finding was the high level of satisfaction (89%) reported with animals as sources of social support. No one reported that they were extremely dissatisfied with their pets.

> Animals may be an especially important source of emotional support during conditions involving social isolation, such as the COVID-19 pandemic when contact with other people is limited, or during experiential conditions such as the loneliness so common in bereavement . . . the adoption of pets could be one avenue by which to promote well-being and reduce loneliness.[101]

99. Joanne Cacciatore et al., "What is Good Grief Support?"
100. Ibid.
101. Ibid.

Besides other loving gestures (meals, financial assistance), the gift of a pet (after getting approval from the future owner) may be considered a practical action to help grieving people in their adversity.

Helping sufferers can be an individual act. Even better are the efforts, care, and support of a loving community of friends.

> *Before my father's decline, he was a preeminent scholar of Black religious history. As brilliant as he'd been, I wasn't sure, at the end of his life, that he recognized me. He had died of dementia . . . In early December, an invitation arrived . . . a Christmas party . . . I was surprised to find my seat at the head, squeezed right next to Ayana's . . . "The reason Emily is seated here in a place of honor," she announced, "is that her father has recently died" . . . Ayana sat beside me and took my hand. I stopped shaking at her touch . . . Though Bev and Naledi came from different tribes with different rites around death, they shared their customs around grief . . . It came as a great comfort to learn this . . . She (Ayana) understood how to make space at her table for grief, to let me find a ritual in the sweetness of community. Another word for that knowledge is grace. Only after that could we—I—make space for hope.*[102]

As children of God, "we must *help* the weak, remembering the words the Lord Jesus himself said: 'It is more blessed to give than to receive.'"[103]

*Empathy.*

Empathy is defined as "the ability to understand and share the feelings of another."[104] Empathy can mean a word of condolence ("I am sorry for your loss," "I am sorry that you are hurting so much"), or a willingness to just sit and listen to the sufferer's thoughts and feelings (e.g., "We can talk if you want but we don't have to," "I am happy to just sit here with you," "I will listen if you want to talk."). Compassion and empathy can alleviate other people's burdens and allay their fears of facing the future alone.

Drs. Paul and Beernink reported on the use of empathy in the resolution of grief: "The empathizer makes no judgments about what the other should feel but solicits the expression of whatever feelings may exist and,

---

102. Emily Raboteau, "How to Rescue a Grieving Friend." https://www.oprahdaily.com/life/relationships-love/a41860406/how-to-rescue-a-grieving-friend-emily-raboteau/

103. Acts 20:35 NIV.

104. https://www.lexico.com/definition/empathy

for brief periods, feels them as his own . . . The empathy relationship is generous; the empathizer does not use the object as a means for gratifying his own sense of importance but is himself principally concerned with encouraging the other."[105] Empathy is not self-seeking but aims to understand and share other people's burdens.

However, like any other sharing, true empathy can be very costly to the empathizer, making the endeavor even more worthwhile. In the COVID-19 pandemic, nurses were on the front line of the battle, caring for patients and consoling distraught families, at great personal expense. "Empathetic nurses connect with patients in a uniquely valuable way and often provide higher quality, more compassionate care because of it. But there's another side to empathy. Nurses and other caregivers who are naturally empathetic (which, for many, is the reason they entered the profession in the first place) run the risk of experiencing compassion fatigue."[106] "As a result of the coronavirus disease 2019 pandemic, more than one half of health care workers report being burned out, approximately 60% indicate the associated stress has harmed their mental health, and 30% have contemplated leaving the profession."[107]

Empathy is costly, yet necessary. It is the tie that binds all of us as humans and children of God.

Ryan (not his real name) was a little six-year-old boy with leukemia. For some reason, he was all alone in the hospital without mom, dad, grandparents, or any other relatives. Nobody ever visited him; so, we (medical students) considered him "our" baby. I can still see him now, big brown eyes in a gaunt face, a sad smile, and pale skin with ugly bruises all over (uncontrolled, advanced leukemia combined with too many blood draws). I loved that little boy and dreaded the moment when I had to come and draw his blood. We became good friends and I tried to bring him some treats as I went through his ward. Personally, I thought that the poor child had suffered enough and that we should temper the blood drawing frequency. Unfortunately, I was not the one who made the decisions about the orphan boy's medical care.

One day, as I came for my dreaded assignment, Ryan looked at me for a long time with his deep brown eyes and then, with a sad smile,

---

105. Norman Paul and Kenneth Beernink, "The Use of Empathy in the Resolution of Grief," 154.

106. Wolters Kluwer, "When Empathy Turns Harmful." https://www.wolterskluwer.com/en/expert-insights/when-empathy-turns-harmful

107. Sandra Galura, "Combating Burnout in Health Care Providers," 3.

wordlessly lifted the sleeve of his drab hospital gown and exposed his bruised and battered little arm for his friend. That simple gesture of trust, resignation, and love pierced my heart to its innermost core, and I cried as I had never cried before! Yes, Ryan, I cried for your lost youth; I grieved for your loneliness in this wretched world; I wept for the peaceful life that you deserved and yet would never have! Ryan, it has been more than forty years. Yet, I have never forgotten you!

Sharing one another's burdens[108] is an honorable venture and the right undertaking in society. "If one part of the body suffers, all the parts suffer with it."[109]

"Empathy is more important than ever to a national population worried about difficult political and socioeconomic situations . . . Empathy is particularly important to social work practice. Clients experiencing empathy through treatment have improved outcomes."[110] Besides its value in clinical and professional settings, empathy is also important in everyday life.

> *I was in downtown Indianapolis for my job, and I was walking out of a restaurant after a meal. I noticed a couple quietly sitting on the sidewalk, with a sign that said, "Homeless vet. No job. No food." So, this time I decided to engage, not avoid. I asked if I could sit down and talk to them for a while. I also had a bag of leftovers and asked if they minded if I left the food. The man immediately gave the leftovers to his wife. As he began to talk, I just listened. He thanked me for the food and just for stopping. He went on to tell me how he had served in Iraq, came home, and worked construction. As the economy tightened, both he and his wife had lost their jobs, their home, and much of their dignity. This young man placed his life in harm's way, for me, and for you. He thanked me repeatedly for the food, for stopping and listening to his story. I thanked him repeatedly for his service. He did not need or deserve my pity, just my respect.*[111]

---

108. Gal 6:2

109. 1 Cor 12:26

110. Karen Gerdes and Elizabeth Segal, "Importance of Empathy for Social Work Practice," 141.

111. Crisis Prevention Institute, "'I Still Matter!' 4 Stories About Empathy." https://www.crisisprevention.com/Blog/Stories-About-Empathy

Not pity, but empathy. Not avoidance but love. As he loved us and died for us,[112] the Lord asked of us, "Love your neighbor as yourself."[113] Watching Lazarus' family and friends mourning his premature death, "Jesus wept."[114] "For we do not have a high priest who is unable to empathize with our weaknesses, but we have one who has been tempted in every way, just as we are—yet he did not sin."[115] Should we not follow our Lord's example and *empathize* with the many sufferers in our path?

*Legitimation.*

A grief-stricken mother needs to have her feelings acknowledged ("I can't imagine what you are going through," "feel free to cry"). A distraught husband wants to be heard and feel validated ("You really miss her," "she genuinely loves you"). Children of aged parents eagerly desire to be reassured ("You have done everything you could"). Sufferers from failed marriages need to have their pains legitimized ("I see that you are hurting. I am listening if you want to talk"). These words of comfort ease the pangs of guilt, lighten the burden of sole responsibility, and provide the needed freedom to express one's pains and emotions.

> *In the first bleak months after my divorce, I returned to my home state of Virginia . . . An old friend from Scotland, Morna, phoned and asked if she could come visit me . . . Huddled on my knees, sobbing, I hadn't noticed Morna had quietly approached me. She sat down on the kitchen floor next to me and softly put her hand on my shoulder. I glanced at her quickly without making eye contact and said, "Now you see what a basket case I really am." "I see someone who is in pain . . . a lot of pain." I wept longer, letting her words sink in. She was right. I felt relief just hearing her say the truth out loud. "Yes, that's right. I've been really, really hurt. I feel so alone. I am so afraid no one wants to be with me anymore." Morna made herself more comfortable on the floor, sitting cross-legged. "I don't mind listening, if you want to talk about this now." I remembered she was a professional counselor and blushed. "You sure you aren't just playing counselor with me? You're supposed to be getting a break from listening to people in pain all the time." She smiled softly and paused. "I'm*

112. John 15:13
113. Matt 22:39
114. John 11:35
115. Heb 4:15 NIV.

> your friend. Why do you think I'm sitting here on the floor with you?" Feeling welcomed to speak from my heart, uncensored, I took the plunge to trust her. The floodgates opened. We sat on the kitchen floor for another hour, until our legs ached, then moved to the sofa and talked nonstop until 3 a.m.[116]

A sympathetic ear, an acknowledgment of grief, and a validation of the sufferers' feelings are balms that heal a broken heart.

In his famous prayer, St. Francis of Assisi asked: "O divine Master, grant that I may not so much seek to be consoled as to console, to be understood as to understand, to be loved as to love."[117] By mourning "with those who mourn,"[118] we *legitimize* their feelings and lighten their heavy loads. "Bear one another's burdens, and thereby fulfill the law of Christ."[119]

*Presence.*

The most important thing we can do for grief-stricken people is to *be there* for them. We tend to gravitate toward joyful situations (e.g., weddings, birthday parties) and avoid events that dampen our spirits (e.g., funerals, hospital vigils).

In a study of families with a child who died of cancer, the physical presence of relatives and friends is a key component in the management of grief. A father related: "It would be almost impossible to survive something that way if you were alone. It was comforting to have others who were always right beside you."[120]

> Interestingly, fathers, more often than mothers, spoke about relying on their spouses for support. One father explained, "I was blessed to have a beautiful spouse . . . When I was up or if she was ever down it always worked that I was up and vice versa." Another shared, "I have a spouse and companion that you wanted to share that with, to weather that with, to lean on. Hopefully, I comforted her too . . . We wanted to be there to console one

---

116. Val Walker, https://thestoriesbetween.com/blog/the-gift-of-comforting/

117. St. Francis of Assisi. https://www.catholicnewsagency.com/resource/55030/peace-prayer-of-st-francis-of-assisi

118. Rom 12:15

119. Gal 6:2

120. Amanda Thompson et al., "A Qualitative Study of Advice from Bereaved Parents and Siblings."

*another no matter what."* In contrast to fathers, mothers discussed the support they received from close friends. One mother put it simply, "Talking to my friends is what pulled me through," while another explained further: "The friends you do have that you can keep close to you, that you have someone to share your emotions, who's still very willing to let you talk about your child and they feel comfortable talking about your child, sharing memories. I think it's important to have someone that you can really just express your emotions with."[121]

The COVID-19 pandemic has greatly disrupted the process of offering support to the bereaved by our physical presence due to the various quarantine protocols and the fear of exposure to the disease. "Persons dying of the virus spend their final days in hospitals and nursing facilities, separated from their families. Their bereaved kin must mourn the loss without the comforting embrace of loved ones, or the support of mourners who show their respect for the deceased at funerals."[122]

With the ebbing of the pandemic, we can again strive to connect with others in their griefs. "Physical presence means so much. Phone calls are good. Video connections can be better. But there is nothing like experiencing physical presence with the potential or reality of a hand on the shoulder, a hand in another's hand, and a body-to-body hug."[123] Dr. Wuthnow observed: "The healing power of touch is part of the gift of our humanity."[124] Christ himself often touched the people he healed, even lepers.[125]

When my son Dan was facing open-heart surgery, while my colleagues were supportive, I noticed that many were avoiding any mention of the situation, especially its emotional ramifications. Sufferers were expected to grit their teeth, carry on with their duties, and bear their private grief alone in silence.

One day, an anesthesiologist (one of our competitors) met me in the hospital hallway. He stopped, looked at my face, and silently gave me a bear hug. I almost cried on his shoulder. For that brief moment, my heavy burden was shared, my feelings were understood, and my

---

121. Ibid.

122. Deborah Carr et al., "Bereavement in the Time of Coronavirus."

123. Greg Adams, "Grief in the Absence of Physical Presence." https://www.opentohope.com/grief-in-the-absence-of-physical-presence/

124. Sara Wuthnow, "Healing Touch Controversies," 221.

125. Matt 9:29, Mark 1:41, Luke 22:51

loneliness assuaged. "A sorrow shared is a sorrow halved."[126] That was more than thirty years ago, yet, I have not forgotten that man's kindness in my time of need.

Our physical *presence* (e.g., a hug) in challenging situations speaks loudly about our commitments to see our grieving brethren through their times of trial and exemplifies the love of Christ to the entire world. "Pure and undefiled religion in the sight of our God and Father is this: to visit orphans and widows in their distress."[127]

*Strengthening.*

Strengthening through encouragement is "the process of facilitating the development of a person's inner resources and courage toward positive movement."[128] The focus is more on enhancing the sufferer's inner motivation and strength than in changing outward behavior.

Edward was born in Halifax, England, in a family of Irish immigrants. As a child, he was bullied for his strange looks and disturbing behaviors (probably from attention deficit disorder). He found solace in playing guitar and singing in the local church choir.

At the age of sixteen, Edward dropped out of high school and moved from place to place looking for musical "gigs, attention, and somewhere to spend the night."[129] He played in small clubs, worked as a guitar tech, knocked "on doors and being told no, over and over again, chasing a seemingly impossible dream. 'The amount of confidence that I'd lost . . . doing the same rounds, over and over again, going into record labels and their going, 'It's not going to happen.'"[130] After three years of futile efforts, Edward left the London music scene and came to Los Angeles.

> "*Scrounging for other gigs led to playing Jamie Foxx's radio show The Foxxhole and a 12-minute set at Foxx's weekly live-music night at a downtown club . . . 'You're incredible,' Foxx recalled telling Sheeran . . . 'I know you don't have anywhere to go, so chill*

---

126. "A common proverb in Western Europe." Silke Hoppe, "A Sorrow Shared Is a Sorrow Halved," 180.

127. Jas 1:27

128. Don Dinkmeyer and Lewis Losoncy, *The Skills of Encouragement*, 7.

129. https://sites.williams.edu/f18-engl117-01/uncategorized/from-homelessness-to-stardom-the-ed-sheeran-phenomenon/

130. https://www.inc.com/jeff-haden/a-penniless-ed-sheeran-once-slept-on-jamie-foxxs-couch-power-of-belief-kindness.html

> here' (six weeks on Jamie Foxx's couch). I was giving him food. My daughter was like, 'Who do you have over here now?'... You don't have to offer your couch. But you can be kind. You can offer a word of encouragement to a struggling friend. You can offer a little help to a struggling connection.[131]

Ed (Edward) Sheeran, one of the world's best-known artists reminisced: "Within a month... of going there with zero confidence, being able to fly to L.A. with nothing and ending up in one of the biggest movie stars in the world's house... in my mind I was like, 'I must have something.'"[132]

We can encourage, strengthen struggling people, and enhance their inner motivation and self-confidence by letting them know that we will help them and support them in their difficult journey ("We will get through this together," "You are not alone").

We can pray with them and for them. "Pray for one another so that you may be healed."[133] Heartfelt prayers show that we genuinely care and will stand with them for as long as necessary.

We can send encouraging notes or cards, especially on significant dates (e.g., anniversary of the death) as pain and grief may resurface during these times. We can affirm them when they share some positive outcome from the loss (e.g., organ donations).

"Encourage them to speak, openly and honestly, about their emotional and physical feelings. Utilize active listening skills and provide a nonjudgmental environment... Encourage loved ones at the bedside to remember to take care of their own health."[134]

There is much we can do to *strengthen* others in their time of need. "Encourage one another and build up one another."[135] "Strengthen the hands that are weak and the knees that are feeble,"[136] so that we may be "built up in him, strengthened in the faith."[137]

---

131. Ibid.
132. Ibid.
133. Jas 5:16
134. Julianne Oates and Patricia Maani-Fogelman, *Nursing Grief and Loss*.
135. 1 Thess 5:11
136. Heb 12:12
137. Col 2:7

## Summary

The "Religious Problem of Evil" (our sixth question) is often deeply personal and heart-wrenching. When we encounter trials and tribulations in this world, (whether of our own doing, other people's twisted wills, or God), we must *refocus* our priorities from the four Ps of this world (Power, Prestige, Pleasures, and Possessions) to the Lord, take the provided way of *escape*, *change* when our weaknesses are revealed, *accept* others in their failings, and *praise* the Lord for his help and guidance (RECAP), knowing that "all things work together for good to those who love God."

In supporting our fellow pilgrims, rather than downplaying, advising, rebuking, evaporating, or sermonizing (DARES), we should offer them much needed help, empathy, legitimation, presence, and strengthening (HELPS). These are the balms that heal the throbbing wounds in this broken and sorrowful world.

Furthermore, we can assist sufferers who claim that a good God can never exist in the presence of so much horrendous evil and suffering (e.g., cancers, murders). In the next section, we will provide some meaningful answers to their agonizing questions. Why does God not intervene to prevent some gruesome calamities in this world (e.g., child abuse, school shootings, Hurricane Katrina, COVID-19)? Does he not care about us? Can a virtuous God exist in the presence of vicious evil? Does this "problem of evil" have a solution?

# PART TWO

## A Novel Solution to the Problem Of Evil

# 7

# Evil, an Insurmountable Problem?

*The problem of evil is not something we will solve in the present world.*

—N. T. Wright[1]

JOSEF WAS AN INTELLIGENT and serious student, learning medicine and anthropology under Dr. von Verschuer, an expert in twin genetics. Early in his career, Josef decided to experiment on human beings to advance his theories.

In 1943, he was appointed chief medical officer of a concentration camp in Poland. Soon after, he conducted barbarous experiments on helpless twins, injecting children with toxic chemicals, jabbing their eyes with color dyes without anesthetic, and dissecting their organs.

A witness at Auschwitz-Birkenau, Vera Alexander, recounted:

> One day, (Josef) Mengele brought chocolate and special clothes. The next day, SS men came and took two children away. They were two of my pets, Tito, and Nino. One of them was a hunchback. Two or three days later, an SS man brought them back in a terrible state. They had been cut. The hunchback was sewn to the other child, back-to-back, their wrists back-to-back too. There was a terrible smell of gangrene. The cuts were dirty, and the children cried every night.[2]

---

1. N. T. Wright, *Evil and the Justice of God*, 11.
2. Gerald Posner and John Ware, *Mengele*, 37.

Another survivor, Annani Pet'ko, described what she saw:

> A large group [of SS officers] arrived on motorcycles, Mengele among them. They drove into the yard and got off their motorcycles. Upon arriving, they circled the flames (of the firepit) . . . After a while, trucks arrived, dump trucks, with children inside. There were about ten of these trucks. After they had entered the yard, an officer gave an order and the trucks backed up to the fire and they started throwing those children right into the fire, into the pit. The children started to scream; some of them managed to crawl out of the burning pit; an officer walked around it with sticks and pushed back those who managed to get out. Hoess and Mengele were present and were giving orders . . . I was told by the zone commanders that it was difficult to poison the children in the gas chambers, therefore they were burned in the pit. They were all under five years old.[3]

Where was God in this holocaust? Can he even exist in the presence of such unspeakable evil?[4] This disturbing question of "the coexistence of God and evil" has plagued humanity since the dawn of time.

Dr. Kreeft acknowledged that "the problem of evil is the most serious problem in the world. It is also the one serious objection to the existence of God."[5] Before proposing a new solution, let us summarize what has been done over the centuries to resolve the conundrum.

The problem of evil is more accurately a family of problems (logical, evidential, religious) dating back to antiquity. Epicurus (ca. 300 BC) questioned the existence of a good and powerful God in the presence of evil.[6] David Hume popularized Epicurus's paradox/riddle in his famous rendition of the problem.

> "Is he [God] willing to prevent evil, but not able? Then he is impotent.
> Is he able, but not willing? Then he is malevolent.
> Is he both able and willing? Whence then is evil?"[7]

---

3. Ibid., 46.

4. "Any fully successful theodicy must account for horrors—even the worst horrors—but horrors appear immune to standard approaches." Vince Vitale, *Non-Identity Theodicy*, 9.

5. Peter Kreeft, *Fundamentals*, 54.

6. "God, he (Epicurus) says, either wishes to take away evils, and is unable; or He is able, and is unwilling; or He is neither willing nor able." Lactantius, *The Works of Lactantius, Vol. 2*, 28. We do not have any surviving Epicurean work mentioning his paradox.

7. David Hume, *Dialogues Concerning Natural Religion*, 196. Dr. Hickson offered a

Aeschylus claimed that evil and suffering are necessary for human learning and progress.[8] The Stoics advocated resigned acceptance of unavoidable misfortunes.[9]

The question of suffering and evil can be addressed by assuming God's existence and then endeavoring to explain why evil is compatible with God's goodness. This approach was used during most of Christianity's history.

The Early Church Father Irenaeus proposed character building as to why a good God would allow evil.[10] Tertullian blamed sin on human actions and denied that God was the author of evil.[11] Origen maintained that wickedness proceeded from blameworthy people, not God.[12]

In the Late Roman period, Augustine argued against the dualistic threat of the Manicheans who, like Plato,[13] advocated an evil essence in opposition to the omnibenevolent (all-good) God.[14] Following Aristotle[15] and Plotinus,[16] Augustine believed that evil is only a privation (lack) of the good[17] and not a separate entity, attributing its cause to humanity's

---

more complete discussion of Hume's adaptation of Epicurus' riddle. Michael Hickson, "A Brief History of Problems of Evil," 6-8.

8. "Man must learn by suffering." Aeschylus, "Agamemnon," 9.

9. Paul Gavrilyuk, "An Overview of Patristic Theodicies," 1.

10. Irenaeus, *Against Heresies,* III.20.

11. "If it is man's sin, it will not be God's fault, because it is man's doing; nor is that Being to be regarded as the author of the sin, who turns out to be its forbidder, nay, its condemner." Tertullian, *Adversus Marcionem,* 2.9.

12. "We ... maintain that evil, or wickedness, and the actions which proceed from it, were not created by God." Origen, *Contra Celsum,* 6.55. "But if it (the good) should fail any one, it must be through his own fault, in being slothful to partake of this living bread and genuine drink." Origen, *Contra Celsum,* 6.44.

13. "There must always be something opposed to the good." *Plato: Complete Works,* 195.

14. "Two beings made the beginning of the world, one Light and the other Darkness. Each is separate from the other." Henry Neumann, "Manichaean Tendencies in the History of Philosophy," 491.

15. "We maintain that a thing may 'come to be from what is not'—that is, in a qualified sense. For a thing comes to be from the privation, which in its own nature is not-being." Aristotle, *Physics,* I.8.

16. "If evil exists at all, that it be situate in the realm of Non-Being, that it be some mode, as it were, of the Non-Being." Plotinus, *Enneads,* I.8.3

17. Augustine, *The Enchiridion on Faith, Hope, and Love,* IV.12.

perverted will.[18] Unfortunately, this explanation did not fully counter the claim that God is the ultimate author of evil.[19]

Following the Patristic period,[20] in the Early Renaissance, the existence of an omnibenevolent Creator was also assumed by Aquinas who taught that evil is the absence of the good, and a defect in the human agent.[21]

In the Reformation and Counter-Reformation, Christian scholars (e.g., Luther, Calvin, Ignatius of Loyola, Francis Xavier) never doubted the existence of an omnipotent Lord[22] while providing explanations for evil.[23]

Sadly, the assumption of God's existence faltered in the Early Modern period. The use of evil as an argument against the existence of God can be traced to David Hume (1711–1776).

> There may four hypotheses be framed concerning the first causes of the universe: that they are endowed with perfect goodness; that they have perfect malice; that they are opposite and have both goodness and malice; that they have neither goodness nor

---

18. Augustine, *The Problem of Free Choice, (De Libero Arbitrio)*, 189.

19. "If the creation of evil in the world was logically necessary to the fulfillment of the divine purposes in creating the world, then of course God not only might have but must have created evil." R. Douglas Geivett, "Augustine and the Problem of Evil," 75. "To ground a denial that God directly created evil on the theory of the nature of evil as privation looks very much like a tour de force of definition." G. Stanley Kane, "Evil and Privation," 55.

20. Dr. Gavrilyuk summarized the "common core of patristic theodicy." "1. God is not the author of evil 2. God prevents or permits evil and draws good out of it. 3. Ontologically, evil is nonbeing: a privation, corruption, and perversion of the good 4. The misuse of angelic and human free will is the cause of evil 5. Salvation history provides a narrative framework that accounts for the origin, spread, and ultimate destruction of evil." Paul Gavrilyuk, "An Overview of Patristic Theodicies," 6.

21. Thomas Aquinas, *Summa Theologica*. 1.49.1.

22. Martin Luther, *On the Bondage of the Will (De Servo Arbitrio)*, section 94. John Calvin, *Institutes of the Christian Religion*, 1.16.3. Ignatius of Loyola, *Ignatius of Loyola: The Spiritual Exercises and Selected Works*, 24. Dominique Bouhours, *The Life of St. Francis Xavier of the Society of Jesus*, 297.

23. Martin Luther affirmed: "In accordance with the Scripture, we should speak fully and bluntly of sin—or guilt, or inward evil—as a universal corruption of nature in all parts." Peter Hodgson and Robert King, "Luther: Sin and Grace," 181. "Such is the depravity of his nature, that he cannot be excited and biased to anything but what is evil." John Calvin, *Institutes of the Christian Religion*, 2.3.5. "It is characteristic of the evil spirit to harass with anxiety, to afflict with sadness, to raise obstacles backed by fallacious reasonings that disturb the soul." Ignatius of Loyola, *The Spiritual Exercises of St Ignatius*, 315. "The devils were created good by God but became evil by their own fault." Henry Coleridge, *The Life and Letters of St. Francis Xavier*, 337.

> *malice. Mixed phenomena can never prove the two former unmixed principles; and the uniformity and steadiness of general laws seem to oppose the third. The fourth, therefore, seems by far the most probable.*[24]

In other words, according to Hume, the omnibenevolent God does not exist for a being with "neither goodness nor malice . . . seems by far the most probable." This was a radical change in thought as God had been portrayed as a good father caring for his creation.[25]

This disbelief in God's existence was carried further by the Australian scholar J. L. Mackie who claimed in the "Logical argument from evil"[26] that "religious beliefs . . . are positively irrational, that the several parts of the essential theological doctrines are *inconsistent* with one another."[27] Christians are deemed irrational in clinging to the (supposedly illogical) belief that an omnipotent and omnibenevolent Creator can coexist with evil.

Dr. Plantinga refuted Mackie in his "Free Will Defense,"[28] showing that it is logically impossible for God to create humans with free will (to do good or evil), and at the same time prevent them from committing evil.[29] In his wisdom, God chooses the "greater good" (i.e., humans with free will)[30] that may result in some evil. Hence, a good God and evil can *logically* coexist. Unfortunately, Plantinga had to contend with the criticism that free will is not worth the price of the gruesome calamities in the world (e.g., genocides, gang rapes, mass shootings). Dr. van Inwagen argued: "The existence of free will may be worth some evil, but it certainly isn't worth the amount we actually observe."[31] Dr.

---

24. David Hume, *Dialogues Concerning Natural Religion*, 114.
25. Matt 6:25-34
26. The argument attempts to prove that "a good God and evil cannot logically coexist" (The "Logical problem of evil").
27. J. L. Mackie, "Evil and Omnipotence," 200.
28. Alvin Plantinga, *God, Freedom, and Evil*.
29. According to Plantinga's concept of "transworld depravity," every potential person (with free will) would do *some* evil in every possible world. "If every essence suffers from transworld depravity, then it was beyond the power of God himself to create a world containing moral good but no moral evil." Alvin Plantinga, *God, Freedom, and Evil*, 53.
30. "A world containing creatures who are significantly free (and freely perform more good than evil actions) is more valuable, all else being equal, than a world containing no free creatures at all." Ibid., 30.
31. Peter van Inwagen, *The Problem of Evil*, 84.

Ekstrom affirmed: "What can one say except that libertarian free will seems *just not worth it.*"[32] Dr. Roth stated: "It (our freedom) is far more an occasion for waste."[33] Nevertheless, "many theists and non-theists came to agree that the free will defense shows that the logical argument against theism, as exemplified in Mackie, fails."[34]

Subsequently, non-theists produced more refined arguments against the existence of an Omnigod (an omnipotent, omniscient, and omnibenevolent being).[35] Dr. Rowe developed a sophisticated "Evidential argument from evil"[36] to disprove God's existence in the presence of gratuitous evil, evil that is not necessary for a greater good[37] (evil without an accompanying greater good).[38] The argument rests on two premises, (1) There are gratuitous evils, and (2) If God exists, there are no gratuitous evils (i.e., God prevents all gratuitous evils).[39] According to Rowe, since there are (probably) gratuitous evils (e.g., child abuses), it is likely that God does not exist.[40]

Christian philosophers and theologians have devised many innovative answers to this "Evidential problem of evil."

32. Laura Ekstrom, "The Cost of Freedom," 77.
33. John K. Roth, "A Theodicy of Protest," 12.
34. Michael Peterson, "Introduction," 4.

35. "As long as there were multiple deities, evil could readily be attributed to one or several of them with little harm to the total worldview. The emergence of belief in only one god who is both good and powerful brought an attendant problem: explaining evil." James Crenshaw, *Defending God,* 54.

36. The argument attempts to prove that "a good God and *gratuitous* evil cannot coexist" (The "Evidential problem of evil").

37. or evil not necessary for "the prevention of an evil at least as bad." Nick Trakakis, "The Evidential Problem of Evil."

38. William Rowe, "The Problem of Evil and Some Varieties of Atheism," 336.

39. "An omnipotent, omniscient, wholly good God would not permit any gratuitous evil." Nick Trakakis, "The Evidential Problem of Evil."

40. Since Rowe used an inductive/probabilistic argument to show that there are (probably) gratuitous evils, he only claimed that gratuitous evil lowers the probability of God's existence. Other versions of the "evidential problem of evil," aimed to show that the presence of evil makes it *improbable* that God exists, have also been proposed, e.g., Dr. Paul Draper's indirect inductive approach ("Pain and Pleasure: An Evidential Problem for Theists," 331–50), Dr. William Rowe's Bayesian probabilistic argument ("The Evidential Argument from Evil: A Second Look," 262–85), and Dr. Michael Tooley's Carnapian construction ("Inductive Logic and the Probability that God Exists," 144–64). They have also met with significant challenges. Daniel Howard-Snyder, "Theism, the Hypothesis of Indifference," 452–66. Michael Bergmann, "Skeptical Theism and Rowe's New Evidential Argument from Evil," 278–96. Richard Otte, "A Carnapian Argument from Evil," 83–97.

# EVIL, AN INSURMOUNTABLE PROBLEM?

In his "Skeptical Theism Defense,"[41] Dr. Wykstra challenged Rowe's claim that there are gratuitous evils. While we do not see any good resulting from some horrendous evils (murders, COVID-19 . . .),[42] we cannot conclude that no such good exists as we cannot fathom God's purposes.[43] There may be goods beyond our knowledge and comprehension, making these evils not gratuitous. Regrettably, the Skeptical Theism Defense is just that, a defense.[44] No reasons are given to explain *why* God would allow such calamities in the world.

Following Irenaeus,[45] Dr. Hick proposed a "soul making" solution, seeing evil as the means to a perfect future in heaven, following a long and painful process of growth ("soul making") in the present realm.[46] The theory was subjected to severe criticisms including the counter-argument that the number of evils observed far exceeded what was needed for "soul making"[47] and might even lead to "soul destroying."[48] Furthermore, Hick's claim of universal salvation for all humans[49] is contrary to traditional Christian doctrines.[50]

Dr. Swinburne offered a "Serious free will" approach, claiming that the exercise of free will to accomplish great goods (Mother Teresa) or to commit great evils (Hitler) was extremely valuable, and that

---

41. "Skeptical Theism" may be a contemporary form of a Butlerian type of theodicy. Joseph Butler, *The Analogy of Religion*.

42. "The first thing that occurs to me is the reflection that I must not be surprised if I am not always capable of comprehending the reasons why God acts as he does." René Descartes, *The Method, Meditations and Philosophy of Descartes*, 251.

43. Stephen Wysktra, "A Skeptical Theist View."

44. "The attempt to defeat or undercut an argument from evil, without seeking to delineate even any possible reasons as to why God permits evil." Nick Trakakis, "Response to Bishop," 59.

45. John Hick, "An Irenaean Theodicy." Hick's theodicy "has more affinity with Origen than with Irenaeus." Mark Scott, "Suffering and Soul-Making: Rethinking John Hick's Theodicy," 314.

46. John Hick, *Philosophy of Religion*, 45.

47. William Rowe, "Paradox and Promise," 120.

48. "Life's pains and agonies, which sometimes help to create stronger and more compassionate men and women, at other times overwhelm and crush, leaving only despair, tragedy and disintegration." John Hick, *An Interpretation of Religion*, 360.

49. "God will eventually succeed in His purpose of winning all men to Himself." John Hick, *Evil and the God of Love*, 342.

50. Louis Berkhof, *Systematic Theology*, 113-18. Wayne Grudem, *Systematic Theology*, 137-41. Millard Erickson, *Christian Theology*, 940-46. Charles Ryrie, *Basic Theology*, 520-21. Thomas Rausch, *Systematic Theology: A Roman Catholic Approach*, 212.

the positive values of the goods outweighed the negative values of the evils.[51] However, this is difficult to believe,[52] considering the profusion of horrendous, heartbreaking evils in this fallen world (e.g., the 2010 Haiti earthquake, the Russia-Ukraine war).

Dr. Plantinga introduced the "Felix Culpa" proposal, asserting that the Fall of humans (with its resulting evils) was a happy fault (felix culpa) as it was necessary for the great good of the incarnation and atonement of Christ.[53] However, intimacy with God could be obtained by incarnation alone, not requiring evil, sin, or atonement.[54] Aquinas asserted: "Even had sin not existed, God could have become incarnate."[55] Dr. Stump stated: "That benefit (union with God) could have been gotten in a world without a Fall and without suffering."[56] If so, the Fall and atonement for sin were unnecessary and detrimental to an unbroken fellowship between God and humans, rather than being a "happy fault." Furthermore, the claim that natural evils were caused by Satan and demons was not well received.[57] Dr. Plantinga admitted: "The Felix Culpa approach does not dispel all the perplexity surrounding human suffering and evil; I suppose nothing can do that."[58]

These theodicies[59] and the "Skeptical Theism Defense" challenged Rowe's claim that there are gratuitous evils (Rowe's first premise, the

---

51. Richard Swinburne, *Providence and the Problem of Evil*.

52. "I don't believe it is possible for Swinburne to show in any rigorous way that this criterion is satisfied in respect of all the world's evils." Paul Draper, "Review: Providence and the Problem of Evil by Richard Swinburne," 466.

53. Alvin Plantinga, "Supralapsarianism or 'O Felix Culpa.'"

54. Kevin Diller, "Are Sin and Evil Necessary for a Really Good World?" 396.

55. Thomas Aquinas, *Summa Theologica*, 3.1.3.

56. Eleonore Stump, *The Image of God*, 6.

57. "This suggestion is not at present widely popular in Western academia." Alvin Plantinga, "Supralapsarianism, or 'O Felix Culpa,'" 377.

58. Ibid., 386.

59. "A theodicy replies to an argument from evil by giving a justifying reason for the existence of the evil in question– a reason such that, if it obtains, the permission of the evil by God is morally justifiable and does not constitute a reason to disbelieve in God's existence or his goodness." William Hasker, "An Open Theist View," 61. Dr. Swinburne argued that "most theists need a theodicy, an account of reasons why God might allow evil to occur. Without a theodicy, evil counts against the existence of God." Richard Swinburne, *Providence and the Problem of Evil*, x. The German theologian Wolfhart Pannenberg differed: "As to the problem of theodicy, I do not think that it is the task of theology to exculpate God theoretically for the evil in the world." Mark Hocknull. *Pannenberg on Evil*, 35.

factual premise). Many theists do not believe that this is a fruitful approach[60] as it is exceedingly difficult (if not impossible)[61] to prove that every evil in the world must lead to (or is necessary for) some "greater good." A more promising path may be to question Rowe's claim that God prevents all gratuitous evils (Rowe's second premise, the theological premise).

Such an attempt was made by Open Theists who "hold that much of the future is known by God as what *might happen,* and as what *will probably happen,* but not as what *will definitely* take place."[62] Hence, some gratuitous evils cannot be prevented by God as humans chart their own independent paths. Furthermore, in a war between good and evil, we "must accept that at least sometimes, God is *unable* to prevent them (gratuitous evils)."[63] Unfortunately, the Open Theism view of God's limited omnipotence and finite omniscience runs counter to most traditional understandings of the divine attributes.[64]

Other solutions advanced by Christian scholars[65] to resolve the "Evidential problem of evil" have not been more successful. This situation has led to the belief that God's motives for allowing gruesome evils in this world cannot be known by mere humans. God may have good reasons to permit evil, reasons that are beyond our understanding (i.e., a mystery).[66] Sadly, "mystery" is not a very helpful answer for suffering

---

60. Michael Peterson, "Christian Theism and the Evidential Argument from Evil." Gregory A. Boyd, *God at War.* William Hasker, "An Adequate God."

61. "The nature of the problem makes it impossible for any theist to show that all actual evil is justified. But it is also true that the nature of these problems makes it impossible for non-theists to show that actual evil is not justified." M. B. Ahern, *The Problem of Evil,* 72.

62. William Hasker, "An Open Theist View," 60.

63. Gregory Boyd, *Satan and the Problem of Evil,* 16.

64. Louis Berkhof, *Systematic Theology,* 52–81. Wayne Grudem, *Systematic Theology,* 185-268. Millard Erickson, *Christian Theology,* 233-71. Charles Ryrie, *Basic Theology,* 35-44.

65. Marilyn McCord Adams, *Horrendous Evils and the Goodness of God.* Eleonore Stump, *Wandering in Darkness.* Laura Ekstrom, "A Christian Theodicy." William Lane Craig, "A Molinist View." John Feinberg, *The Many Faces of Evil,* and many others.

66. The appeal to mystery is prevalent among scholars. "As I read them, the other essayists provide partial solutions and appeal to mystery in the crucial issue of God preventing evil." Thomas Jay Oord, "The Essential Kenosis Response," 163.

believers and non-believers who question the existence of a good God in the presence of horrendous evils.

Elie Wiesel, the 1986 Nobel Peace Prize laureate, bitterly recounted his crisis of faith at Auschwitz and Buchenwald where his parents and younger sister were murdered:

> *For the first time, I felt anger rising within me. Why should I sanctify His name? The Almighty, the eternal and terrible Master of the Universe, chose to be silent. What was there to thank Him for? . . . Never shall I forget the small faces of the children whose bodies I saw transformed into smoke under a silent sky. Never shall I forget those flames that consumed my faith forever. Never shall I forget the nocturnal silence that deprived me for all eternity of the desire to live. Never shall I forget those moments that murdered my God and my soul and turned my dreams to ashes. Never shall I forget those things, even were I condemned to live as long as God Himself. Never.*[67]

Can a good and virtuous God exist in the presence of such vicious evils? Does this problem of evil have a solution?

Dr. Trakakis declared: "The problem of evil often strikes people as *irresolvable*. No adequate or convincing solution to the problem seems forthcoming, and this despite numerous and often sophisticated attempts over the centuries and from highly trained and gifted philosophers and theologians."[68] Dr. Bishop affirmed: "No satisfactory explanation of evil can be provided that fits with key theist values."[69] Dr. Oord stated: "For many believers, a solution to this age-old challenge is beyond hope."[70] Dr. Erickson acknowledged: "A total solution to the problem of evil is beyond human ability."[71] Dr. Grudem asserted: "We have to agree with Berkhof that ultimately 'the problem of God's relation to sin remains a mystery.'"[72] Dr. Plantinga, the 2017 Templeton Prize laureate, concluded: "A Christian must therefore admit that he doesn't know why God permits the evils this world displays."[73]

---

67. Elie Wiesel, *The Night Trilogy*, 51-52.
68. Nick Trakakis, "Anti-theodicy," 94.
69. John Bishop, "Response to Oppy," 84.
70. Thomas Jay Oord, "An Essential Kenosis View," 77.
71. Millard Erickson, *Christian Theology*, 394.
72. Wayne Grudem, *Systematic Theology*, 437. Louis Berkhof, *Systematic Theology*, 175.
73. Alvin Plantinga, "Self-Profile," 35.

Watching the grim situation,[74] Dr. Speak wondered: "Where does this leave us? Not, I hope, with simple cynicism about the project of theodicy or about the prospects for its future development."[75]

In agreement, this work will present a novel solution to the problem of evil. We will contend that, in tough love (a morally justifying reason),[76] God does *not* prevent all evils (moral and natural, gratuitous or otherwise), a direct rebuttal of the evidential argument from evil/evidential problem of evil's claim that God prevents all gratuitous evils.[77] In the broader context, this "Tough Love Theodicy" will also resolve Epicurus's paradox and the logical problem of evil as to how an omnipotent, omniscient, and omnibenevolent being can exist in the presence of evil (moral, natural . . .).

## Summary

The "coexistence of a virtuous God and vicious evil" is an enigma, eluding a satisfactory resolution since time immemorial, despite numerous efforts by countless theologians and philosophers over the millennia. Dr. Stump affirmed: "The problem of evil is so perennial a topic in philosophy that it sometimes seems an icon for philosophical puzzles that cannot be solved."[78] "To this day, there is no universally accepted solution to the theodicy problem even among philosophers. Indeed, for quite a number, the unsolved problem is a reason not to believe in an almighty and benevolent God at all."[79]

In response, we will introduce the Tough Love Theodicy, our answer to the age-old quandary. We will also address the seventh question of our project, "What is God's response to people who deny him and commit evil?"

74. After reviewing the numerous attempts to resolve the problem of evil and suffering, Dr. Ekstrom concluded: "We have not identified a convincing reason or set of reasons that could justify a perfect God in causing or allowing such suffering." Laura Ekstrom, *Evil and Theodicy*, 50.

75. Daniel Speak, *The Problem of Evil*, 114.

76. We do not claim that "tough love" is God's actual reason, only as a probable reason. "It is unnecessary, and often unwise, for the theodicist to claim that the reason given is the actual reason God has permitted the evil; this might or might not be the case." William Hasker, "An Open Theist View," 61.

77. Rowe's Theological Premise.

78. Eleonore Stump, *The Image of God*, 2.

79. Johannes Grössl, "Introduction," 4-5.

# 8

# What Is God's Response to People Who Deny Him and Commit Evil?

*I don't want there to be a God; I don't want the universe to be like that.*

—Thomas Nagel[1]

A CERTAIN FARMER WAS very rich, with much land and many possessions. One exceptional year, he was blessed with such a great harvest that he had no place to store his crops. Of course, he could sell the grain immediately since his barns were bursting with the fruits of the land. However, the price he could obtain would necessarily be low as he had to compete with all the other farmers eager to sell at harvest time!

Or he could be a good neighbor and give the surplus to the poor. "One who is gracious to a poor man lends to the Lord, and he will repay him for his good deed."[2] Rather than obeying God's command, "You shall freely open your hand to your brother, to your needy and poor in your land,"[3] he decided to ignore the Lord, act as if God does not exist, and keep the riches for himself.

So, he built bigger barns to hoard all his God-given crops, enough to eat, drink, and be merry for many years to come. The Lord's disapproval

---

1. Thomas Nagel, *The Last Word*, 130.
2. Prov 19:17
3. Deut 15:11

of the rich man's action was swift. "You fool! This very night your soul is required of you; and now who will own what you have prepared?"[4]

In this chapter, we will show that God disapproves of humans (e.g., "The rich farmer") who insist that "God is dead,"[5] God is a "benign, absentee landlord of the universe,"[6] "God is indifferent to our suffering,"[7] or "God does not exist"[8] (e.g., Benito Mussolini).[9] We will also introduce our Tough Love Theodicy, a novel approach to the problem of evil.

## Definitions

Contra Open Theism, God is defined as a being with absolute omnipotence,[10] unlimited omniscience,[11] and infinite omnibenevolence[12] (among his many other attributes).[13]

"Tough love" is defined as the "promotion of a person's welfare, especially that of an addict, child, or criminal, by enforcing certain constraints on them, or requiring them to take responsibility for their actions"[14]— with the goal of reconciliation[15] and restoring loving relationships.

4. Luke 12:20
5. "Gott ist tot." Friedrich Nietzsche, *The Gay Science (Die Fröhliche Wissenschaft)*, 181.
6. Roger Olson, *The Mosaic of Christian Belief*, 190.
7. László Bernáth and Daniel Kodaj, "Evil and the God of Indifference," 259-72.
8. Victor Stenger, *God, The Failed Hypothesis. How Science Shows That God Does Not Exist*.
9. "'God does not exist—religion in science is an absurdity, in practice an immorality and in men a disease.' Benito (Mussolini) upheld the affirmative (statement) before a huge Socialist audience." https://content.time.com/time/subscriber/article/0,33009,846545,00.html
10. "Omnipotence means that God is all-powerful and able to do anything consistent with His own nature." Charles Ryrie, *Basic Theology*, 40. Many people deny God's omnipotence. "God would like people to get what they deserve in life, but He cannot always arrange it." Harold Kushner, *When Bad Things Happen to Good People*, 42. Thomas Jay Oord, *God Can't*.
11. "The knowledge of God is not only perfect in kind, but also in its inclusiveness. It is called *omniscience*, because it is all-comprehensive . . . He knows all things as they actually come to pass, past, present, and future." Louis Berkhof, *Systematic Theology*, 67.
12. "All-loving, or infinitely good, usually in reference to a deity or supernatural being." https://www.yourdictionary.com/omnibenevolent
13. The Tough Love Theodicy does not adopt an alternative concept of God. See Andrei Buckareff and Yugin Nagasawa, eds. *Alternative Concepts of God*.
14. https://en.oxforddictionaries.com/definition/tough_love.
15. United Nations Office on Drugs and Crime, *Drug Counsellor's Handbook*.

Harsh treatment (physical violence, verbal and emotional abuse, coercion, blackmail, threats . . .)[16] is *not* what we mean by "tough love."[17]

Tough love takes concrete, caring steps to improve the situation, not giving in, giving up, disowning, shaming, guilting, enabling, or bailing out the immature person.

> *Saying "no" to a young adult may mean calling the police if you believe your grown son or daughter is headed for the street or a car and is impaired. Will that adult child be mad at you? A good chance of this in the short run. Will you have saved their life and their future? Possibly. Regardless of the outcome, you will be able to look in the mirror and say you took the loving and right action . . . A juvenile had gotten into lots of problems with drugs and the law. At one point in a counseling session, the young man looked over and asked his father—"would you cry for me if I died?" The father, a big burly man who had been angry and frustrated with his son, said without hesitation—"There are not enough buckets in the world to hold the tears I would cry if something happened to you." Do our young adults know that there are not enough buckets to hold the tears we would cry for them?*[18]

Likewise, God weeps and mourns for his wayward people. "Let my eyes overflow with tears night and day without ceasing, for the Virgin Daughter, my people."[19] The Lord *ceaselessly* calls his errant people to return, offering forgiveness and reconciliation. "Return to the Lord your God, for He is gracious and compassionate, slow to anger, abounding in lovingkindness."[20]

Tough love emphasizes *love*, a key ingredient in a balanced blend of warmth and firmness. It is to say to one's child: "You may hate my guts, but I love you, and I'm doing this because I love you."[21] Like the father of

16. "The study found that the substance abuse education/treatment programs actually implemented in boot camp facilities are not likely to result in the rehabilitation of boot camp participants." US Department of Justice, "'Boot Camp' Drug Treatment and Aftercare Interventions: An Evaluation Review."

17. "Treating someone harshly in hopes to improve behavior is ineffective at best." https://www.psychologytoday.com/us/blog/pulling-through/202007/dismantling-the-myth-tough-love

18. Jack Stoltzfus. https://parentslettinggo.com/try-love-tough-instead-of-tough-love-with-your-young-adult/

19. Jer 14:17 NIV.

20. Joel 2:13

21. Bill Milliken, *The Last Dropout*, 62. Bill Milliken coined the phrase "tough love" in 1968.

the Prodigal Son,[22] in tough love, God neither bails out his self-seeking creatures,[23] nor enables them in their path of self-destruction, but patiently[24] and longingly awaits their return!

## The Tough Love Solution to the Problem of Evil

The Tough Love Theodicy consists of three premises leading to the conclusion that a good God and evil (moral, natural . . .) coexist on earth.

1. If God exists, he disapproves[25] of humans claiming that he does not exist (Ps 14:1, Ps 10:4, Rom 1:21–22).

2. The disavowed[26] God reluctantly lets humans separate themselves from him and, in love, patiently calls them to return. In his disapproval and tough love, God does not intervene to prevent all moral evils, gratuitous or otherwise (Rom 1:28–31, Luke 15:11–32, Job 21:14–16).

3. In his disapproval and tough love, God does not intervene in humans' environment to prevent all natural evils, gratuitous or otherwise (Rom 8:20–22, Gen 3:17–18, Isa 24:5–6).

4. Therefore, if God exists, then God and evil (moral and natural evils, gratuitous or otherwise) coexist (Isa 45:7, Amos 3:6, Matt 6:13).

The valid deductive argument[27] is sound if the premises are true.

---

22. Luke 15:11-32

23. And "if he did, what would happen next? What would prevent the fall from immediately recurring?" Peter van Inwagen, "The Magnitude, Duration, and Distribution of Evil," 380.

24. "The Lord is not slow about His promise, as some count slowness, but is patient toward you, not wishing for any to perish but for all to come to repentance" (2 Pet 3:9).

25. "To think (something) wrong or reprehensible; censure or condemn in opinion; to withhold approval from; decline to sanction." https://www.dictionary.com/browse/disapprove.

26. "To disclaim knowledge of, connection with, or responsibility for; disown; repudiate." https://www.dictionary.com/browse/disavow

27. If God exists, he disapproves of humans claiming that he does not exist.
If he disapproves of humans claiming that he does not exist, then, in tough love, he does not intervene to prevent all evils (moral and natural evils, gratuitous or otherwise).
If, in tough love, he does not intervene to prevent all evils (moral and natural evils, gratuitous or otherwise), then God and evil coexist.
Therefore, if God exists, then God and evil coexist.

## Support for the First Premise of the Tough Love Theodicy

Secular support for the first premise.

The first premise of the Tough Love Theodicy states: "If God exists, he disapproves of humans claiming that he does not exist." No one likes to be treated as a non-person; everyone likes to be recognized and acknowledged. Dale Carnegie advocated: "Remember that a man's name is to him the sweetest and most important sound in any language."[28] "Remember that name and call it easily, and you have paid him a subtle and very effective compliment. But forget it . . . and you have placed yourself at a sharp disadvantage."[29] Likewise, God, as a person,[30] wants to be addressed as a real being and not treated as a non-entity.

Ludwig was a professor of physics in Austria. His work demonstrated that the second law of thermodynamics could be reduced to a probabilistic law of collision of atoms. Unfortunately, most scientists at the time disbelieved the existence of atoms, preferring the electromagnetic view of nature. Ludwig tried to suggest a compromise, to no avail.

At a major conference, he was shunned by his colleagues who would not allow his research to be presented in the physics section of the meeting.[31] Despite a spirited defense of his theory, he continued to be ignored by the scientific community.

On September 5, 1906, while on vacation with his wife and daughter, he committed suicide by hanging himself. Ludwig Boltzmann was only 62 years old. His contributions to science included the Maxwell-Boltzmann distribution, the Boltzmann equation, and the Boltzmann constant. A brilliant career was unfortunately cut short by a lack of acknowledgment of one's worth and existence.

Being snubbed and "ignored is a hurtful experience that can make you feel anxious, angry, or sad. But no one deserves this treatment."[32] "Think of the last time you sent an important email and didn't get a response. Your first reaction was probably, '*He's just busy*.' After a few days, you wonder,

---

28. Dale Carnegie, *How to Win Friends and Influence People*, 84.

29. Ibid., 80.

30. "Since everything that is perfect must be attributed to God, forasmuch as His essence contains every perfection, this name 'person' is fittingly applied to God." Thomas Aquinas, *Summa Theologica*, 1.29.3

31. John Blackmore, *Ludwig Boltzmann*, 115.

32. Melody Causewell, "What Does It Mean to Ignore Someone?" https://oureverydaylife.com/mean-ignore-someone-5384614.html

'*Did he get my email?*' A few days later, '*What did I do wrong?*'"[33] This is not how we should treat other people, dismissing them as unimportant, bothersome non-entities. Hence, we should not be surprised that God (if he exists) disapproves of humans dismissing him as a Santa Claus-like myth[34] and spurning his repeated calls through the Church!

In 2020, Christians and Jews accounted for only 31.2 percent of the world population,[35] leaving 68.8 percent not believing in the Judeo-Christian God. Furthermore, "in the United Kingdom . . . there are roughly three times as many non-practicing Christians (55%) as there are church-attending Christians (18%)."[36] In the US, only "9% of those identifying as Christians possess a biblical worldview, believing the Bible to be accurate and reliable."[37] God's displeasure is therefore justified as only a small minority of humanity acknowledges his existence and biblical precepts.

People who deny God's existence can only rely on themselves to manage the many evils in this world. Paul Tillich observed: "Since the beginning of the 18th century, God has been removed from the power field of man's activities. He has been put alongside the world *without permission to interfere* with it because every interference would disturb man's technical and business calculations. The result is that God has become superfluous, and the universe left to man as its master."[38]

Self-seeking humans choose to disavow God, reject his offered love, and break his fatherly heart as he aims for nothing but the well-being of his children. "God grants us freedom,[39] even to reject his love . . . the father still holds out his broken end of the rope of the relationship hoping that the other end can yet be joined. In so doing, he suffers."[40]

We have all experienced the agonizing torment of unreciprocated love, whether from a potential mate, a parent, or a child.

---

33. Tasha Eurich, "The Hidden Costs of Ignoring Email." https://www.entrepreneur.com/article/244751

34. Nigel Barber, "Why Believe in God but Not Santa Claus?" https://www.huffpost.com/entry/why-believe-in-god-but-not-santa-claus_b_4816026

35. https://worldpopulationreview.com/country-rankings/religion-by-country

36. https://www.pewresearch.org/religion/2018/05/29/being-christian-in-western-europe/

37. https://julieroys.com/george-barna-survey-biblical-worldview/

38. Paul Tillich, *Theology of Culture*, 43-44.

39. "God surely approves of the conditions of cognitive freedom within which some persons conclude that he does not exist." Michael Peterson, personal communication.

40. Kenneth Bailey, *The Cross & the Prodigal*, 47.

> *At 5 years old, my son thought he was Michelangelo from Teenage Mutant Ninja Turtles. He used to run around the house with an orange bandanna tied around his head, brandishing plastic weapons and fighting evil. When we look at our children with addiction, at times we see that 5-year-old and mourn the loss of a child. We would try anything to get them back. My son is now a 21-year-old man. He is an adult, with a child's maturity at times. However, our world recognizes chronological age, not maturity level. Parents must learn to do that, too. I will always believe that Michelangelo is lost inside of him. Those that are lost sometimes find their way back, but some do not. I can grieve this loss, but it will not help either of us if we don't move forward.*[41]

Likewise, God's fatherly heart aches, mourning the lost relationships, the denials of his existence,[42] and the repeated rejections[43] of his appeals through the Church to reconcile and accept his love!

## Biblical support for the first premise.

In Romans 1:21–22, the apostle Paul asserted: "For even though they knew God, they did not honor Him as God or give thanks, but they became futile in their speculations, and their foolish heart was darkened. Professing to be wise, they became fools." The word "fool" here is the Greek "moraino," meaning "dull, silly, to play the fool, to be foolish."[44] Thus, God disapproves of humans who do not honor him as God.

In Psalm 10:4, the psalmist declared, "The wicked, in the haughtiness of his countenance, does not seek Him. All his thoughts are, 'There is no God.'" The word "wicked" here is the Hebrew "rasha" meaning "criminal, guilty of hostility to God, of crime, of sin, deserving of punishment."[45]

---

41. Ron Grover, "7 Truths about My Son's Addiction That Took 5 Years to Learn." https://drugfree.org/parent-blog/7-truths-about-my-addict-that-took-5-years-to-learn/

42. "There is no God. No one created the universe, and no one directs our fate." Stephen Hawking, *Brief Answers to the Big Questions*, 38. "The whole conception of God is a conception derived from the ancient Oriental despotisms. It is a conception quite unworthy of free men." Bertrand Russell, *Why I Am Not a Christian*, 23.

43. Christopher Hitchens, *God Is Not Great: How Religion Poisons Everything.* "One of the truly bad effects of religion is that it teaches us that it is a virtue to be satisfied with not understanding." Richard Dawkins, *The God Delusion*, 152. "Christianity will go . . . It will vanish and shrink." John Lennon, https://www.britannica.com/story/did-the-beatles-really-say-they-were-more-popular-than-jesus

44. https://biblehub.com/greek/3471.htm

45. F. Brown, S. Driver, and C. Briggs. *The Brown-Driver-Briggs Hebrew and English*

God pronounced those who denied his existence guilty of hostility to him and deserving of punishment. "'When I called, they did not listen; so, when they called, I would not listen,' says the Lord Almighty."[46] People who deny God's existence should *not* expect God to intervene and prevent moral and natural evils in their lives (no bailing out or enabling).

Through King David, God affirmed in Psalm 14:1, "The fool has said in his heart, 'There is no God.'" The word "fool" here is the Hebrew "nabal" meaning "senseless, foolish, ignoble, disgraceful."[47] Did David remember a certain person when he wrote this psalm?

When David was on the run from King Saul who wanted to kill him, he needed provisions to feed his six hundred men in the wilderness. Hoping to earn goodwill, he faithfully protected the servants and the property of the rich "Nabal" from any danger.

At the festive time of sheep shearing, when the fruit of one's long labor was finally gathered and the hearts of men were joyful and inclined to be generous, David, the future king of Israel, humbly asked Nabal for some donations. "Please give whatever you find at hand to your servants and to your son David."[48]

Rather than granting that reasonable and polite request, Nabal foolishly chose to insult the future king (anointed by God),[49] ignoring the obvious danger of revenge and disaster to his whole household. "Who is David? And who is the son of Jesse? There are many servants today who are each breaking away from his master. Shall I then take my bread and my water and my meat that I have slaughtered for my shearers, and give it to men whose origin I do not know?"[50]

As expected, David angrily gathered his troops and set out to murder Nabal! God, in his mercy, intervened through the entreaty of Abigail, Nabal's wife, and prevented David from committing a great sin (murder for revenge) that could have later repercussions for his royal rule.[51] Then,

---

*Lexicon*, 957.

46. Zech 7:13 NIV.

47. F. Brown, S. Driver, and C. Briggs. *The Brown-Driver-Briggs Hebrew and English Lexicon*, 614-15.

48. 1 Sam 25:8

49. 1 Sam 16:12

50. 1 Sam 25:10-11

51. 1 Sam 25:31

"the Lord struck Nabal, and he died."[52] His wife Abigail became David's wife, a sad ending[53] for a "nabal" who did not acknowledge his maker.

"My people are determined to turn from me . . . How can I give you up, Ephraim? How can I hand you over, Israel? . . . My heart is changed within me; all my compassion is aroused."[54] God mourns as he watches his beloved people mired in evil. He is not indifferent to their sufferings. Though he disapproves of their stubborn denial of his existence, he still yearns for them in heartbreak and sorrow. Will his creatures ever return and accept his steadfast love?

## Summary

In this chapter, we have introduced the Tough Love Theodicy consisting of three premises leading to the conclusion that God and evil coexist on this earth. In answer to the seventh question of our journey, using secular evidence, case studies, and Scriptures, we have shown that God disapproves of humans claiming that he does not exist. With great sadness, he mourns the broken relationships and grieves in his unreciprocated love for his wayward children!

Yet, if he genuinely cares for us, why does he not intervene to prevent all the moral evils in the world (the eighth question of our project and the second premise of the Tough Love Theodicy)?

---

52. 1 Sam 25:38

53. It is the practice of victorious conquerors to take over the wives of the defeated. "He (Emperor Wu) acquired the harem of a defeated ruler." Keith McMahon, "The Institution of Polygamy in the Chinese Imperial Palace," 925. "They (the Romans) sent a general against the Greeks and attacked them. Many of them were wounded and fell, and the Romans took captive their wives." 1 Maccabees 8:10. http://www.pseudepigrapha.com/apocrypha_ot/1macc.htm

54. Hos 11:7-8 NIV.

# 9

# Why Does God Not Intervene to Prevent All Moral Evils?

*God does not intervene to prevent man from doing evil. To do so would be to remove from man that which makes him human.*

—Abraham Cohen[1]

Iosif was the only surviving offspring of a poor, wife-beating, alcoholic shoemaker, and a laundress. Having contracted smallpox as a boy, he was left with a pockmarked face. His mother finally escaped from the abusive relationship and moved to the house of a priest who arranged for the child to attend a church school. Fortunately, Iosif excelled in his studies and earned a scholarship to the Spiritual Seminary.

However, his ideas about God changed from reading Darwin's *Origin of Species*. He professed to a friend: "They are fooling us. There is no god."[2] Iosif declared himself an atheist, got involved in Marxist propaganda, and was expelled from the seminary. He became a political activist against the government and raised funds for the communist party by staging robberies, running protection rackets, counterfeiting currencies,[3] and kidnapping children for ransom. He was arrested many times and sentenced to prison and Siberian exiles.

---

1. Abraham Cohen, "Theology and Theodicy," 235.
2. https://www.marxists.org/archive/murphy-jt/1945/stalin/01.htm
3. Robert Service, *Lenin: A Biography*, 74.

After the Russian revolution of 1917 and the death of his protégé Lenin, Iosif outmaneuvered his rivals and became the dictator of the Soviet Union. He followed in the footsteps of Lenin who once declared: "'Religion is the opium of the people'—and this postulate is the corner stone of the whole philosophy of Marxism with regard to religion."[4]

In 1932, Iosif promulgated "The five-year plan of atheism" with the stated goal that "not a single house of prayer shall remain in the territory of the USSR, and the very concept of God must be banished from the Soviet Union."[5] The target of the campaign was the Russian Orthodox Church. Clergy and believers were killed or sent to the gulags. By 1939, only 1% of the churches remained open.

Iosif also orchestrated the "Great Purge" of 1936–1938, resulting in the murder of 600,000 people, including members of the Communist party, government officials, and Red Army leadership.

The estimated death toll from his hands was twenty million people, the entire population of New York State. Where was God in this mass murder? Why did he not intervene and end the wholesale butchery? Iosif Dzhugashvili (code name "Stalin" meaning "man of steel") boldly declared: "God is not unjust; he doesn't actually exist."[6]

In this chapter, we will show that God, in tough love and disapproval of humans who deny his existence, does not intervene to prevent all moral evils (murders, wars . . .). Pains and sufferings in this world are due to human actions as they insist on fulfilling their desires.[7]

## Support for the Second Premise of the Tough Love Theodicy

Secular support for the second premise.

The second premise of the Tough Love Theodicy states: The disavowed God reluctantly lets humans separate themselves from him and, in love, patiently calls them to return. In his disapproval and tough love, God does not intervene to prevent all moral evils, gratuitous or otherwise.[8]

---

4. Paul Dixon, "Religion in the Soviet Union." https://www.bolshevik.info/religion-soviet-union170406.htm

5. Ibid.

6. Simon Montefiore, *Young Stalin*, 40.

7. Rom 3:10-18

8. The Tough Love Theodicy rebuts Rowe's Theological Premise that God prevents *all* gratuitous evils.

People who deny God's existence and *separate themselves* from him[9] are free[10] to act as they see fit, doing good (Warren Buffett gave more than $51 billion to charitable causes)[11] as well as evil (Stalin's horrendous crimes). Moral goods and evils are the consequences of human actions or inactions. Billy Graham affirmed: "God is not responsible for what evil men do; they alone are responsible, and they are accountable to God for their evil actions . . . When men allow sin to take over their souls and live without any restraints, they end up doing terrible things to others."[12] The German philosopher Immanuel Kant declared: "We are accountable for the propensity to evil; for as this concerns the morality of the subject and is consequently found in him as a freely acting being, it must be imputed to him as his own fault."[13] Since people are in full control of their lives and (most of) their environment, they must bear total responsibility for their deeds.[14] If they do well and solve all the troubles in the world, they can congratulate themselves for a job well done. However, if they struggle with horrendous evils and unmanageable problems, they have two options to consider.

They can decide to seek help from God as did the Russians after Stalin's "reign of terror" and the demise of communism. "Between 1991 and 2008, the share of Russian adults identifying as Orthodox Christian

---

9. Addressing Dr. Daniel Speak's comment (personal communication), humans deny God's existence and *separate themselves* from God, rather than God separating himself from them (e.g., the parable of the Prodigal Son in Luke 15).

10. Both compatibilists and libertarians agree that humans have free will (compatibilist versus libertarian free will), and that humans are responsible for their actions, whether good or evil. The Tough Love Theodicy can accommodate both compatibilists and libertarians. Contrary to some greater good theodicies, the Tough Love Theodicy does not claim that free will is a "greater good" outweighing (or justifying) all the evils in the world. Rather, free will is a *logical requirement* of a true love relationship between Creator and creatures. Since God desires freely given love from his creatures, he must *logically* accept freely given rejection (possibly resulting in much evil and no greater good).

11. https://www.reuters.com/markets/us/warren-buffetts-charitable-giving-tops-51-billion-2023-06-22/

12. Billy Graham. https://billygraham.org/answer/if-god-is-in-control-why-did-he-make-people-like-hitler-or-stalin-who-caused-the-deaths-of-millions-doesnt-that-make-god-responsible-for-those-deaths/

13. Immanuel Kant, *Kant's Critique of Practical Reason (Kritik der Praktischen Vernunft)*, 342.

14. "God, being wholly good, has created humans with free will and we are responsible for evil by the exercise of our free will." Adam Willows, "Augustine, The Origin of Evil, and The Mystery of Free Will," 256.

rose from 31% to 72%."[15] Contrary to Stalin's belief, religious convictions have been associated with better physical[16] and mental health. Dr. Freud, the Austrian neurologist and father of psychoanalysis, declared: "The true believer is in a high degree protected against the danger of certain neurotic afflictions."[17] Dr. Koenig, a professor of psychiatry at Duke University, affirmed: "A large volume of research shows that people who are more R/S (religious/spiritual) have better mental health and adapt more quickly to health problems compared to those who are less R/S."[18] Thus, religion can serve a very useful role in society.

These positive benefits require acknowledging that God exists, for how can one ask for support from a non-existent being? If humans *freely* choose to take this path, the tough love approach (no bailing out or enabling, with God's ceaseless call to reconcile) will be successful in bringing them back to God.

On the other hand, if people are happy with their decision to pursue their own desires, if they do not mind occasional reversals in their lives, they are free to persist in their conviction that God is non-existent.

When non-theists encounter evils, such calamities are often deemed products of random chance or of other people's twisted wills. In that environment, there is no God, religion is a pox of humanity (according to Hitler and Richard Dawkins),[19] and evils are just the normal consequences of life, serving no defined purpose and having no redeeming value. "There is, at the bottom, no design, no purpose, no evil and no good. Nothing but blind, pitiless indifference."[20]

Amid random adversities, people can choose to tough it out and continue to go it alone. The reasoning may be that God is a human

---

15. Pew Research Center. "Russians Return to Religion." http://www.pewforum.org/2014/02/10/russians-return-to-religion-but-not-to-church/

16. "People who regularly attend religious services tend to have lower rates of mortality and hospital admissions in any given period, as well as better cardiovascular function." David DeSteno, "Is Religion Good for Your Health?" https://www.wsj.com/articles/is-religion-good-for-your-health-921814a7

17. Sigmund Freud, *The Future of an Illusion (Die Zukunft Einer Illusion)*, 76–77.

18. Harold Koenig, "Religion, Spirituality, and Health: The Research and Clinical Implications."

19. "The reason why the ancient world was so pure, light, and serene was that it knew nothing of the two great scourges: the pox and Christianity." Adolf Hitler, *Hitler's Table Talk (Tischgespräche im Führerhauptquartier)*, 48. "I think a case can be made that faith is one of the world's great evils, comparable to the smallpox virus but harder to eradicate." Richard Dawkins, "Is Science a Religion?" 26.

20. Richard Dawkins, *River Out of Eden*, 133.

invention and seeking help from that quarter is totally illogical,[21] a delusion,[22] and a fool's errand.

Humans may also think that inviting God to the table will require giving up too much control for too little gain as no one likes to be told what to do and few people delight in giving someone else veto power over their lives. The Brazilian novelist Paulo Coelho asserted:

> *Surrendering completely to love, be it human or divine, means giving up everything, including our own well-being or our ability to make decisions. It means loving in the deepest sense of the word. The truth is that we don't want to be saved in the way God has chosen; we want to keep absolute control over our every step, to be fully conscious of our decisions, to be capable of choosing the object of our devotion.*[23]

Besides the fear of losing control, non-theists are also deterred by hypocritical Christians[24] who often act contrary to their stated beliefs and go through lives in the same manner as their non-Christian brethren.

The reasons given by non-theists for keeping their cherished independence are numerous.[25] One cannot say that they are unreasonable or illogical in their decisions. After all, God gives everyone the freedom to acknowledge his existence or not.

Christians may face the same difficulties as their non-theist brethren (e.g., thefts, cancer). However, the evils are now thought to be intended for good as God is believed to be alive and active, bringing good out of evil with an eye toward a positive outcome!

People can live their lives as they see fit. They may believe or disbelieve God's existence. They may choose to relish in the here and now without any thought for the hereafter, or they may decide to soldier on in this fleeting and often challenging existence, looking forward to the rewards in the world to come. Everyone is free to make his or her own

---

21. Jason Sylvester, "Christianity: Fundamentally Illogical." https://www.atheistalliance.org/blog/christianity-fundamentally-illogical/

22. Richard Dawkins, *The God Delusion*.

23. Paulo Coelho, *The Witch of Portobello (A Bruxa de Portobello)*, 18.

24. Lee Goff. "The church is full of hypocrites. Yes, it is . . . The church wants hypocrites, adulterers, thieves, and more, for the church is where we receive healing. To condemn the church because it has failed members is to condemn a hospital because it's full of sick people." https://www.goodreads.com/quotes/845932-the-church-is-full-of-hypocrites-yes-it-is-and

25. Bertrand Russell, *Why I am Not a Christian*. Daniel Dennett, *Breaking the Spell*. Sam Harris, *The End of Faith*.

decision. May we do so wisely and live at peace with one another as we (theists and non-theists) must share a common abode!

Some non-theists have claimed in the "Evidential argument from evil/evidential problem of evil" that there are gratuitous evils in this world, evils that lead to no greater goods or do not prevent worse evils. Are there such things as gratuitous evils? While we cannot be dogmatic about the matter, the answer would have to be "possibly yes."[26] The assertion that the innumerable horrendous evils in this realm (e.g., rapes, murders) *all* lead to greater goods is hard for most people to believe and accept.[27]

If one maintains that sufferings on earth happen for a good reason, the good may be the opportunity for the prodigal sons and daughters to reconcile with their heavenly Father, when they realize that they need help with their dire problems. The evils and pains they suffer will be redeemed by the "greater good" of an eternal fellowship with God.

However, if they decide not to avail themselves of the opportunity to reconcile with their maker, or if they decide to do so only after much adversity, the calamities they endure may well be gratuitous as the "ultimate good" of a relationship with God is not achieved or only obtained after much unnecessary suffering.

Hence, evils in a person's life (e.g., a drunk driving accident) may turn out to be gratuitous or non-gratuitous, *depending on the person's response*. Dr. Crummett observed: "Achieving the goods in question requires a particular free response on the part of the sufferer, and some people, believe it or not, may ultimately be so perverse as to not love God no matter how horrific the torments he allows to befall them."[28]

---

26. For the sake of discussion, we will grant the claim that there are gratuitous evils (Rowe's factual premise). The Tough Love Theodicy can accommodate both the presence and absence of gratuitous evils.

27. "I believe almost any of us would naturally tend to agree with Oord that there are many, many instances of genuine (gratuitous, unjustified) evil in our world." William Hasker, "The Open Theist Response," 158.

28. Dustin Crummett, "Sufferer-Centered Requirements on Theodicy and All-Things-Considered Harms," 75.

Contrary to the Greater Good Theodicy's[29] claim that evil *always* leads to a "greater good,"[30] the Tough Love Theodicy acknowledges that the evils self-seeking humans commit may not bring any greater good (e.g., child abuse, murder).

In his disapproval of creatures who deny his existence and perpetrate wrongdoing, in tough love, the disavowed Creator—aiming for their return and reconciliation—refuses to enable them in their errant paths (e.g., drug addiction) and does *not* intervene to prevent all moral evils, gratuitous or otherwise (e.g., drug overdose).

Enabling

> *refers to the act of helping someone in such a way that rather than solving a problem, it is, in fact, being perpetuated... It is common for family members to believe they are helping their addicted loved ones when, in reality, they are acting as enablers. To truly help an addict or an alcoholic, you should be ready, willing, and prepared to address the consequences of substance abuse. Your approach will require honesty and boundaries while being able to enforce consequences and accountability.*[31]

Likewise, God holds self-declared independent creatures accountable for their actions and the resulting consequences (e.g., diseases from drug abuse, jail time for robbery and murder). In the words of Dr. van Inwagen, after much pain and suffering from our ill-advised deeds, we may become "*dissatisfied* with our state of separation from Him."[32] We can then choose either to return to God, acknowledge his existence, and seek his help, or we can continue in our way of "freedom and independence" and live with the outcome, whether good or evil.

---

29. The Greater Good Theodicy "states that God allows only the evil from which He can bring about a greater good or prevent a worse evil." Bruce Little, *God, Why This Evil*, 2. Greater Good Theodicies claim that evil always leads to (or follows) a "greater good" (e.g., Felix culpa, Soul-making, Free will, Molinism, Divine intimacy, Relationship building, God's justice in punishing sin, Heaven swamps everything . . .). In the Tough Love Theodicy, greater goods may not happen for all people.

30. A specific-benefit theodicy "requires that there be a specific benefit from the particular evil under consideration." In contrast, a general-policy theodicy "justifies God's permission of certain evils as being the consequence of a general policy that a wise and benevolent might well adopt." William Hasker, "An Open Theist View," 61-62.

31. Family First Intervention. https://family-intervention.com/blog/the-truth-about-enabling/

32. Peter van Inwagen, "The Magnitude, Duration, and Distribution of Evil: A Theodicy," 381.

With this tough love approach, humans should not be surprised that God *appears* to be a hidden,[33] indifferent landlord,[34] an imaginary being,[35] or a dead deity.[36]

In long-suffering, the heavenly Father perseveres in the tough love path to bring his children back into a relationship with him. Similarly, fathers and mothers hold fast in hope, refusing to give in, bail out their kids, and allow them to go down the spiral of self-destruction (e.g., alcohol abuse).

> *Erin Brockovich, the famed environmental crusader played by Julia Roberts in a 2000 movie, faced a similar situation with her own daughter. Elizabeth, then 16-years-old, was addicted to drugs and alcohol. Her $500 a week drug habit was funded by money stolen from the family. "As a parent, you want to believe your kid, yet you know something's wrong," Brockovich said. "I've cried myself to sleep. And I've honestly sat and shook in a corner." Elizabeth refused to admit to her mother the seriousness of the problem, but*

---

33. Dr. Hick proposed the concept of "a distance in the dimension of knowledge" ("epistemic distance"), the "hiddenness" of God to preserve human freedom and "soul making." John Hick, *Philosophy of Religion*, 44. Dr. Schellenberg argued that, if God exists, there should not be any "reasonable non-believers," people who would be willing to believe in God if he had been less "hidden." J. L. Schellenberg, *Divine Hiddenness and Human Reason*. However, short of a blatant display of power, there will always be "insufficient evidence," and "too much hiddenness." The French theologian Blaise Pascal asserted: "There is enough light for those who only desire to see, and enough obscurity for those who have a contradictory disposition." Pascal, *The Thoughts of Blaise Pascal (Pensées)*, Pensée # 430. "Determined skeptics might not be persuaded regardless of the type or amount of evidence." Tyler Taber, "Divine Hiddenness and the Problem of Evil," 23. Furthermore, would God consider non-belief in his existence a "reasonable non-belief" after expending incredible amounts of money (billions of dollars), time, effort, and lives of his followers (and his own involvement through the Holy Spirit) to spread the message far and wide about his existence?

34. The "hypothesis of indifference" claims that if supreme beings exist, they are indifferent to human suffering. Supposedly, this hypothesis explains the presence of pain and suffering better than the belief in the existence of a good God. Paul Draper, "Pain and Pleasure: An Evidential Problem for Theists," 331-50. In the Tough Love Theodicy, God is not indifferent to our sufferings. He endeavors to help (The Salvation Army, World Relief, Children's Hunger Fund . . .) and ceaselessly calls humans to return to him for a better future.

35. Paul Pardi, "Jesus, the Easter Bunny, and Other Delusions: Just Say No!" https://www.philosophynews.com/post/2012/02/14/Jesus-the-Easter-Bunny-and-Other-Delusions-Just-Say-No.aspx

36. Friedrich Nietzsche, *The Gay Science (Die Fröhliche Wissenschaft)*, 181. The saying is not original to Nietzsche. "'God is dead!' . . . appears in Hegel at least three times." Eric Von Der Luft, "Sources of Nietzsche's 'God is Dead!' and its Meaning for Heidegger," 263.

> Brockovich knew she had to take action. Not wanting to completely isolate her daughter, Brockovich continued to offer emotional support to Elizabeth, but cut the financial purse strings from her daughter. This kind of financial tough love approach is one of the best ways parents can reach out to a child in trouble.[37]

"Tough love takes courage. Some of the children clear out. This is hard on parents, but they accept the risk because the alternative of continuing to support irresponsible behavior is worse."[38] "There's ultimately only one person who can help your loved one get better: the addict himself or herself. You didn't cause it, you can't control it, and you can't cure it."[39] In long-suffering, parents (and God) continue to offer an avenue for reconciliation in the face of persistent denial and rejection! As parents extend love and emotional support, God also holds out the promise of complete forgiveness, a restored loving relationship, and abundant help to sort out one's problems.

Thus, tough love is a reasonable approach for God to adopt with humans. It has been used widely in the fields of medicine,[40] economics,[41] education,[42] politics,[43] social work,[44] altruism,[45] criminal justice,[46] psychology[47] . . .

While tough love is not a panacea, God does not have any other (loving and non-coercing) alternative if people demand their rights to go their own way. Dr. Hasker affirmed: "If the children insist on making

---

37. https://abcnews.go.com/WN/tough-love-families-dealing-drug-addiction/story?id=9841591

38. Garrett Hardin, "The Toughlove Solution," *Newsweek* Oct 26, 1981, 45.

39. Promises Treatment Centers, "Using Phrases Like 'Rock Bottom' Is Easy; Living with Them Is Hard." https://www.promises.com/articles/addiction-intervention/using-phrases-like-rock-bottom-easy-living-hard/

40. Ron Zodkevitch MD, *The Tough Love Prescription*.

41. Beata Javorcik and Mariana Spatareanu, "Tough-love: Do Czech Suppliers Learn from their Relationships with Multinationals?" 811–33.

42. Frederick Hess, *Tough love for Schools*.

43. Steven Blockmans, *Tough Love: The European Union's Relations with the Western Balkans*.

44. Bill Jordan and Charlie Jordan. *Social Work and the Third Way: Tough-love as Social Policy*.

45. Spiros Bougheas et al., "Tough-love or Unconditional Charity?" 561–82.

46. Stacey Burns and Mark Peyrot, "Tough-love: Nurturing and Coercing Responsibility and Recovery in California Drug Courts," 416-38.

47. Lisa Stiepock, Amy Lorio, and Lori Gottlieb, eds. *Tough Love: Raising Confident, Kind, Resilient Kids; 18 Top Experts Share Proven Parenting Strategies*.

*really big* mistakes (the biblical story of the Prodigal Son may serve as an example), the parents may have no choice but to stand back, despite their own pain and foreboding, and let the child experience the consequences of the course he has chosen."[48] Likewise, the disavowed Father reluctantly lets his wayward children leave and do what they desire. In love, he patiently awaits their return and a blessed reconciliation.

This is not to say that he is doing nothing in the meantime. Contrary to deism,[49] God ceaselessly calls his errant children to acknowledge his existence through the tireless, persuasive work of the churches (sermons, evangelistic rallies, billboards . . .).[50] The benevolent Creator never gives up on his creatures. He actively undertakes *numerous* positive endeavors on various fronts (Food for the Hungry, Catholic Medical Mission, Christian orphanages, clean water projects . . .) to redress the situation (i.e., "love"). He also lets humans exercise their free will on earth and live with the consequences (i.e., "tough"). The combination of "love" and "tough consequences" provides a constructive path for people to come to their senses and return to their maker.

Since we are not born knowing God,[51] he uses various means to make his creatures aware of his existence. Astounding numbers of Bibles are freely distributed worldwide in (almost) all languages. Religious books are widely available everywhere at low (or no) cost to anyone willing to read and ponder God's existence. Internet postings, radio and television broadcasts spread the message far and wide. Furthermore, friends, co-workers, relatives, acquaintances, and even strangers are more than willing to share their knowledge of God with anyone who would show the least bit of interest (or even no interest at all)! God is investing enormous amounts of money (in 2021, American churches received 135.78 billion dollars),[52] prodigious volumes of time (more than 2000 years), incalculable measures of talent (medical, engineering, business, musical . . .) and untold lives (900,000 Christian martyrs

---

48. William Hasker, "God and Gratuitous Evil," 475.

49. Clarification following a comment by Dr. Bruce Reichenbach—personal communication. Deism is defined as "the belief in a single god who does not act to influence events, and whose existence has no connection with religions, religious buildings, or religious books, etc." https://dictionary.cambridge.org/us/dictionary/english/deism.

50. and the conviction of the Holy Spirit.

51. "The newborn child has no conscious conviction of the existence of God." Charles Hodge, *Systematic Theology*, Vol. 1, 93. "We had, by nature, no knowledge of God." John Wesley, *The Works of the Rev. John Wesley*, 191.

52. https://www.churchtrac.com/articles/the-state-of-church-giving

## WHY DOES GOD NOT INTERVENE TO PREVENT ALL MORAL EVILS?

over the last decade, one every six minutes)[53] of his followers to let the entire world know about his existence.

Is that massive endeavor bringing satisfactory results? In 2023, according to the Pew Research Center, "28% of U.S. adults are religiously unaffiliated, describing themselves as atheists, agnostics, or 'nothing in particular' when asked about their religion,"[54] up from 16% in 2007, despite monumental evangelistic efforts and immense financial expenditures. So, it should not be surprising that God would adopt a tough love approach *in addition to* his other means (evangelistic rallies, medical missions, TV and radio programs, internet websites . . .) to bring people to himself.

Is tough love going to be ultimately successful? The French Jesuit priest Jean-Pierre de Caussade affirmed: "Crosses and afflictions are such great graces that the wicked are rarely converted without them, and good people are only made perfect by the same means."[55] Parents using tough love with drug addicted children always hope that their offspring will soon hit "rock bottom" and "see the light." However, as we all know, the results of tough love are not uniformly positive. People may still decide to persist and die in their destructive paths rather than come to their senses, no matter how much help they receive to overcome their problems. For example, according to Dr. Dodes, a psychiatry professor at Harvard Medical School, a 12-step recovery program like Alcoholic Anonymous has a success rate of only between "5 and 10 percent."[56] "Of the 23.5 million teenagers and adults addicted to alcohol or drugs, only about 1 in 10 gets treatment, which too often fails to keep them drug-free."[57]

A tough love approach (letting people live with the consequences of their actions, no bailing out or enabling) is often the only avenue left to salvage a tragic situation. Dr. Stump observed: "No amount of moral or natural evil, of course, can *guarantee* that a man will seek God's help. If it could, the willing it produced would not be free. But evil of this sort is the best hope, I think, and maybe the only effective means, for bringing men

---

53. Peter Walker, "900,000 Christians were 'martyred' over last decade, says Christian research." https://www.independent.co.uk/news/christians-killed-martyred-900000-last-decade-africa-boko-haram-al-shabaab-study-of-global-a7526226.html

54. https://www.pewresearch.org/religion/2024/01/24/religious-nones-in-america-who-they-are-and-what-they-believe/

55. Jean-Pierre de Caussade, *Abandonment to Divine Providence (L'Abandon à la Divine Providence)*, 287.

56. Lance Dodes and Zachary Dodes, *The Sober Truth*, 1.

57. Jane Brody, "Effective Addiction Treatment," *The New York Times*, February 4, 2013.

to such a state."[58] God's tough love, combined with his countless other evangelistic efforts, offers only a modest hope of bringing humanity back into a relationship with him.

Hence, many non-theists have steadfastly denied the existence of a good and virtuous God by citing various cases of vicious moral evils.

## The Case of Five-year-old "Sue"

> *A report in the Detroit Free Press of January 3, 1986, runs as follows:*
>
> *The girl's mother was living with her boyfriend, another man who was unemployed, her two children, and her 9-month-old infant fathered by the boyfriend. On New Year's Eve, all three adults were drinking at a bar near the woman's home. The boyfriend had been taking drugs and drinking heavily. He was asked to leave the bar at 8:00 p.m. After several reappearances he finally stayed away for good at about 9:30 p.m. The woman and the unemployed man remained at the bar until 2:00 a.m. at which time the woman went home and the man to a party at a neighbor's home. Perhaps out of jealousy, the boyfriend attacked the woman when she walked into the house. Her brother was there and broke up the fight by hitting the boyfriend who was passed out and slumped over a table when the brother left. Later, the boyfriend attacked the woman again, and this time she knocked him unconscious. After checking the children, she went to bed. Later, the woman's 5-year-old girl went downstairs to go to the bathroom. The unemployed man returned from the party at 3:45 a.m. and found the 5-year-old dead. She had been raped, severely beaten over most of her body and strangled to death by the boyfriend.*[59]

Dr. Rowe declared: "The idea that none of those instances of suffering (from evils) could have been prevented by an all-powerful being without the loss of a greater good must strike us as an extraordinary idea, quite beyond our belief."[60] Dr. Oppy asserted: "Nothing could justify inaction . . . (or) permission, by an omnipotent, omniscient, and perfectly good god, of the rape, torture and murder of five-year-old girls."[61] Is God to blame for not preventing Sue's rape and murder?

58. Eleonore Stump, "The Problem of Evil," 409.
59. Nick Trakakis, "The Evidential Problem of Evil."
60. William Rowe, "Evil, Evidence, and Skeptical Theism—A Debate," 133.
61. Graham Oppy, "Rowe's Evidential Arguments from Evil," 59.

In the Tough Love Theodicy, the disavowed God lets headstrong people separate themselves from him and cause much pain and suffering. In his disapproval and tough love, God does not intervene to prevent all moral evils, gratuitous or otherwise. Self-governing humans should not expect some miraculous intervention from God to hinder the drinking, drug taking, and fighting, culminating in rape and murder. For good or evil, all the adults in the heartbreaking events freely chose to do what they did. Sue's mother agreed to have the boyfriend live with her children. She also allowed another unemployed man to stay with them. They all decided to go drinking at a bar (leaving the children home alone?). After fighting with the woman and her brother, the drug-taking boyfriend decided to rape and murder the five-year-old girl. Who was responsible for these vicious evils? Mark Twain famously declared: "There are many scapegoats for our blunders, but the most popular one is Providence."[62] We cannot blame God as he is *not obligated* to intervene and save us from the consequences of our ill-considered actions.

> *The notion that God will bail us out of the consequences of our own bad decisions is not one taken seriously by any religion I am familiar with, and as a pastor's daughter, I am confident that I never learned that one in Sunday school. Instead, the Bible and many scriptures from other faiths are full of stories of otherwise decent, even holy people making selfish decisions they repeatedly have been warned against and facing inevitable consequences as judgment. They can be forgiven, they can be healed, and they can repent and take instead a different path. But as long as they persist in their destructive behavior, there is a price to be paid.*[63]

Thus, we can either choose to repent, return to God, and acknowledge his existence or we can insist on doing whatever we desire and live with the consequences, *without* blaming God for our misfortunes. The choice is ours to make for God does not coerce anyone to believe in him.

Furthermore, if we believe that God is "dead" or just a figment of our imagination, why should we waste our breath to denounce him for our troubles? Pastor Alcorn quipped: "I don't believe in leprechauns, but I haven't dedicated my life to battling them . . . I would *not* get angry

---

62. Mark Twain, *Mark Twain's Notebook*, 347.

63. Melanie Scruggs, Texas Campaign for the Environment. https://www.texasenvironment.org/scruggs-we-should-heed-popes-climate-change-stance/

with leprechauns. Why not? Because I can't get angry with someone I know doesn't exist."[64]

If we live as if God does not exist, then it is *our* responsibility to deter the evils in the world. It is irrational to assert our rights to do whatever we want (e.g., to drink, take drugs) and yet expect that (a non-existent) God will somehow rescue us from our self-caused disasters. It is unreasonable to allow a non-related, drug-addicted person to live with our defenseless children and rely on God to protect them from harm (and blame him when he doesn't).

Moreover, we cannot demand that God must intervene worldwide on a massive scale to prevent the adults' damaging behaviors from affecting their children. Dr. van Woudenberg observed: "If God were to prevent bad actions from having bad consequences, God would constantly have to perform miracles, which would mean that the natural world would become massively irregular."[65]

Letting humans live with the outcomes of their ill-conceived deeds, God does not hinder every drunk from driving. God does not thwart every pregnant woman from using drugs. God does not restrain all gamblers from spending the family food budget. God does not prevent all mothers with young children (e.g., Sue) from having live-in boyfriends.

Was the outcome of Sue's tragedy surprising? "Mothers' boyfriends were responsible for 64 percent of non-parental abuse in single-parent families, despite performing less than 2 percent of non-parental child care."[66] "Children who had a father surrogate living in the home were twice as likely to be reported for maltreatment after his entry into the home than those with either a biological father . . . or no father figure in the home."[67] In 1994, "children residing in households with adults unrelated to them were 8 times more likely to die of maltreatment than children in households with 2 biological parents."[68] In 2010, the rate of *physical abuse* was ten times higher in a "single parent with partner"

---

64. Randy Alcorn, *If God Is Good*, 136.

65. René van Woudenberg, "A Brief History of Theodicy," 178.

66. Samantha Allen, "Why Are 'Mothers' Boyfriends' So Likely to Kill?" https://www.thedailybeast.com/why-are-mothers-boyfriends-so-likely-to-kill

67. Radhakrishna et al., "Are Father Surrogates a Risk factor for Child Maltreatment?" Abstract.

68. Stiffman et al., "Household Composition and Risk of Fatal Child Maltreatment," 617.

environment than in a household with "married biological parents." The rate of *sexual abuse* was seventeen times higher![69]

Unfortunately, the frontline workers tasked with managing the problem are overwhelmed. Low political and societal priorities, resulting in budget cuts and excessive caseloads, make it impossible for social workers to keep track of all the endangered households. "When children die in Pennsylvania, a lot of times, these are families that were on someone's radar . . . We know they're under stress, but we don't connect them to proven services that potentially help to mitigate or resolve that stress. Then we all act a little surprised and outraged when something bad happens to that child. But we knew."[70] When we ignore our societal responsibilities to protect the innocents, we cannot blame God for the evils befalling Sue and other children like her.

No one lives in a vacuum. Our ill-considered actions (or inactions) can bring severe consequences for many people in our family, workplace, and society. "No man is an island, entire of itself; every man is a piece of the continent."[71] The British philosopher John Cottingham acknowledged: "Whether we like it or not, (we need) to come to terms with our own 'evil doings'. . . and to realize how these impact the lives of others."[72]

Hence, we should not expect God to miraculously intervene and prevent the natural consequences of our ill-advised deeds (e.g., drinking, drug taking) from falling on our innocent children (e.g., Sue's death).[73] Nor should we blame him for failing to save us from our self-inflicted disasters (e.g., jail for rape and murder). In tough love, the all-wise God

---

69. Andrea Sedlak et al. (2010). Fourth National Incidence Study of Child Abuse and Neglect, 5-32. https://www.acf.hhs.gov/sites/default/files/opre/nis4_report_congress_full_pdf_jan2010.pdf

70. Eleanor Klibanoff, "Proactive Child Abuse Prevention Gets Increased Attention as Fatalities Rise in PA." http://wesa.fm/post/proactive-child-abuse-prevention-gets-increased-attention-fatality-rate-rises-pa#stream/0

71. John Donne, *Devotions upon Emergent Occasions and Death's Duel*, 102.

72. John Cottingham, "Evil and the Meaning of Life," 26.

73. "I want to suggest that Christian doctrine is committed to the claim that a child's suffering is outweighed by the good for the child which can result from that suffering." Eleonore Stump, "The Problem of Evil," 410. "Children who die . . . will go straight to heaven." Pastor David Jeremiah. https://davidjeremiah.blog/do-children-go-to-heaven-what-happens-to-the-souls-of-little-ones-when-they-die/ The Tough Love Theodicy does *not* claim that Sue's sufferings are *necessary* for any greater good. Rather, Sue's "eternal felicity" in heaven is God's *redeeming work* (i.e., turning human evil into good for the sake of the innocent party *without* excusing or condoning the evil that was done, Gen 50:20).

neither bails out his prodigals nor enables them on their destructive paths, but *ceaselessly* urges them to return and get help from their Creator!

## The Case of "The Brothers Karamazov"

In *The Brothers Karamazov*, Dostoevsky related a tense scene between the two siblings. Ivan challenged his brother Alyosha, a novice monk, on the excruciating problem of evil.

> *"Tell me frankly, I appeal to you—answer me: imagine that it is you yourself who are erecting the edifice of human destiny with the aim of making men happy in the end, of giving them peace and contentment at last, but that to do that it is absolutely necessary, and indeed quite inevitable, to torture to death only one tiny creature, the little girl who beat her breast with her little fist, and to found the edifice on her unavenged tears—would you consent to be the architect on those conditions? Tell me and do not lie!"*
> *"No, I wouldn't consent," said Alyosha softly.*[74]

Dr. Fales contended: "For me, Alyosha's answer is moral bedrock. Any theodicy that answers 'yes' to Ivan's questions is unworthy of serious consideration."[75] Dr. Markham stated: "Ivan rejects completely and categorically all attempts at a means-end theodicy: for Ivan, the end of freedom or character-building cannot justify the means of the suffering of children."[76]

Contrary to the claim of the Greater Good theodicies (means-end theodicies), in the Tough Love Theodicy, God is *not* "erecting the edifice of human destiny" on the little girl's unavenged tears. Evil (e.g., torture and murder of a child) must not be done for the sake of any "greater good," as the (good) end does not justify the (evil) means.[77] Immanuel Kant advocated: "Act in such a way that you treat humanity. . . *never merely as a means to an end."*[78]

Humans are on the path of independence from their Creator and insist on fulfilling their own selfish desires. Hence, there is *no* intent on

---

74. Fyodor Dostoevsky, *The Brothers Karamazov*, 287.
75. Evan Fales, "Theodicy in a Vale of Tears," 349.
76. Ian S. Markham, *Understanding Christian Doctrine*, 98.
77. The Catholic Church, *Catechism of the Catholic Church*, 434.
78. Immanuel Kant, *Grounding for the Metaphysics of Morals (Grundlegung zur Metaphysik der Sitten)*, 30.

God's part to give self-declared independent people "peace and contentment at last."[79] The torture and death of the little girl are strictly humans' evil doings as they ignore the moral precept "Do not murder."[80] Like Ivan and Alyosha, God never consents to the killing of even one of his innocent children and does not condone evil as the means for a "greater good" (e.g., "making men happy in the end").

Rather, God patiently calls his wayward creatures to return and will eagerly help them sort out their problems.

## The Case of the New York Murders

David was born out of wedlock to a poor woman who was involved with a married man. The infant was given up for adoption to a Jewish couple of moderate means. He was a troubled child growing up, variously described as a loner with a mean streak, a bully indulging in lawless behavior which got worse when his adoptive mother died of breast cancer. He did not have a good relationship with his adoptive father's second wife and joined the army when he turned eighteen. After his discharge, he worked for the US Postal Service.

David started out his criminal career by setting "1488 fires in New York City by his own account and (pulling) several hundred false alarms."[81] He kept a journal of his exploits and proudly referred to himself as "The Phantom of the Bronx."[82] His killing spree began on July 29, 1976, with the shooting of two teenage girls. By the time of his arrest on August 10, 1977, he had killed six people and wounded seven. He claimed that the killings were ordered by a demon-possessed dog owned

---

79. "God promises a new creation of all things in righteousness and peace." Jürgen Moltmann, *Theology of Hope (Theologie der Hoffnung)*, 23. "My conclusion is—to a universalism of hope which is not a doctrine or a certainty but is a presupposition." Jürgen Moltmann, "Talk-back Session with Jürgen Moltmann," 41. "The theology of the cross is the true Christian universalism." Jürgen Moltmann, *The Crucified God (Der Gekreuzigte Gott)*, 194. "By the power of redemption, a general restoration of all human souls would eventually occur." Friedrich Schleiermacher, *Christian Faith: A New Translation and Critical Edition (Der Christliche Glaube Nach den Grundsätzen der Evangelischen Kirche im Zusammenhange Dargestellt)*, 998.

80. Besides Judaism and Christianity (Ex 20:13), the precept "Do not murder" also appears in Buddhism (Paul Dahlke et al., *The Five Precepts*, 4), Islam (*The Quran*, Sura 4:92, 4:93), Hinduism (Nathaniel Altman, *Ahimsa: Dynamic Compassion, A Nonviolence Anthology*), and Shintoism (W. G. Ashton, *Shinto: The Way of the Gods*, 241).

81. Mary Mavromatis, "Serial Arson," 89.

82. Paul Brody, *Son of Sam: A Biography of David Berkowitz*, 9.

by his neighbor Sam. Nevertheless, he was deemed mentally competent and sentenced to six consecutive 25 years to life terms. The real reason for the murders might have been his anger against women.[83]

In 1987, a fellow inmate gave David a Bible. After reading Psalm 34:6, "This poor man cried, and the Lord heard him and saved him out of all his troubles," he turned to God and Christianity. Instead of "Son of Sam," he chose the name "Son of Hope." He refused to be paroled, saying: "In all honesty, I believe that I deserve to be in prison for the rest of my life. I have, with God's help, long ago come to terms with my situation and I have accepted my punishment."[84] David Berkowitz (aka "Son of Sam") stayed active in prison ministry, counseled inmates, and contributed articles on repentance and redemption to various Christian websites.

Tough love can bring wayward people back to God. However, for every David Berkowitz, there are many more Jack the Ripper (5+ murders), John Wayne Gacy (33+ murders), and Ted Bundy (30–100 murders). Everyone is free to go his own way and do what is right in his own eyes. No one is forced to acknowledge God or coerced to believe in his existence. Yet, in tough love, God stands ready to welcome back his prodigal son/daughter whether his/her name is "the Zodiac killer" or "the Son of Sam."

## Biblical support for the second premise.

In his disapproval of humans denying his existence and going their own way, God, in tough love, does not intervene to prevent all moral evils (gratuitous or otherwise). This biblical truth can be seen in both the Old and the New Testaments.

"He (God) let all nations go their own way. Yet, he has not left himself without testimony: He has shown kindness by giving you rain from heaven and crops in their seasons; he provides you with plenty of food and fills your hearts with joy" (Acts 14:16–17 NIV). Though the disavowed God reluctantly lets humans separate themselves from him, in love, he still kindly provides for them,[85] giving them time and opportunity to return and reconcile.

Yet, self-declared independent humans said to God: "Depart from us! We do not even desire the knowledge of your ways. Who is the

---

83. Elliott Leyton, *Hunting Humans: The Rise of the Modern Multiple Murderer*, 203.
84. https://usatoday30.usatoday.com/news/world/2002/07/09/son-of-sam.htm
85. Luke 6:35

Almighty, that we should serve Him, and what would we gain if we entreat Him?" (Job 21:14–15). Creatures repudiated their Creator, denying that he is the omnipotent Lord and the provider of all the good things they enjoyed.[86] They refused to serve their God or come to him in worship and prayer. They expected nothing from him, and he should expect nothing from them! In tough love, the disavowed God gave them their wish to depart and do what their hearts desire. However, God's warning was clear. Without his help, they would be like "straw before the wind," "chaff which the storm carries away," "their prosperity is not in their hands."[87] Should they then complain and blame God for not helping them when they encountered "the day of calamity"?[88]

In Romans 1:28, as people "did not see fit to acknowledge God any longer, God gave them over to a depraved mind, to do those things which are not proper." As the result of God letting them go, handing them over (Greek "paradidomi")[89] to the powers of this world,[90] and, in tough love, not intervening to prevent evils, "unrighteousness, wickedness, greed . . . envy, murder, strife, deceit, malice"[91] proliferated, bringing much pain and suffering in this world! Should self-governing humans then blame God for the horrendous evils they perpetrated in this fallen realm?

In Luke 15:11–32, Jesus told a parable about a son who disowned his father. The Prodigal Son demanded his inheritance money (while his dad was still alive)[92] and decided to *separate himself* from his family. He went to "a distant country, and there he squandered his estate with loose living . . . he began to be in need. And he went and attached himself to one of the citizens of that country" who sent him into the fields to feed pigs, a shameful task for a good Jewish boy![93] He was starving as "no one was giving anything to him."

86. Job 21:8-13
87. Job 21:16,18
88. Job 21:30
89. https://biblehub.com/greek/3860.htm
90. Beverly Gaventa, "God Handed Them Over," 44-45.
91. Rom 1:29
92. "This request means *he wants his father to die!*" Kenneth Bailey, *The Cross & the Prodigal*, 41.
93. "The intensity of this climax could only be duly felt by Jews, who had such a loathing and abhorrence for swine that they would not even name them, but spoke of a pig as dabhar acheer, 'the other thing.'" Frederic Farrar, *The Gospel According to St. Luke*, 258.

In tough love, his father did not come with food or money to save him from his self-inflicted miseries and enable him in his path of self-destruction! He could easily have perished in that foreign country, far away from the love and protection of his family.

Fortunately, that was not how the parable of the Prodigal Son ended. After much evil, pain, and suffering (the father's tough love approach, requiring the son to take responsibility for his actions),[94] the prodigal finally came to his senses, returned home, and reconciled with his dad. Forgiveness and full restoration of the relationship were immediately bestowed. "Quickly bring out the best robe and put it on him and put a ring on his hand and sandals on his feet, and bring the fattened calf, kill it, and let us eat and be merry; for this son of mine was dead, and has come to life again; he was lost, and has been found."[95]

The choice of outcome was up to the Prodigal Son. He could persist in his estrangement with his dad and live with the consequences (e.g., starvation)—without blaming his father. Or he could decide to go home, acknowledge his dad's existence, and seek reconciliation.

The father did not facilitate his son's degenerate life. He patiently waited,[96] in love and long-suffering, for his son to change his mind and return willingly, without any coercion or recrimination.

Was there a possibility that the son might never return? Sadly, yes. However, the father had no other (non-coercing) alternative in the face of the Prodigal Son's stubborn resistance! "If you love something, set it free. If it comes back, it's yours. If not, it was never meant to be."[97]

God's love and compassion for his wayward creatures compel him to watch for the blessed day when they reconsider and acknowledge his existence. Pope Francis proclaimed: "God is father, and he awaits our return up to the last moment."[98]

---

94. The father also carried his own burden of pain and suffering as parents of drug addicted children well know.

95. Luke 15:22-24

96. "Therefore, the Lord longs to be gracious to you, and therefore He waits on high to have compassion on you" (Isa 30:18).

97. Jonathan Munn, *Whom Seek Ye?* 42.

98. Pope Francis, quoted by Carol Glatz, "In the End, Everyone Faces God with 'Empty Hands,' Pope Says." https://www.ncronline.org/news/vatican/end-everyone-faces-god-empty-hands-pope-says

## Summary

Using secular evidence, case studies, and Scriptures, in answer to our eighth question, we have shown that the disapproving God, in tough love, does not intervene to prevent all moral evils (gratuitous or otherwise). He neither bails his wayward creatures out of their self-created disasters nor enables them in their destructive paths. Moral evils on this earth are perpetrated by humans who insist on ignoring their heavenly Father's commands (e.g., honor your father, do not murder), and doing whatever they please.

Yet, God, in love, unceasingly calls and offers forgiveness and reconciliation to his errant people who choose to return and acknowledge his existence, as he "desires all men to be saved and to come to the knowledge of the truth"[99] without any coercion. Hence, humans are free to choose their paths and live with the consequences, whether good or evil.

If all moral evils are not prevented by God, does he intervene to thwart all natural evils (our ninth question and the third premise of the Tough Love Theodicy)?

---

99. 1 Tim 2:4

# 10

## Why Does God Not Intervene to Prevent All Natural Evils?

> *I believe the universe is governed by the laws of science . . . the laws may have been decreed by God, but God does not intervene to break the laws.*
>
> —STEPHEN HAWKING[1]

MAIKEL SIREGAR, A 15-YEAR-OLD boy, recounted his ordeal in the 2004 Indonesian tsunami.

> Suddenly, I felt the house and the ground shaking. I felt everything swaying from side to side with the rocking movement of the ground. Immediately I realized what was happening and I shouted, "Earthquake! Earthquake!" . . . The tremor lasted about 40 minutes. But for me it seemed like it was four hours . . . People were running and shouting at the top of their voices, "Run! Water! Flood!" . . . We found ourselves trapped by the oncoming gigantic waves that were about 40 ft. high. It looked like a dragon about to swallow its prey . . . With a tremendous roaring sound, it smashed into us. There was no time to think. The next thing I knew, we were completely engulfed and swallowed up by this massive wall of black, muddy, and oily water. . . I thought this was the end of our

---

1. Stephen Hawking quoted by Phil Stewart. https://www.reuters.com/article/us-pope-hawking/pope-sees-physicist-hawking-at-evolution-gathering-idUSTRE49U6E220081031

lives on earth; that the end of the world had come. Indeed, many had shouted as the wave approached, "It's doomsday!"[2]

The tsunami killed at least 225,000 people, did 10 billion dollars in damage, and left behind 150,000 orphaned children.[3] Where was God in such a disaster?

In this chapter, we will show that, in tough love, the disavowed God does not intervene to prevent all the natural evils in this fallen world. Natural disasters (tsunamis, hurricanes, COVID-19 . . .) are the consequences of a creation prone to vagaries and corruption.[4]

## Support for the Third Premise of the Tough Love Theodicy

Secular support for the third premise.

The third premise of the Tough Love Theodicy states: "In his disapproval and tough love, God does not intervene in humans' environment to prevent all natural evils, gratuitous or otherwise." On this earth governed by natural laws, commonplace events (e.g., forest fires, monsoons) will continue, bringing both good and evil outcomes to people's lives. The British theologian Robert Tennant stated: "Physical (natural) evil is the necessary accompaniment of a structured world."[5] Dr. Hasker affirmed: "The natural evils should be allowed to exist; they are, so to speak, the price of admission for the existence of such a world."[6] Hence, living in an environment "designed to make intelligent life with free will possible,"[7] humans must accept natural evils, "the price of admission" to this world with its vagaries (e.g., tornadoes, hail storms).[8]

---

2. Maikel Siregar, *Morning Walk*. https://thoughts-about-god.com/stories/siragar_walk.htm

3. https://www.cemex.com/w/cemex-and-sos-children-s-villages-partner-to-provide-long-term-care-for-orphans-of-the-indonesia-tsunami

4. Rom 8:19-22

5. Robert Tennant quoted by Martin Gardner. *The Whys of a Philosophical Scrivener*, 265.

6. William Hasker, "An Open Theist View," 63.

7. Johannes Grössl, "Introduction," 5.

8. This world is "a fallen and broken world." Millard Erickson, *Christian Theology*, 398. In stark contrast to philosophers and theologians who bemoan the natural evils of death and suffering, scientists are very pleased with the "red in tooth and claw" of this world. For example, Dr. Soulé, the father of conservation biology, affirmed that "evolution is good," "diversity of organisms is good," "ecological complexity is good,"

Miraculous interventions by God to prevent earthquakes, tsunamis, diseases . . . cannot be presumed, nor can these catastrophes be blamed on him. "Unless God micromanages nature so as to destroy its autonomy, such things (natural evils) are going to occur."[9] In tough love, God lets humans' environment proceed according to its innate criteria and does not "micromanage" by suspending natural laws (e.g., global warming from greenhouse effect), causing harmful organisms to self-destruct (e.g., COVID-19), altering physiological parameters by giving people an on/off button to control their pains (e.g., back pain),[10] or providing unlimited natural resources (e.g., unlimited amount of clean water).[11] Humans are confined by the boundaries of their universe, the scant reserves of the earth, and the whims of the environment.

The disavowed God gave self-declared independent people the earth and its finite assets to manage, and it is up to them to do it with or without God's help. "In the West, our blessings have left us content without revival . . . But when he (man) is desperate for a touch from heaven, then God will bring brokenness."[12] Hence, natural evils (e.g., droughts, floods) are often God's "megaphone to rouse a deaf world."[13] In his desire to awaken his "deaf" creatures and make them aware of their ill-considered ways (e.g., deforestation), God—aiming for reconciliation and restoration—does not prevent all natural evils, gratuitous or otherwise (no bailing out or enabling).

These natural calamities are often the results of humans insisting on their rights to build houses in flood prone areas, trash their environment, poison their land, befoul their water, and pollute their air. The outcomes of such ill-advised decisions are catastrophic. For example, relentless global warming threatens the already dire world food supply. "Increasing temperatures, sea-level rise, and extreme weather, such as droughts, floods, and storms, will further undermine food security. Crop yields will

---

and "biotic diversity has intrinsic value." Michael Soulé, "What is Conservation Biology?" 727-34.

9. Karl Giberson and Francis Collins, *The Language of Science and Faith*, 137.

10. This on/off pain button scheme is counterproductive and downright dangerous. Pain in the body can be likened to a brake warning light in the car. Does anyone really want to turn off the brake warning light without fixing the brakes? In any case, we already have a pain on/off button: drugs.

11. Michael Tooley, "The Problem of Evil."

12. Kevin Turner, "Why Isn't the American Church Growing?" http://www.swi.org/through-kevins-eyes/featured-articles/why-isnt-the-american-church-growing/

13. C. S. Lewis, *The Problem of Pain*, 91.

be diminished by rising temperatures, changes to precipitation, the expansion of the reach of crop pests (which currently account for 25–40% of all crop loss) and shifts in predators that keep crop pests in check."[14]

Despite numerous warnings by scientists,[15] precious little has been done to remedy these human-caused disasters. People's impact on the environment (greenhouse gases, plastic wastes . . .) is their responsibility to solve and mitigate. Their short-sighted decisions (houses built on seismic fault lines, water pollution . . .) may bring dire consequences for their lives, the well-being of their children, and the survival of the living creatures on this earth.

Animal pains, sufferings, and deaths will continue unabated. Humans can take some measures to alleviate such afflictions (e.g., adopt a pet), or they can choose to assert their dominant status on earth (e.g., dog fighting).

God's intervention to protect animal species from eradication should not be expected. "The total weight of Earth's wild land mammals—from elephants to bisons, and from deer to tigers—is now less than 10% of the combined tonnage of men, women and children living on the planet . . . The natural world and its wild animals are vanishing."[16] "A new United Nations report warns that more diseases that pass from animals to humans, such as COVID-19, are likely to emerge as habitats are ravaged by wildlife exploitation, unsustainable farming practices and climate change. These pathogens, known as zoonotic diseases, also include Ebola, MERS, HIV/AIDS, and West Nile virus. They have increasingly emerged because of stresses humans have placed on animal habitats."[17]

"In 'A Joint Message for the Protection of Creation,' Pope Francis, Archbishop of Canterbury Justin Welby, and Orthodox Ecumenical Patriarch Bartholomew asked Christians to pray that world leaders . . .

---

14. Robert Glasser, *Preparing for the Era of Disasters*, 10.

15. In 2023, "Scientists warned that human-induced climate change is warming the planet to the point where it is causing irreversible damage in some parts of the world. The report was released by the United Nations Intergovernmental Panel on Climate Change." https://www.pbs.org/newshour/show/un-scientists-warn-drastic-steps-needed-to-prevent-climate-change-catastrophe

16. https://www.theguardian.com/environment/2023/mar/18/a-wake-up-call-total-weight-of-wild-mammals-less-than-10-of-humanitys

17. Scott Neuman, "U.N. Predicts Rise in Diseases That Jump from Animals to Humans Due to Habitat Loss." https://www.npr.org/sections/coronavirus-live-updates/2020/07/06/888077232/u-n-predicts-rise-in-diseases-that-jump-from-animals-to-humans

make courageous choices"[18] to protect their fragile God-given abode. Pope Francis implored: "Let us not leave in our wake a swath of destruction and death which will affect our own lives and those of future generations."[19] Let us "repent and modify our lifestyles and destructive systems."[20] In long-suffering, God is patiently awaiting his headstrong people to return. In love, he stands ready to help them solve their many urgent ecological problems and restore their ravaged earth for the sake of future generations. "God loves and cares for all creation" as "creation reveals the nature of God."[21]

Yet, the existence of a loving and caring God has been questioned by various scholars who cited cases of horrendous natural evils.

## The Case of "Bambi"

"In some distant forest, lightning strikes a dead tree, resulting in a forest fire. In the fire, a fawn is trapped, horribly burned, and lies in terrible agony for several days before death relieves its suffering."[22] Dr. Lynch opined: "The existence of any natural evil, including animal pain, is evidence against theism."[23] Dr. Tooley asserted: "An omnipotent and omniscient being is never justified in not preventing the undeserved suffering of sentient nonpersons."[24] Is God to blame for Bambi's suffering and death?

Forest fires have occurred since time immemorial. "We often regard fire as an agent of destruction, but to Nature, it is an agent of necessary change."[25] Hence, forest fires are natural occurrences that serve a great purpose in the ecological balance. After much effort to prevent *all* fires,

---

18. Philip Pullella, "World's Top Three Christian Leaders in Climate Appeal Ahead of U.N. Summit." https://www.reuters.com/business/environment/worlds-top-three-christian-leaders-climate-appeal-ahead-un-summit-2021-09-07/

19. Pope Francis, *The Joy of the Gospel*, 108.

20. Pope Francis. https://www.americamagazine.org/politics-society/2022/09/01/pope-francis-prayer-creation-climate-change-243665

21. US Conference of Catholic Bishops. https://www.usccb.org/beliefs-and-teachings/what-we-believe/catholic-social-teaching/care-for-creation

22. William Rowe, "The Problem of Evil," 336.

23. Joseph Lynch, "Theodicy and Animals," 9.

24. Michael Tooley, *The Problem of Evil*, 27.

25. http://www.freshfromflorida.com/Divisions-Offices/Florida-Forest-Service/Wildland-Fire/Prescribed-Fire/The-Natural-Role-of-Fire

people have finally learned to allow nature to proceed,[26] resulting in occasional fawns being trapped and killed in wildfires. Animals' pains and sufferings are the results of natural laws in effect in the universe, for "a world without natural laws would be a much worse world."[27]

The Tough Love Theodicy can accommodate a fawn's death as either a gratuitous or non-gratuitous evil. Bambi's demise may not be gratuitous due to the necessary preservation of natural laws for the welfare of all earthly creatures.[28] A fawn's suffering may be gratuitous, the result of people's ill-considered actions (e.g., a lingering and painful death from sport arrows or arson-caused forest fires).

Furthermore, human-caused global warming has bred frequent cataclysmic wildfires. "Greenhouse gas emissions continue to drive changes in the climate, contributing to warmer-than-average surface temperatures and shifting precipitation patterns—trends that are expected to increase the frequency, intensity and duration of wildfires across the U.S. Climate change is creating the perfect conditions for larger, more intense wildfires."[29]

Are we trying to reverse the trend or are we blithely doing whatever we please? What will it take for us to realize that we are going down the wrong path? Can we blame God for climate-change-driven calamitous forest fires trapping and killing "Bambis"?

## The Case of the 1755 Lisbon Earthquake

The 1755 Lisbon earthquake on All Saints' Day with its subsequent fires and a twelve-meter-high tsunami brought a death toll of sixty thousand

---

26. "After a three-year, on-the-ground assessment of the park's Illilouette Creek basin (Yosemite National Park), UC Berkeley researchers concluded that a strategy dating to 1973 of managing wildfires with minimal suppression and almost no preemptive, so-called prescribed burns has created a landscape more resistant to catastrophic fire, with more diverse vegetation and forest structure and increased water storage." https://news.berkeley.edu/2016/10/24/wildfire-management-vs-suppression-benefits-forest-and-watershed

27. Michael Tooley, "The Problem of Evil."

28. "They (natural evils) are the by-products made possible by that which is necessary for the greater good." Bruce Reichenbach, *Evil and a Good God*, 101–102. "The actual universe is a complex, multileveled natural world, containing creatures that are sentient as well as some that are intelligent . . . It also unavoidably contains a great deal of suffering and death." William Hasker, "An Open Theist View," 69.

29. Andrew Moore, "Climate Change Is Making Wildfires Worse—Here's How." https://cnr.ncsu.edu/news/2022/08/climate-change-wildfires-explained/

people. The 8.5 to 9 Richter scale convulsion destroyed 85 percent of the buildings in the Portugal capital.

Was God to blame for this destructive earthquake? The historian Mark Molesky decried: "How could a Creator, both beneficent and all-powerful, have permitted such a catastrophe?"[30] Dr. Moltmann declared: "With the Lisbon earthquake, confidence in the harmony of the world and a gracious ruler of it was shattered."[31]

This tragedy prompted the French poet Voltaire to compose *Poem on the Lisbon Disaster*,[32] questioning the existence of a good, intervening God and Leibniz's view that our world is "the best of all possible worlds."[33]

However, the French philosopher Jean-Jacques Rousseau countered in a letter to Voltaire: "It was hardly nature who assembled there twenty-thousand houses of six or seven stories. If the residents of this large city had been more evenly dispersed and less densely housed, the losses would have been fewer or perhaps none at all."[34]

Ample warnings had been given to Lisbon residents over the years. Records showed that Lisbon earthquakes also happened in 1309, 1337, 1340, 1344, 1350, 1355, 1356 . . .[35] with the 1531 earthquake and tsunami causing thirty thousand deaths.[36] Sadly, no precautions were taken to mitigate the subsequent 1755 disaster (e.g., dispersed, less dense housing).

According to scientists, "the offshore 1755 earthquake actually triggered an onshore rupture on the LTV fault (Lower Targus Valley fault passing through Lisbon). Thus, the return period of magnitude 6 to 7 earthquakes along the LTV could be as short as 150 to 200 years, making Lisbon the highest risk area in Portugal."[37]

30. Mark Molesky, *This Gulf of Fire*, 19.
31. Jürgen Moltmann, "Theodicy," 565.
32. Voltaire, *Poèmes sur le Désastre de Lisbonne et sur la Loi Naturelle*.
33. "This universe must be in reality better than every other possible universe." Gottfried Leibniz, *Leibniz Selections*, 96.
34. Jean-Jacques Rousseau, *Correspondence Complète de Jean Jacques Rousseau*, vol. 4, Letter 424, 18 August 1756.
35. Chronology of Calamities in Portugal (14th–20th century). http://pwr-portugal.ics.ul.pt/wp-content/uploads/Chronology_of_Calamities.pdf
36. Richard Hoffman. *An Environmental History of Medieval Europe*, 309.
37. Guillermo Franco and Bingming Shen-Tu, "From 1755 to Today—Reassessing Lisbon's Earthquake Risk." https://www.air-worldwide.com/publications/air-currents/from-1755-to-today-reassessing-lisbons-earthquake-risk/

How prepared is Lisbon for the next devastating earthquake? "This seismic source zone, with its proximity to Lisbon, the large number of old masonry buildings and a fraction of reinforced concrete frames designed with limited lateral resistance, presents the most significant potential for large loss earthquakes in Portugal."[38] However, people are still living and building in this disaster-prone area despite all the warnings. Dr. Bezzegoud, the lead scientist on earthquakes at Evora University in Portugal, declared: "I am trying to say we are very close to an earthquake of the same magnitude of the one registered in 1755. I cannot say when and how it will manifest. It could repeat itself in various forms, even with two or three earthquakes of different intensities."[39]

At 7:44 am on August 17, 2017, an earthquake measuring 4.3 on the Richter scale shook Lisbon and its surrounding areas. "Its epicenter was 23 miles north-west of Lisbon and the estimated population in the area which felt the tremors is around 3.5 million people."[40] On March 18, 2021, a 3.3 magnitude tremor jolted Lisbon again. On January 7, 2023, Lisbon experienced another 4.1 convulsion. Seismic data obtained on January 1, 2024, revealed 142 earthquakes in the Lisbon area in 2023.[41] Is anybody listening to the warnings?

## The Case of the Great Sparrow Campaign

Once upon a time, in the land of the "Great Wall," as part of the "Great Leap Forward," the "Great Sparrow Campaign" was introduced with lavish fanfare. The "Great Leader" had been warned by his court sycophants that the innocent sparrows subsisted on a diet of fruit and grain seed, eating up some the "Great Helmsman's" crops. Consequently, the "Great Chairman" was worried about the dent the little creatures were making into his private "Gross National Product." Rather than reckoning that it was just "for the birds," and that all of God's creatures had to eat, he wisely decided to take some drastic measures to preserve what was rightfully his.

38. Ibid.

39. Shareit, "New 'Earthquake Probability' Map Highlights Risks of Lisbon and Algarve." https://www.portugalresident.com/new-earthquake-probability-map-highlights-risks-of-lisbon-and-algarve/

40. Ravneet Ahluwalia, "Portugal Earthquake." http://www.independent.co.uk/travel/news-and-advice/portugal-earthquake-lisbon-magnitude-seismic-richter-scale-institute-sea-atmosphere-epicentre-a7897891.html

41. https://www.volcanodiscovery.com/region/7839/earthquakes/lisboa.html

Since private farming was banned and all products (grains or otherwise) belonged to the state (aka the "Great Supreme Commander"), sparrows were "stealing from the people" and consequently declared to be "enemies of the proletariat" and sentenced to be eradicated as a species.

No sooner ordered than done. Millions and millions of "volunteer citizens" chased the poor beasts around day and night, banging pots, pans, drums . . . to scare them into flying all over the vast country until they were exhausted from all the enforced exercise and dropped dead from the sky! Eggs and chicks that could not fly were summarily executed and their abode razed to the ground. Recalcitrant specimens that managed to stay aloft were shot down by designated marksmen. When some of the desperate feathered creatures asked for asylum and took refuge in the Polish embassy, the "Revered Leader's" henchmen demanded the immediate extradition of the convicted criminals. Abruptly rebuffed, the "Great Teacher's" stooges besieged the building and proceeded to terrify the hapless escapees by a steady bedlam of banging and drumming. After two days of constant cacophony, there were so many dead refugees in the embassy that the Poles had to use shovels to clear them.[42]

The sparrow population was driven to near extinction as hundreds of millions of the birds were exterminated. The God-like Mao Zedong's scheme succeeded beyond any wild expectation for the population of insects and locusts (previously held in check by the sparrows) borrowed a page from the "Great President's" divine "Little Red Book," took a "Great Leap Forward," ballooned to biblical proportions, ravaged the crops, and contributed to the "Great Chinese Famine" of 1960 when 15 to 78 million people died of starvation.

In tough love, the disavowed God lets self-declared independent people freely make decisions about their earthly abode and choose among options that may impact the cleanliness of its air, the purity of its water, the richness of its soil, and the balance of its ecology. Since independence entails responsibility and consequences for one's actions, humans must live and die in an environment of their own making whether it is Blessed Eden or Blighted Hades!

Pope Francis implored people to come to their Creator and "ask forgiveness for sins committed against the environment and our 'selfish' system motivated by 'profit at any price.'"[43] In love, God stands ready

42. https://www.unbelievable-facts.com/2017/10/acts-of-mass-stupidity.html

43. Josephine McKenna, "Pope Francis Says Destroying the Environment Is a Sin." https://www.theguardian.com/world/2016/sep/01/pope-francis-calls-on-christians-

to help *if and when* humans decide to acknowledge his existence rather than insist that they are their own little deities and that all it takes for a "Great Leap Forward" on earth is a "Little Red Book" written by the "Great Teacher" of the "Land of the Red Dragon"!

## Biblical support for the third premise.

"God created Man in his own image," and gave humans dominion over the whole earth, the authority to "fill it and subdue it."[44] As part of his stewardship of the Lord's creation, Adam was tasked with the care and cultivation of the lush and well-watered Garden of Eden.[45]

The Lord also gave Adam two options concerning the tree of the knowledge of good and evil: "Obey, not eat of the tree, and live" or "disobey, eat of the tree, and die."[46] Sadly, Adam and Eve believed Satan and chose to transgress God's command. While Adam himself was not cursed, his dominion, the earth, was cursed. "Cursed is the ground (Adamah) because of you (Adam); in toil you shall eat of it all the days of your life. Both thorns and thistles it shall grow for you."[47]

The word "curse" is the Hebrew "arar," meaning "bitterly curse, to put a curse on, lay under a curse, to be made a curse."[48] The whole earth was made a curse because of Adam's sin. "Through one man sin entered into the world, and death through sin."[49] Besides the death of all humans, this world of universal death also abounds in dead plants (plant fossils), dead animals (dinosaur fossils), and demise of the unfit (nature red in tooth and claw). The earth no longer surrenders its bounties without much pain, suffering, and labor. People must toil by the sweat of their brow, being subject to the numerous vagaries of nature (droughts, floods). In the end, humans must return to the dust from which they were made.[50]

---

to-embrace-green-agenda

44. Gen 1:27-28
45. Gen 2:15
46. Gen 2:16-17
47. Gen 3:17-18
48. https://www.bibletools.org/index.cfm/fuseaction/Lexicon.show/ID/H779/arar.htm
49. Rom 5:12
50. Gen 3:19

This fallen world continues to bear the dreadful consequences of the curse. "For the creation was subjected to futility, not willingly, but because of Him who subjected it, in hope that the creation itself also will be set free from its slavery to corruption into the freedom of the glory of the children of God. For we know that the whole creation groans and suffers the pains of childbirth together until now."[51]

The word "futility" is the Greek "mataiotes," meaning "frailty, want of vigor."[52] Our cursed world is very frail and easily spoiled by abuse (global warming, deforestation). Recognizing this dire situation, the British physicist Stephen Hawking bemoaned: "I don't think we will survive another 1,000 years without escaping beyond our fragile planet."[53]

"Corruption" is the Greek "phthora" meaning "internal decay, rottenness, decomposition, deterioration."[54] This world of death is enslaved to decay and rottenness (aging, diseases), unable to escape from decomposition and deterioration (chaos and disorderliness).

The whole creation "groans and suffers together" in this universe of death for "heavens and earth will pass away."[55] The fallen world longs in hope for its eventual freedom and redemption from the primordial curse, "looking for new heavens and a new earth in which righteousness dwells."[56]

In the meantime, rather than faithfully preserving their God-given abode, self-seeking humans persist in their destructive behaviors. "The earth is also polluted by its inhabitants, for they transgressed laws, violated statutes, broke the everlasting covenant. Therefore, a curse devours the earth."[57] Ever increasing short-sighted human actions despoil the earth and add to its scourge.[58] People poison the soil with toxic wastes; they contaminate the water with sewage and chemicals; they release

---

51. Rom 8:20 22
52. https://biblehub.com/greek/3153.htm
53. Stephen Hawking, quoted by Elizabeth Ford and Deborah Mitchell, *Apocalyptic Visions*, 2.
54. https://biblehub.com/greek/5356.htm
55. Luke 21:33
56. 2 Pet 3:13
57. Isa 24:5-6
58. "In biblical times, modern toxic chemical and biological pollutants, of course, were unknown. But biblical law did express concerns about other ways by which human actions could pollute the land." Richard Hiers, "Reverence for Life and Environmental Ethics in Biblical Law and Covenant," 171.

enormous amounts of pollutants into the air. How much longer can people survive on this earth is open to question!

**Summary**

Using secular evidence, case studies, and Scriptures, in answer to our ninth question, we have shown that God, in his disapproval and tough love, does not intervene to prevent all natural evils (gratuitous or otherwise). Self-declared independent humans must live in an environment of their own making, whether good or evil.

Yet, in long-suffering, God patiently calls his creatures to return and will eagerly help them solve their many urgent ecological problems! "Call upon Me in the day of trouble; I shall rescue you, and you will honor Me."[59]

If God is intimately involved with his people on this earth, can a good God coexist with evil (our tenth question and the conclusion of our Tough Love Theodicy)?

59. Ps 50:15

# 11

# Can a Good God Coexist with Evil?

> *It is necessarily true that God coexists with gratuitous evil in some world.*
>
> —MICHAEL ALMEIDA[1]

ON OCTOBER 2, 2006, Charlie Roberts, a 32-year-old milk truck driver went to a schoolhouse in Nickel Mines, Pennsylvania, shot ten Amish girls (ages 6 to 13), killing five, and then committed suicide. His mother Terri reminisced about the nightmare.

> *I heard sirens and wondered what could be happening in our small rural community. Just as I got back to my desk, my husband, Chuck, called. He asked me to come immediately to Charlie and Marie's home. As soon as I got to his house and pushed through the crowd of police and reporters, I asked a trooper if my son was alive. "No, ma'am," he responded somberly. I turned to my husband. With pain in his eyes, he choked out, "It was Charlie. He killed those girls" . . . Later, anger set in, mixing with my pain. Where were you, God? I found myself screaming out in my head. How could you let this happen? I didn't understand how Charlie could leave his children fatherless, to face the shame and the horror. And the gentle Amish families—what darkness had so possessed Charlie that he would want to rip away daughters as precious as his own?*[2]

1. Michael Almeida, "On Necessary Gratuitous Evils," 120.
2. Terri Roberts, "My Son Shot 10 Amish Girls in a Pennsylvania Schoolhouse." https://www.womansday.com/life/inspirational-stories/a53626/terri-roberts-forgiven-

Can a virtuous God exist in the presence of such vicious evils? Sadly, in this fallen creation inhabited by imperfect humans,[3] a good God and evil coexist.

## Support for The Conclusion of the Tough Love Theodicy

Secular support for the conclusion.

If we accept the three premises of the Tough Love Theodicy, the deductive argument leads to the conclusion that, if God exists, God and evil[4] coexist on earth. God is not to blame for the atrocities in the world since people deny his existence and insist on doing whatever they desire. Naturally, God is not pleased with the horrendous calamities perpetrated over the centuries with no sign of abatement (the Holocaust, the 9/11 terrorist attack, the Russia-Ukraine war, the Israel-Hamas war . . .). Nevertheless, in tough love, he does not coerce humans to acknowledge his existence as he wants a voluntary relationship with his creatures, just as parents desire true and willingly offered love from their children.

With great patience and long-suffering, God beseeches his people to come to their senses and return to him, as he yearns for them in love and bears them no ill will. The French bishop Francis de Sales lamented in God's behalf:

> But I grieve for their misfortune, that having left me, they have chosen for themselves wells that have no water. And if, by supposition of an impossible thing, they could have met with some other fountain of living water, I would lightly bear their departure from me, since I aim at nothing in their love, but their own good. But to forsake me and perish, to fly from me headlong, is what astonishes and offends me in their folly.[5]

Tough love emphasizes *love*, a desire to help and to promote the beloved's well-being by encouraging responsibility-taking.

---

excerpt/

3. Eph 2:3

4. Evil includes moral and natural evils (gratuitous or otherwise), evils of various kinds, amounts, intensities, distribution . . . Rowe mentioned four problems of evil (the coexistence of God with any evil, with diverse kinds of evils, with various amounts of evils, and with some particular evils, e.g., the Holocaust). William Rowe, "Paradox and Promise," 111-24.

5. Francis de Sales, *Treatise on the Love of God (Traité de l'Amour de Dieu)*, 445.

In substance abuse situations, parental tough love strives for the children's freedom from drug addiction and a restoration of warm family relationships. "Take the car, take the money, take the phone, remove all privileges . . . Giving natural consequences a push in the right direction can go far in helping your child, while you're still there for emotional support."[6] In long-suffering love, parents stand ready to assist if and when their prodigal sons and daughters decide to return.

In education, the teacher's tough love[7] aims to help the students understand their responsibilities and recognize the dire consequences of their ill-considered actions. No loving teacher wants to see his/her students fail in school or even worse, in life.

In marriage, spousal tough love (e.g., a temporary separation) endeavors to bring the partner back to his/her senses and foster a return to a jointly avowed commitment.[8]

In sports, using tough love, the coach seeks to help his/her players reach their full potential as athletes and well-rounded citizens in society. "Many of us that have played or coached this great sport (football) would have gladly thrown in the towel when things got tough, but those of us lucky enough to have someone administer some tough love pushed through the situation and came out better men because of it in the long run."[9]

Likewise, God uses tough love to bring his creatures to a recognition of his existence and an appreciation of his benevolence as it is in their best interests to do so.

Unfortunately, tough love is not a magic formula; children may choose to persist in their destructive drug habits; students may refuse to take responsibility for their education and drop out of school; spouses may insist on continuing their extramarital affairs and wrecking their marriages; athletes may reject their coach's discipline and never reach their potential; God's creatures may disavow their Creator and assert their right to do whatever they want.

---

6. Teicher, "What Is Tough Love and When to Use It." https://wholisticfitliving.com/what-is-tough-love-and-when-to-use-it

7. Izhak Berkovich and Yael Grinshtain, "Typology of 'Tough Love' Leadership in Urban Schools Facing Challenging Circumstances."

8. James Dobson, *Love Must Be Tough: New Hope for Marriages.*

9. Doug Samuels. "Are We Witnessing the End of the Tough Love Coaching Approach?" http://footballscoop.com/news/are-we-witnessing-the-end-of-tough-love-coaching/

In these circumstances, wayward children cannot blame their tough love parents for not preventing drug overdoses. Illiterate students cannot blame their teachers for being unable to read or write. Unfaithful spouses cannot blame their mates for the acrimonious divorces. Undisciplined athletes cannot blame the coaches for their poor performances. Self-seeking people cannot blame God for not preventing the evils perpetrated in the world.

> It's time to stop playing the blame game . . . blaming God. The author Philip Yancey writes of being contacted by a television producer after the death of Princess Diana to appear on a show and explain how God could have possibly allowed such a tragic accident. "Could it have had something to do with a drunk driver going 90 miles-an-hour in a narrow tunnel?" he asked the producer.[10]

In the Tough Love Theodicy, the disavowed God reluctantly lets self-declared independent humans separate themselves from him and go their own way (e.g., driving drunk), resulting in much evil. Without any coercion from God (therefore he appears to be absent or dead), people are free to insist on living independently, or they can choose to respond to their Creator's *ceaseless* call to return, acknowledge his existence, and develop a relationship with him. Whichever option they select, they must live with the consequences.

Tough love (an appeal to reconcile, with no physical violence, verbal or emotional abuse, disowning, coercion, blackmail, threats . . . but also no bailing out or enabling) is a *morally justifying reason* for God not to prevent all the moral and natural evils, gratuitous or otherwise.

Dr. Stump asserted: "A successful theodicy or defense is one that can explain why God was (or could have been) justified in allowing human suffering."[11] Dr. Trakakis affirmed: "A theodicy elucidates *plausible* reasons as to why God permits evil, where 'plausibility' amounts to an account which 'is true for all we know.'"[12] Dr. Bishop declared: "They (the theists) must provide theodicies that exemplify what, for all we know, God's morally adequate reasons for causing or permitting evil could

---

10. Chris Witts, "Hating and Blaming God," https://hope1032.com.au/stories/faith/2023/hating-blaming-god/
11. Eleonore Stump, *The Image of God*, 4.
12. Nick Trakakis, "Response to Bishop," 59.

possibly be."[13] Dr. Tooley advocated: "To be successful, a theodicy must appeal only to beliefs that it is reasonable to accept."[14]

Tough love is intuitively plausible as it is used widely in many fields of human endeavor (medicine, education, economics, social work, criminal justice, altruism, organizational management and government, psychology. . .) and supported by much evidence in science[15] and history.[16] It is a belief commonly held in many cultures (Eastern, Western, African), and espoused by all the major world religions (Christianity, Judaism, Buddhism, Hinduism, and Islam).

For example, tough love has been practiced in child rearing since antiquity. "At the age of seven, Spartan boys were removed from their parents' homes and began the 'agoge,' a state-sponsored training regimen designed to mold them into skilled warriors and moral citizens."[17] All Spartan males were lifelong soldiers and fully expected to die for the state. "According to Plutarch, these 'tough-love' parenting techniques were so admired by foreigners that Spartan women were widely sought after for their skill as nurses and nannies."[18] Tough love, balancing love with discipline and responsibility-taking (e.g., Chinese tiger moms[19] and traditional Nigerian parenting style),[20] is well-accepted in history and in many cultures.

In medicine, physicians are often required to use tough love and speak the hard truth that may not please their listeners. Dr. Richard Colman said it well.

13. John Bishop, "Response to Trakakis," 110.

14. Michael Tooley, "The Problem of Evil."

15. "Tough love is never comfortable. But it usually leads to change for the better. And in the case of nanotechnology, getting health and safety research right will mean that everyone benefits in the end." Andrew Maynard, "Tough Love for Science and Technology Innovation." https://2020science.org/2008/12/10/tough-love-for-science-and-technology-innovation/

16. Claire Clark. "Tough Love: A Brief Cultural History of the Addiction Intervention," 233-46. Alexander Livingston, "Tough Love: The Political Theology of Civil Disobedience," 851-66.

17. Evan Andrews, "8 Reasons It Wasn't Easy Being Spartan." http://www.history.com/news/history-lists/8-reasons-it-wasnt-easy-being-spartan

18. Ibid.

19. Amy Chua, "Tough Love, The Tiger Mom's Tale." https://archive.shine.cn/feature/Tough-Love-the-tiger-moms-tale/shdaily.shtml

20. "The old school or traditional Nigerian parenting style includes: tough love, discipline, instilling a sense of responsibility and diligence at home." Yetty, "What Is the Nigerian Parenting Style?" https://lagosmums.com/what-is-the-nigerian-parenting-style/

> *He (the physician) considers a professional's duty is not primarily to please but to do or advise the 'right' thing. Usually, this does please as well as alleviate the problem but at times what is said or advised is not what the patient wants to hear . . . Doctors are in a privileged position and the concept of professionalism as described above is perhaps subconsciously recognized by society in awarding that privilege. With that privilege comes a responsibility to always act professionally by being well informed and being able and prepared to provide 'tough love' if necessary. In my opinion, the reason we are prepared to do this is because we CARE.*[21]

In ministering to sufferers, physicians must be willing to use tough love as well as tender love and compassion. Medicine, besides a science, is also an art, the art of balancing love and truth, of striving to heal and not to harm, of caring but not fostering codependency.

Tough love is widely adopted in the terrain of education. "A positive alternative to detention and suspension, 'Tough love' meetings held at schools help troubled teens learn personal accountability."[22] "Tough love . . . properly applied—with high expectations . . . is the highest vote of confidence anyone can offer."[23] Encouragement and accountability used judiciously together bring the best results for children at risk of failing academically.

Tough love is applied in the field of economics, where companies are allowed to directly compete for foreign investment, with the successful firms having a higher capital-labor ratio, higher wages, and a higher productivity level.[24] Companies that take responsibility for their actions and make the correct tough love changes to their business models survive and thrive. Those who do not, suffer the consequences in the free market.

The tough love concept is used in the United Kingdom's social work and social policy to implement a New Labor's program "of reform of the welfare state." The policy adopts "tough-love" as the "central principle, the idea of a welfare system which demands more of those who receive

---

21. Richard Colman, "The Role of the Doctor—Tough Love," 335.

22. Rita Roberts, "Tough Love for Kids at Risk." http://www.ascd.org/publications/educational-leadership/nov93/vol51/num03/Toughlove-for-Kids-at-Risk.aspx

23. Joanne Lipman, "The Fine Art of Tough Love," https://hbr.org/2013/12/the-fine-art-of-tough-love

24. Beata Javorcik and Mariana Spatareanu, "Tough-love: Do Czech Suppliers Learn from Their Relationships with Multinationals?" 811-33.

assistance—no rights without responsibilities—and which in exchange improves their incentives and opportunities."[25]

Tough love is advocated in the field of criminal justice. "Drug courts signal a move away from a 'get tough' retributive approach to criminal justice and toward a 'tough-love,' rehabilitation and treatment-oriented approach." Offenders have a choice between persisting in their destructive paths (and being held fully responsible for their misdeeds) or submitting to the judge who will "exercise enhanced supervision, monitoring and control over their lives."[26]

Tough love is also employed in the field of altruism. "Charitable giving has increasingly become 'tough-love'—it has come to require recipients to undertake costly prior action. A common justification is that of greater efficiency: willingness to undertake costly actions signals greater productivity from transfers."[27] Potential recipients of charitable giving are given two choices: proceed independently without help or accept the donation at the cost of making some required constructive changes.

Tough love is a concept fostered in organizational management. "One of the most-pervasive debates in literature on managing people is whether using 'hard' or 'soft' approaches produces better organizational performance . . . it appears that cultures characterized by 'tough-love' perform better than those with only 'hard' or 'soft' features by themselves."[28] A combination of "hard/tough" (accountability, responsibility) and "soft/love" (consensus decision making, warm climate, acceptance) features used together fosters the best results.

Tough love is well-known in psychology as it is often the bedrock of healthy relationships. "No one likes critical feedback. We often avoid criticism by discouraging those who give it or dismissing it as invalid. It's hard to hear that someone feels mistrust, disappointment, or anger toward us. But avoiding 'tough love' denies us the opportunity to enhance respect and trust in our relationships and our lives."[29]

25. Bill Jordan and Charlie Jordan, *Social Work and the Third Way: Tough-love as Social Policy*, 1-4.

26. Stacey Burns and Mark Peyrot, "Tough-love: Nurturing and Coercing Responsibility and Recovery in California Drug Courts," 416-38.

27. Spiros Bougheas et al., "Tough-love or Unconditional Charity?" 561-82.

28. Steven Kelman and Sounman Hong, "Hard, Soft, or Tough-love: What Kinds of Organizational Culture Promote Successful Performance in Cross-Organizational Collaborations?"

29. Linda and Charlie Bloom, "Why Tough Love Can Be the Best Thing for Your Relationship." https://www.psychologytoday.com/us/blog/stronger-the-broken-places/

Tough love also appears prominently in all the major world religions. In his classic work *Love Must Be Tough*, Dr. Dobson, an influential protestant leader, popularized the concept of tough love.[30] Father Moloney, a Catholic priest, described God's dealings with his beloved people as tough love. "Sometimes, the most loving route to take in truly loving your children and bringing them to their ultimate good is through the course of tough love."[31] Father Allen, a Greek Orthodox priest, affirmed that "the Church uses tough love to save souls for eternity."[32] Rabbi Kligler clarified the concept of tough love in Torah relationships, "Love demands that we sometimes must risk all, even the relationship itself, in order to try to help someone we love."[33] The Buddhist monk Jack Maguire explained the idea of karuna (compassion) promulgated by Buddha: "Often when karuna is enacted . . . it can even seem stern: what modern psychology calls 'tough love.'"[34] Dr. Lamb, a Hindu sadhu (religious ascetic), recounted his teaching of tough love to jailed convicts: "I could speak with them about the doctrine of karma . . . 'There is no one else to blame. You have to take responsibility, and you will never grow spiritually or emotionally until you own up to your own choices.'"[35] Dr. Speight, an Islamic scholar, affirmed: "There is another kind of love between (Muslim) believers that is sometimes called 'tough love,' the love that holds another to the highest standards of moral behavior."[36] In the Wiccan tradition, the African/Caribbean/South American god Eleggua "treats his devotees with what can be best summed up as tough love."[37]

Thus, tough love is not a concept foreign to history, science, education, economics, religion . . . It has been widely used in many fields of human undertaking over the centuries. A combination of love and personal accountability is an ideal mix in child rearing and in numerous other societal endeavors.

---

201505/why-tough-love-can-be-the-best-thing-your-relationship

30. James Dobson, *Love Must Be Tough*.

31. Daniel Moloney, *Mercy: What Every Catholic Should Know*, summary.

32. Steven Allen, "Orthodox Truth." http://orthodoxtruth.org/uncategorized/tough-love/

33. Jonathan Kligler, "The Mitzvah of Tokhekha: Tough Love." https://www.wjcshul.org/sharing/kedoshim-mitzvah-of-tokhekha-tough-love/

34. Jack Maguire, *Essential Buddhism*, 148.

35. Randas Lamb, "Tough Love: Prisons, Hinduism, and Spiritual Care," 204-205.

36. R. Marston Speight, "The Practical Moral Values of Karbala," 152.

37. A. J. Drew, *A Wiccan Bible*, 30.

It is therefore not surprising that God would use the same approach with humans, balancing love with responsibility-taking. People are free to come to God for help (responding to his call to return)[38] or they can deny his existence and accept full responsibility for the calamities on earth. The disavowed Creator does not intervene to prevent all evils, neither bailing out his self-declared independent creatures nor enabling them in their ill-conceived paths (e.g., the Prodigal Son). Tough love is a plausible, God-justifying reason that is morally adequate, "true for all we know," and very reasonable to accept.

In tough love, God lets humans separate themselves from him, follow their hearts' desires, and live with the consequences of their ill-advised actions (e.g., murders, water pollution causing cancers). Thus, contrary to some people's assertions,[39] a good God and evil (moral and natural evils, gratuitous or otherwise) coexist on earth.

### Biblical support for the conclusion.

God said of himself: "I form the light, and create darkness: I make peace, and create evil."[40] The word "evil" is the Hebrew "ra" meaning "evil, distress, misery, calamity"[41] the same word used for the tree of the knowledge of good and evil (ra).[42] God also declared: "Is it not from the mouth of the Most High that both good and ill (ra) go forth?"[43] "Shall there be evil (ra) in a city, and the Lord hath not done it?"[44] God allowed evil, wickedness,

---

38. Humans want to live as they please without God's interference until they need his help (e.g., cancer, robberies). They also want the right to blame him when he does not comply with their demands or meet their expectations. Unfortunately, this option of humans being the bosses and God the employee is not available.

39. Epicurus, J. L. Mackie, William Rowe, and others.

40. Isa 45:7, KJV. "Evil, as opposed to 'peace' or prosperity, is suffering, but not sin." *Ellicott's Commentary for English Readers.* https://biblehub.com/commentaries/isaiah/45-7.htm

41. F. Brown, S. Driver, and C. Briggs. *The Brown-Driver-Briggs Hebrew and English Lexicon,* 948-49.

42. Gen 2:17

43. Lam 3:38. "Evils here design the judgments of God, or punishment inflicted on sinners, and chastisement on his own people." *Gill's Exposition of the Entire Bible.* https://biblehub.com/commentaries/lamentations/3-38.htm

44. Amos 3:6 KJV. Evil "is not to be understood of the evil of sin, of which God is not the author, it being contrary to his nature and will; and though he permits it to be done by others, yet he never does it himself, nor so much as tempts men to it." *Gill's Exposition of the Entire Bible.* https://biblehub.com/commentaries/amos/3-6.htm

and darkness[45] to engulf the whole land[46] in the crucifixion of Jesus for the salvation of his wayward people. God forthrightly acknowledges that he coexists with evil in this fallen world.[47]

In God's wisdom, Christians are exhorted to "take up the full armor of God, so that you will be able to resist in the evil day."[48] With the Lord's presence (the indwelling of the Holy Spirit)[49] and help amid our evil calamities, we can overcome the malevolent enemy for "greater is He who is in you than he (Satan) who is in the world."[50] As God indwells and helps his people by restraining evil,[51] God and evil coexist in the present realm.

**Summary**

The Tough Love Theodicy provides a compelling response to the "Evidential problem of evil"[52] by asserting that God, in tough love, does *not* intervene to prevent all gratuitous evils, whether moral or natural. Thus, the claim that "no remedy is possible, other than the fundamental one of abandoning the entire enterprise of theodicy-construction"[53] may be unwarranted, and the suggestion that "the only rational course of action left for the theist to take is to abandon theism and convert to atheism"[54] may be premature.

Can a good God coexist with evil (the tenth question of our odyssey)? While God is benevolent and loving, he cannot be expected to bail wayward creatures out of their self-inflicted disasters or enable them in their destructive paths. Self-declared independent humans are responsible

45. "This corner of the world in which so wicked an act was committed was covered over with great darkness." *Geneva Study Bible*. https://biblehub.com/commentaries/mark/15-33.htm

46. Mark 15:33

47. "God made evil possible by creating free creatures; they are responsible for making it actual." Norman Geisler, *If God, Why Evil?* 31.

48. Eph 6:13

49. 1 Cor 3:16

50. 1 John 4:4

51. 2 Thess 2:7, Thomas Constable, "2 Thessalonians," 719.

52. The "Evidential problem of evil" claims that God and gratuitous evil do not coexist (God prevents all gratuitous evils). "An omnipotent, omniscient, wholly good God would not permit any gratuitous evil." Nick Trakakis, "The Evidential Problem of Evil."

53. Nick Trakakis, "Anti-theodicy," 97.

54. Nick Trakakis, *The God Beyond Belief*, 341.

for their behaviors and must live with the consequences, whether good or evil. They cannot blame their Creator for the horrendous calamities they perpetrate in this fallen world (e.g., the Holocaust). Contrary to Epicurus's paradox and the "Logical problem of evil," the omnipotent, omniscient, and omnibenevolent God coexists with evil (moral and natural evils, gratuitous or otherwise) on this earth, with a *morally justifying reason* (tough love) for not preventing all the pains and sufferings.[55]

Yet, in his mercy and compassion, the Lord does not leave his errant people in their predicament. He ceaselessly calls them to return through the Holy Spirit and the countless efforts of the Church (with massive expenditures of money, time, talents, and lives). In love, God provided a rescue plan, a path of salvation and eternal life for his fallen creatures. To that "way of escape,"[56] the final question of our journey, we now turn!

---

55. In the Tough Love Theodicy, pains and sufferings in this world do not "favor Naturalism over Theism." "Considerations about intense suffering decisively favor Naturalism over Theism." Graham Oppy, "Rowe's Evidential Arguments from Evil," 63.

56. 1 Cor 10:13

# 12

# Is There a Way of Escape from This World Full of Evil and Suffering?

> *Christianity is the only faith whose founder died for His followers in order to enable them to escape the consequences of their sins.*
>
> —Tim LaHaye[1]

ON JUNE 27, 1976, an Air France flight with 246 passengers and 12 crew members was hijacked by terrorists who diverted the flight to Entebbe, Uganda. Under the protection of General Idi Amin, the hijackers demanded five million dollars in ransom, and the release of 53 Palestinian prisoners. After allowing the non-Israelis to leave, the terrorists threatened to kill the remaining Jewish hostages if their requirements were not met.

Diplomatic attempts involving the US, Egypt, and Israel failed to resolve the crisis. The only remaining option was to attempt an extremely risky rescue operation that might involve a pitched battle with Idi Amin's soldiers guarding the prisoners.

A commando group led by Lt. Col. Yonatan Netanyahu, the older brother of the Israeli Prime minister Benjamin Netanyahu, was tasked with the assault to rescue the captives. In an effort to deceive the guards, a black Mercedes resembling Idi Amin's car and several Land Rovers for his supposed escort were brought on the transport planes.

---

1. Tim LaHaye, *The Popular Handbook on the Rapture*, 30.

However, unbeknownst to the task force, Idi Amin had switched to a white Mercedes. The wrong-colored car was stopped by the Ugandans, leading to a premature discovery of the scheme. Undaunted, the commandos fought their way into the airport terminal and rescued the hostages. In the firefight, the leader of the assault unit, Yonatan Netanyahu, was killed.

In a letter to a friend, Yonatan had pondered about life and death. "Death does not frighten me . . . I do not fear it because I attribute little to a life without purpose. And if it is necessary for me to lay down my life to attain an important goal, I will do so willingly."[2]

For the vital goal of rescuing his people from the clutches of the evil one,[3] Jesus (Hebrew Yehoshua, meaning "God/Yahweh saves")[4] willingly laid down his life. Even though humans freely chose to separate themselves from their Creator, God did not want to leave them to their fate, unveiling the protoevangelium (the first hint of the Good News) of Genesis 3:15, later mentioned in Romans 16:20. The omniscient Lord was not caught off-guard by humanity's decision to deny him. In God's wisdom, the forbidden path of death had always included a plan of redemption for his creatures. A disobedient choice, if made, would not be final.

After the fall of humans with its untold pains and sufferings (Dr. Stump's "problem of mourning"),[5] in compassion for his wayward creatures, God endeavored a rescue operation, a means of forgiveness and reconciliation to bring people back into fellowship with him. What is the "safe exit" path that helps us escape from this world of death to the promised land of eternal life?

---

2. https://thejewishnews.com/2021/07/07/yoni-netanyahu-a-heros-story/

3. 2 Tim 2:26

4. "The modern name 'Jesus' comes from the Latin Iesus, which comes from the Greek Iesous, which comes from the Aramaic Yeshu'a and the Hebrew Yehoshu'a." https://www.ancient-hebrew.org/hebrew-names/from-where-did-the-name-jesus-come.htm

5. According to Dr. Stump, even defeated or redeemed evils in the post-Fall world would "count as somehow a disappointment" against God. "Would it not have been better if the first heaven and earth had remained in their original goodness, if there had not been the intervening apocalypse?" Eleonore Stump, *The Image of God*, 4. In the Tough Love Theodicy, the fall of humans was *not* necessary, neither part of God's perfect plan, nor his mandated path for Adam. The omnibenevolent Creator is not to blame for human sufferings in the post-Fall world ("life is still a depressing version of what it might have been" without a Fall, a reason for "mourning," ibid., 9).

## Is It the "Forgive and Forget Path"?

Dr. van Inwagen raised the question: "Why didn't God immediately restore his fallen creatures to their original union with him?"[6] Could God just forgive his creatures, forget the trespasses, move on, and live with them as before?

Since justice is one of God's attributes, he cannot ignore wrongdoings, live and let live. "Shall not the Judge of all the earth deal justly?"[7] As we discipline our children for disobedience, we should not expect anything less from God.[8]

Furthermore, a holy God cannot live in close communion with unholy people. "But your iniquities have made a separation between you and your God."[9] "Without holiness no one will see the Lord."[10] God cannot condone evil, "for what partnership have righteousness and lawlessness, or what fellowship has light with darkness?"[11] God, in his justice and holiness, cannot overlook humanity's transgressions. "And, we may add, if he did, what would happen next? What would prevent the fall from immediately recurring?"[12]

## Is It the "Enabling Path?"

Dr. van Inwagen asked a second question: "Why doesn't God protect his fallen creatures from the worst effects of their separation from him: the horrible pain and suffering?"[13]

Since most people live far away from God, a good life without much pain and suffering will just perpetuate the unsatisfactory situation, keeping them from seeking God and returning to a close relationship with him. C. S. Lewis declared: "Pain insists on being attended to. God whispers to us in our pleasures, speaks in our consciences, but shouts in our pains. It is his megaphone to rouse a deaf world."[14] Pains

---

6. Peter van Inwagen, "The Magnitude, Duration, and Distribution of Evil," 379.
7. Gen 18:25
8. Heb 12:9-10
9. Isa 59:2
10. Heb 12:14 NIV.
11. 2 Cor 6:14
12. Peter van Inwagen, "The Magnitude, Duration, and Distribution of Evil," 380.
13. Ibid., 379.
14. C. S. Lewis, *The Problem of Pain*, 91.

and sufferings are God's tools to bring people back to him. The removal of torments and miseries through God's miraculous intervention will just allow creatures to move further away from their Creator. After all, why should we change course when everything is going well and to our liking? "If we are satisfied with our existence, why should we even consider turning to God and asking for his help?"[15]

As shown in the Tough Love Theodicy, God loves us too much to enable us on our path of self-destruction. In his wisdom, he lets us discover for ourselves that a world without God lacks meaning and is subject to human vagaries and horrendous evils. Maybe then, we would consider giving up our self-declared independence and turning to him for help.[16]

### Is It the "Substitution Path"?

Since gruesome evils are committed on earth (e.g., Pol Pot's killing fields in Cambodia), the Lord must render righteous judgment. Yet, he is unwilling to let humanity perish far away from his presence. Sin and disobedience require a separation from the holy God, but mercy and love demand a close communion between a benevolent Creator and his creatures. What can be done to resolve the conundrum?

On September 5, 1972, eight members of the Palestine Liberation Organization scaled the chain-link fence surrounding the Olympic village in Munich. Using stolen keys, the gunmen entered the Israeli apartments, killed two members of the team, and captured nine.

"Soon after, the terrorists threw a note out of a window with their demands—the release of 236 prisoners within 4 hours and safe passage out of Germany. They threatened to kill two of their hostages every half hour after the 9 a.m. deadline."[17] "Golda Meir, the Israeli prime minister, was absolutely firm. 'If we should give in, then no Israeli anywhere in the world can feel that his life is safe.'"[18]

However, refusing the terrorists' demands would certainly mean violence and bloodshed. The German government and the Olympic organization negotiated with the kidnappers, offering them unlimited

---

15. Peter van Inwagen, "The Magnitude, Duration, and Distribution of Evil," 381.
16. Acts 3:19
17. Edward Mickolus and Susan Simmons, *The 50 Worst Terrorist Attacks*, 17.
18. Simon Burnton, "The Terrorist Outrage in Munich in 1972." https://www.theguardian.com/sport/blog/2012/may/02/50-stunning-olympic-moments-munich-72

amounts of money. They tersely replied: "Money means nothing to us; our lives mean nothing to us."[19] What was left to be done to resolve the stalemate, short of violence?

To safeguard the lives of the Israeli athletes, the German Federal Minister of the Interior Hans-Dietrich Genscher offered himself as a substitute hostage. Unfortunately, the offer of substitution was turned down. The terrorist attack ended up in mayhem. All the hostages perished in a rescue attempt along with five of their captors.

In his memoirs,

> *Genscher describes at length his efforts to win the hostages' freedom, including direct talks with the terrorists and his offer to substitute himself as a hostage in place of the athletes. He concludes: "The president of the German Red Cross even planned to confer the golden pin of honor on me for offering myself in exchange for the hostages. I assured him that what I had done was nothing out of the ordinary and I did not deserve to be honored."*[20]

Since only a non-hostage person can substitute himself/herself for a hostage person, only a non-sinful individual can substitute for a sinful one. A non-sinner may be exceedingly difficult to uncover on this earth.[21] A non-sinner who would be willing to take our deserved punishment for sins (death, separation from the holy, living God)[22] would be impossible to find.

Due to the dearth of such a candidate in this fallen world, is it surprising that the benevolent God, in love, took the form of a man and substituted himself for us? "The Word was God . . . And the Word became flesh, and dwelt among us, and we beheld his glory."[23] The sinless God took our sins and punishments on himself and paid the death penalty for us on the cross (substitution), as there was no other viable way to bring us back into a holy relationship with him. Jesus declared: "I am the way, and the truth, and the life; no one comes to the Father but through me."[24] Christ is the only "safe exit" path, the only "escape route" from this world of evil and death to the world of eternal life. By trusting in Christ for the

19. Edward Mickolus and Susan Simmons, *The 50 Worst Terrorist Attacks*, 17.

20. Philip Zelikow, "After the Wall." http://www.nytimes.com/books/98/03/01/reviews/980301.01zelikot.html

21. "All have sinned and fall short of the glory of God" (Rom 3:23).

22. Rom 6:23

23. John 1:1,14

24. John 14:6

forgiveness of our sins, we will be able to be united with him in heaven, forever free from sin, death, and evil.[25]

However, no one is forced to accept the substitution. It is there, available to all comers. Through Christ the Savior, we can be free from the penalty of sin and return to a close relationship with the Creator. The offer still stands, and the choice is ours to make!

### The Age of Evil

Dr. van Inwagen raised a third question: "Why has God allowed 'the age of evil' to persist for thousands and thousands of years?"[26] God's reasons may not be completely known. However, we can venture some opinions concerning the extended length of the age of evil.

First, in the Tough Love Theodicy, the disavowed God lets self-governing people separate themselves from him, go their own way, explore their options, develop their own solutions, learn from their successes and failures, and decide without any coercion to either pursue their independent paths or turn back to God and seek his help (acknowledge his existence and accept his offer of substitution). Since humans are slow learners, this process may easily take centuries, for people always hope that the solutions to their many problems are just around the corner. "Hope springs eternal in the human breast."[27] Independent creatures believe that they can manage everything without the need to surrender their autonomy. However, is the overall situation improving or deteriorating?

"According to a survey (done at the end of 2016) of more than 21,000 people from 36 countries in all regions of the world, about 60 percent agree that the world has become worse in the past year."[28] In 2022, 56 percent of US voters surveyed "said that, financially, things are 'getting worse,' the highest percentage on record."[29] Runaway inflation, crippling shortages, soaring oil prices, and recession fears are daily concerns. Wars

---

25. Rev 21:4, 27
26. Peter van Inwagen, "The Magnitude, Duration, and Distribution of Evil," 379.
27. Alexander Pope, *Essay on Man*, 1.95.
28. Deidre McPhillips, "The World Has Taken a Turn for the Worse." https://www.usnews.com/news/best-countries/articles/2017-05-31/most-think-the-world-has-gotten-worse-in-the-last-year-survey-says
29. Max Greenwood, "Majority of Americans Say They Are 'Getting Worse' Financially: Poll." https://thehill.com/homenews/campaign/3499302-majority-of-americans-say-they-are-getting-worse-financially-poll/

IS THERE A WAY OF ESCAPE FROM THIS WORLD FULL OF EVIL AND SUFFERING? 197

and their accompanying evils (e.g., atrocities and deaths in the Russia-Ukraine and Israel-Hamas wars) dominate the airwaves.

Are genocides horrendous evils only found in the distant past, in the dusty, arcane books of yesteryear or are they common fare in our instant messages and digital news?

The list of genocides in the history of humanity, ranked by death toll, is as follows: 1. The Holocaust (1933–1945, up to 17 million deaths). 2. The Ukrainian genocide (1932–1933, up to 7.5 million deaths). 3. The Cambodian genocide (1975–1979, up to 3 million deaths). 4. The Kazakh genocide (1931–1933, up to 1.75 million deaths). 5. The Armenian genocide (1915–1922, up to 1.5 million deaths). 6. The Rwandan genocide (1994, up to 1 million deaths). 7. The Zunghar genocide (1755–1758, up to 800,000 deaths). 8. The Circassian genocide (1941–1945, up to 600,000 deaths). 9. The Croatian genocide (1941–1945, up to 600,000 deaths). 10. The Bangladesh Genocide (1971, estimate 300,000 to 3 million deaths).[30] With the exception of the Zunghar genocide (18th century), all the remaining genocides in the top ten list occurred in the 20th century.

How about US mass shootings (defined as the killings of three or more people, not including the shooter)? Have they disappeared following gun control measures?

In 1982, there was only one incident in Miami with 8 killed, 3 wounded. In 2018, 12 mass shootings were recorded with 80 killed, 66 wounded. By July 5, 2022, "there have already been more than 300 mass shootings this year in the United States . . . Not a single week in 2022 has passed without at least four mass shootings."[31] The data from 2023 was even worse. By July 23, 2023, "US surpasses 400 mass shootings so far in 2023 . . . With a little over five months still to go in the year, the number of mass shootings is up 9% from 365 mass shootings that occurred as of this time in 2022—a year in which a total of 647 mass shootings unfolded."[32]

How about the worldwide data? The list of worldwide mass shootings, ranked by death toll, is as follows: 1. The Garissa University College Attack in Kenya (2015, 148 deaths). 2. The Peshawar School Massacre

---

30. https://www.worldatlas.com/articles/most-horrific-genocides-in-human-history.html

31. https://www.washingtonpost.com/nation/2022/06/02/mass-shootings-in-2022/

32. https://abcnews.go.com/US/us-surpasses-400-mass-shootings-2023-national-gun/story?id=101588652

in Pakistan (2014, 141 deaths). 3. The Paris Terrorist Attack (2015, 130 deaths). 4. The Oslo Attack in Norway (2011, 67 deaths). 5. The Westgate Shopping Mall Attack in Kenya (2013, 67 deaths). 6. The Las Vegas Shooting (2017, 58 deaths). 7. The South Korea Shooting (1982, 56 deaths). 8. The Orlando Nightclub Shooting (2016, 49 deaths). 9. The Sousse Beach Mass Shooting in Tunisia (2015, 38 deaths). 10. The Virginia Tech Shooting (2007, 32 deaths).[33] Of the top ten mass shootings, only one occurred prior to 2000. The other nine happened between 2007 and 2017 with the US leading with three incidents followed by Kenya with two occurrences.

Is the US drug problem abating after intensive public education, expensive rehabilitation programs, and severe penalties for drug traffickers? "In 2014, 27.0 million people aged 12 or older used an illicit drug in the past 30 days, which corresponds to about 1 in 10 Americans (10.2 percent)."[34] In 1980, the drug overdose deaths in the US were around 7000. In 2016, it has ballooned to an approximate 64,000 deaths. On October 26, 2017, the president "declared the opioid epidemic a national public health emergency . . . Nobody has seen anything like what is going on now."[35] Yet, the grim toll continues to increase with no end in sight. "Drug deaths nationwide hit a new record in 2022. 109,680 people died as the fentanyl crisis continued to deepen."[36]

Are there less suicides among teenagers in the US as the result of better prevention and advanced treatments? "The suicide rate for white children and teens between 10 and 17 was up 70% between 2006 and 2016 . . . Although black children and teens kill themselves less often than white youth do, the rate of increase was higher—77%."[37] "The number of kids hospitalized for thinking about or attempting suicide doubled in less

---

33. http://www.worldatlas.com/articles/the-deadliest-mass-shootings-in-history.html. The list must now include the 2024 Moscow concert hall attack (143+ deaths).

34. Center for Behavioral Health Statistics and Quality, "Behavioral Health Trends in the United States," 1.

35. http://www.cnn.com/2017/10/26/politics/donald-trump-opioid-epidemic/index.html

36. https://www.npr.org/2023/05/18/1176830906/overdose-death-2022-record

37. Jayne O'Donnell and Anne Saker, "Teen Suicide Is Soaring. Do Spotty Mental Health and Addiction Treatment Share Blame?" https://www.usatoday.com/story/news/politics/2018/03/19/teen-suicide-soaring-do-spotty-mental-health-and-addiction-treatment-share-blame/428148002/

than a decade,"[38] from "0.66% in 2008 to 1.82% in 2015."[39] Suicide was the second leading cause of death in 2021 among young Americans.[40]

Considering the above facts, are people convinced that they need help from God with their dire problems, or do they believe that they should persist in their self-determined paths?

Rather than acknowledging humanity's shortcomings, the German philosopher Rudolf Eucken struck a different tone in his 1908 Nobel Prize speech: "In former ages . . . there was no hope of either tearing up evil by the root or making life richer and more joyous . . . The impossibilities of a former age have been realized in ours. We have witnessed surprising breakthroughs in our own age and can see no limit to this progressive movement."[41]

In 2017, Max Roser, an Oxford economist, opined:

> The last 200 years brought us to a better position than ever before to solve problems. Solving problems—big problems—is always a collaborative undertaking. And the group of people that is able to work together today is a much, much stronger group than there ever was on this planet. We have just seen the change over time; the world today is healthier, richer, and better educated.[42]

In the presence of such views, should people be surprised that the age of evil continues unabated? What would it take for humans to finally turn back to God?

The second reason why the age of evil is extended over many centuries may be God's desire to be patient and long-suffering toward his creatures. "With the Lord, one day is like a thousand years, and a thousand years like one day. The Lord is not slow about his promise, as some count slowness, but is patient toward you, not wishing for any to perish

---

38. Jamie Ducharme, "More Kids Are Attempting and Thinking About Suicide, according to a New Study." http://time.com/5279029/suicide-rates-rising-study/

39. Gregory Plemmons et al., "Hospitalization for Suicide Ideation or Attempt," abstract.

40. https://www.cbsnews.com/news/suicide-homicide-rates-young-americans-increased-sharply-cdc-report/

41. Rudolf Eucken, "Naturalism or Idealism?" (Naturalismus oder Idealismus?) https://www.nobelprize.org/prizes/literature/1908/eucken/25766-rudolf-eucken-nobel-lecture-1908/

42. Max Roser, "The Short History of Global Living Conditions and Why It Matters That We Know It." https://ourworldindata.org/a-history-of-global-living-conditions-in-5-charts

but for all to come to repentance."[43] Should we not take advantage of this reprieve to turn back to him? Furthermore, as we all face death, should we not be concerned about the afterlife? "And inasmuch as it is appointed for men to die once and after this comes judgment."[44] Either at our death or when Christ returns, it will be too late to repent and accept his gift of substitution. While we still have life and breath, it is still possible to change our mind and acknowledge him. The decision is ours to make for the loving God does not coerce anyone to love him.

Third, God may desire a large and diverse community of believers from all nations gathered over a lengthy period (rather than from just a few tribes clustered around the Middle East in the first century). God declared to Abraham: "By your descendants all the nations of the earth shall be blessed."[45] "A comprehensive demographic study of more than 200 countries finds that there are 2.18 billion Christians of all ages around the world, representing nearly a third of the estimated 2010 global population of 6.9 billion."[46] However, the Christian statistical center of gravity has shifted from Turkey in 1000 AD, to Italy in 1700, to Spain in 1900, and to Mali, West Africa, in 2023.

Finally, God may want to teach his people patience, endurance, trust, and love amid prolonged pain and suffering in this age of evil. True love demands sacrifice, a sacrifice of oneself to one's beloved. "Walk in the way of love, just as Christ loved us and gave himself up for us as a fragrant offering and sacrifice to God."[47] In view of Christ's love and sacrifice, Paul declared: "I urge you, brethren, by the mercies of God, to present your bodies a living and holy sacrifice, acceptable to God, which is your spiritual service of worship."[48]

Philip was raised in a Christian family, the third of four siblings. In high school, he showed a great flair for acting, impressing his teachers who suggested that he should become an actor. However, after meeting a missionary who told him about some tribe in the Ecuadorian jungle, he

---

43. 2 Pet 3:8-9
44. Heb 9:27
45. Gen 26:4
46. Pew Research Center. http://www.pewforum.org/2011/12/19/global-christianity-exec/
47. Eph 5:2 NIV.
48. Rom 12:1

contemplated mission work. In 1952, he "waved goodbye to his parents and boarded a ship ... to Quito, Ecuador."[49]

Three years later, many Quichuas had been converted and discipled. Philip then decided to reach out to the Huaorani deep in the Ecuadorian jungle. Unfortunately, they were violent people who had murdered several workers of an oil company, forcing the closure of a drilling site because everyone was afraid to work there. Undaunted, five missionaries were dropped off by plane and built a tree house by the river.

> Two Auca (Auca meaning "savage," is a pejorative used for the Huaorani by the Quichua) women walked out of the jungle. Jim (Philip James Elliot) and Pete (Pete Fleming) excitedly jumped in the river and waded over to them. As they got closer, these women did not appear friendly. Jim and Pete almost immediately heard a terrifying cry behind them. As they turned, they saw a group of Auca warriors with their spears raised, ready to throw. Jim Elliot reached for the gun in his pocket. He had to decide instantly if he should use it. But he knew he couldn't. Each of the missionaries had promised they would not kill an Auca who did not know Jesus to save himself from being killed. Within seconds, the Auca warriors threw their spears, killing all the missionaries,[50]

leaving behind five widows and nine fatherless children.

Jim (Philip James) Elliot had written in his journal: "He is no fool who gives what he cannot keep to gain that which he cannot lose."[51] "For whoever wishes to save his life will lose it, but whoever loses his life for my sake, he is the one who will save it."[52] "I have been crucified with Christ; and it is no longer I who live, but Christ lives in me; and the life which I now live in the flesh I live by faith in the Son of God, who loved me and gave himself up for me."[53] As Christ was crucified for us in love, so should his followers willingly put down their lives for him in full trust and love.

The age of evil will continue until the time of Christ's return.[54] Hopefully, by then, humans will recognize that they have been on the wrong

49. https://www.christianity.com/church/church-history/church-history-for-kids/jim-elliot-no-fool-11634862.html
50. Ibid.
51. http://www2.wheaton.edu/bgc/archives/faq/20.htm
52. Luke 9:24
53. Gal 2:20
54. Heb 9:28

path and will turn back to God. On that day, people from all nations shall praise God for his long-suffering and patience. The faithful believers will be rewarded for their endurance and true love in sacrifice. "This gospel of the kingdom shall be preached in the whole world as a testimony to all the nations, and then the end will come."[55]

## The Distribution of Evil

Dr. van Inwagen asked a final question: "Why do the innocent suffer and the wicked prosper?"[56] Why does evil fall indiscriminately on good and bad people?

In the Tough Love Theodicy, the disavowed God reluctantly lets people separate themselves from him, go their own way, and do what they desire. The wicked (e.g., Hitler and Stalin) may abuse their power to oppress the weak. Of course, the rich and powerful may also use their resources for the good of humanity (e.g., Bill Gates and Warren Buffett). The innocents do *not* always suffer, nor do the wicked always prosper. Yet, they all experience untold miseries in this fallen realm.

"Incredible amounts of pain and suffering fall equally on the innocent and the guilty . . . (whether saints or sinners)."[57] In the novel *The Plague*, the French philosopher Albert Camus, the 1957 Nobel Prize in Literature laureate, recounted the indiscriminate deaths from the bubonic plague of "saints" (the priest, Father Paneloux) and "sinners" (the atheist Jean Tarrou).[58]

Several explanations can be given for such a puzzling situation. As God desires all humans to love him for himself and not for the benefits he can provide, sparing "saints" from evil and suffering would be an underhanded incentive on God's part to lure people back to him (conversion to avoid pain).

God also does not want his believers to follow him for the sake of personal profit. "Does Job fear God for nothing? Have you not made a hedge about him and his house and all that he has on every side? You have blessed the work of his hands, and his possessions have increased in the land. But put forth your hand now and touch all that he has; he will

---

55. Matt 24:14
56. Peter van Inwagen, "The Magnitude, Duration, and Distribution of Evil," 379.
57. William Rowe, "Paradox and Promise," 117.
58. Albert Camus, *The Plague (La Peste)*.

surely curse you to your face."⁵⁹ Job's possessions were taken away to strengthen and purify his commitment.

A case can also be made that Christians are expected to suffer *more* than non-Christians. Besides the evils (moral, natural . . .) that befall all people who live in this broken world, believers may experience additional pain and suffering in their quest for Christlikeness.

In the pursuit for perfection, the 13th century craftsman Masamune fashioned a renowned samurai sword by heating the tamahagane (jewel steel) in the forge (at 1400 degrees F) and removing it just before it could reach a molten state. "The next step involves folding the metal over itself using a technique called mizu-uchi (water striking). The main purpose of folding and hammering the steel is to force all the impurities and voids out of the metal. The force of the hammer blow, along with the thermal shock of the cool water, draws the impurities toward the surface."⁶⁰ This process of "burns and blows" was repeated over and over until the master swordsmith was satisfied that the metal had no remaining impurity. This exquisite Japanese national treasure Honjo Masamune sword belonged to the Tokugawa shogunate and was composed of over 30,000 layers of steel from the repeated hammering, folding, and heat forging.

Likewise, to become the mature, Christlike people the Lord desires, vessels "for honor, sanctified, useful to the Master, prepared for every good work,"⁶¹ Christians must undergo trials and tribulations ("burns and blows") as part of God's process of Rehabilitation, Edification, Shielding, and Training (REST) to make them "perfect and complete, lacking in nothing."⁶²

In his wisdom, God does not entice people to follow him by promising an easy life without pain and suffering. "In the world, you have tribulation"⁶³ is true for both believers and non-believers. In this realm replete with torments and afflictions, people are free to reject God or accept him, without any coercion or bribe.

Mary was a "Navy brat" moving from place to place during her childhood while her father fought in Korea, Vietnam, and the Cold War, earning a Distinguished Flying Cross as a spy plane pilot. She remembered

---

59. Job 1:9-11
60. Michael Smathers, "Iron Sand to Honed Steel." https://www.thecollector.com/how-to-make-a-real-katana-samurai-sword/
61. 2 Tim 2:21
62. Jas 1:4
63. John 16:33

the stress of being constantly uprooted, of missing her absentee dad, and having to attend many soldiers' funerals.

Deciding on a legal career, Mary earned a law degree and married Johnny, a fellow student. They were blessed with a boy named Wade.

At the age of 16, on spring break, Wade was driving his Jeep Grand Cherokee to their beach house when a "gust of wind" blew him off the road. Wade overcorrected and flipped the SUV, causing it to roll twice, land upside down and catch on fire. Wade was trapped and died as he had "to be cut out of the Cherokee."[64]

Mary was heartbroken and reflected about the circumstances of her son's death. "I had to think about a God who would not save my son. Wade was—and I have lots of evidence; it's not just his mother saying it—a gentle and good boy . . . You'd think that if God was going to protect somebody, he'd protect that boy. But not only did he not protect him, the wind blew him from the road."[65]

After Wade's death, Mary decided to have more children. Almost past childbearing age, she underwent fertility treatments and had a girl at age 48 and a boy at 50.

After a successful legal career, Mary's husband Johnny decided to run for public office. While on the barnstorming trail, Mary discovered a lump in her breast. Undaunted, she continued campaigning for her husband until he conceded defeat in 2004. She then underwent treatment for stage 2 breast cancer, receiving chemotherapy, a lumpectomy, and radiation therapy.

In December 2006, Johnny announced another run for political office. In March 2007, Mary's cancer came back with a vengeance as she was diagnosed with stage 4 breast carcinoma and metastases to her bones. Nevertheless, she soldiered on for her husband and the crusade proceeded without interruption. Johnny "continued to use his wife to boost his campaign, saying 'there is no one I admire more than my wife' and calling her 'my hero.'"[66]

However, the *National Enquirer* soon revealed that Johnny was having an affair with a film producer on his payroll, and that she was carrying his child. John (Johnny Reid) Edwards's effort to gain the democratic

64. https://www.washingtonpost.com/wp-dyn/articles/A40174-2001Aug6.html

65. http://www.newsweek.com/elizabeth-edwards-realistic-about-her-prognosis-97625

66. http://abcnews.go.com/Politics/john-edwards-mistress-breakdown-americas-sensational-scandals/story?id=20854336

US presidential nomination imploded under the weight of the salacious news. Elizabeth (Mary Elizabeth) Edwards's world collapsed as she considered the shattering of their political dream, her husband's betrayal, her impending death, and the future of her motherless children. What could be done to remedy all these heartbreaking evils? Was it time to reconsider one's position about God and ask for his help?

Elizabeth Edwards decided: "I'm not praying for God to save me from cancer . . . The hand of God blew him (Wade) from the road. So, I had to think, what kind of God do I have that doesn't intervene—in fact, may even participate—in the death of this good boy?"[67] "I have, I think, somewhat of an odd version of God. I do not have an intervening God. I don't think I can pray to him—or her—to cure me of cancer."[68] She died of metastatic breast cancer on December 7, 2010, at the age of 61.

Charles was born in Boston to a family of Swedish and British descent. After receiving his degree in history from Brown University, he did a two-year stint in the Marine Corps before getting a law degree from George Washington University. In 1968, he left his legal practice for a government job.

Charles was known as the "hard man," the "hit man," or "hatchet man." He reminisced in his memoir about his father meeting President Nixon at the White House. Charles's dad was so proud of him that he thought his "father's chest would explode." "I knew, as Dad did not, that if I was as valuable to the President as he said I was, it was because I was willing at times to blink at certain ethical standards, to be ruthless in getting things done. It was earning me status and power."[69]

This questionable behavior got him entangled in the Watergate scandal as he was indicted for conspiring to cover up the burglaries. Charles recounted the bitter experience: "I was stripped of everything, public enemy number one."[70] With the loss of status and power, the threat of being disbarred, the mounting legal fees, and the specter of a long prison sentence, was it time to reconsider one's position concerning the existence of God and seek his help? Could God do anything at

---

67. http://www.newsweek.com/elizabeth-edwards-dies-after-cancer-struggle-69041

68. Adele Stan, "The Original Theology of Elizabeth Edwards," *The American Prospect*, July 30, 2007. http://prospect.org/article/original-theology-elizabeth-edwards

69. Charles Colson, *Born Again*, 57.

70. https://www1.cbn.com/content/chuck-colson-35-years-faith

this late date when one's back was against the wall, staring at disaster in the face?

The chairman of the board of Raytheon gave Charles a copy of C. S. Lewis' *Mere Christianity*. Subsequently, Chuck (Charles Wendell) Colson became a born-again Christian. After serving seven months of a one-to three-year sentence, he was released and founded Prison Fellowship, "an outreach to prisoners and their families . . . the largest prison ministry in the United States . . . active over 125 countries worldwide."[71]

In the Tough Love Theodicy, "saints or sinners" must live with the evils in this world and the consequences of their actions. Facing heart-wrenching pain and suffering, Elizabeth Edwards and Chuck Colson made their choices about the existence of an omnipotent, omniscient, and omnibenevolent God, the same choice open to every one of us when we consider our troubles and turmoil on this earth!

People are free to follow God or not. If they choose to return to their Creator and obey his commandments (e.g., "You shall not murder," "You shall not steal," "You shall not commit adultery," "You shall not covet"),[72] the world would be a better place for all. Who is responsible when the innocents suffer and the wicked prosper? Besides the steadfast work of the Holy Spirit,[73] and the tireless efforts of the Church, what more can God do (short of coercion) to get humans to follow what he declares in his commandments?

**Summary**

In answer to our final question, "Is there a way of escape from this world full of evil and suffering?" God provides a rescue/salvation plan through his offer of substitution,[74] a "safe exit" path to eternal life, available to all comers. They can return to him and voluntarily obey, making a better life for themselves and their children. However, the decision is theirs for God does not coerce love from anyone. In this "age of evil," with its miseries falling on both "saints and sinners," the world is whatever people make of it, as they consider their options concerning a virtuous God's existence in the presence of vicious evil!

71. https://www.prisonfellowship.org/2016/03/new-honor-chuck-colson/
72. Ex 20:13-17
73. John 16:8-11
74. 1 Pet 2:24

# Conclusion: Vicious Evil! Virtuous God?

*The problem of tragedy, suffering, and injustice is a problem for everyone.*

—Timothy Keller[1]

"Why doesn't a virtuous God prevent vicious evil?" In tough love, the omnibenevolent and virtuous Father does not intervene to thwart all evils, neither bailing out his self-declared independent creatures from the consequences of their actions, nor enabling them in their self-destructive paths (e.g., the Prodigal Son).

Humans are now in God's non-recommended/forbidden path, the world of death (e.g., cancer) where they can deny his existence, separate themselves from him, and perpetrate vicious evils (e.g., child abuse). Over the millennia, the long-suffering Father has been calling his prodigal sons and daughters back to him through the promptings of the Holy Spirit (contra deism) and the tireless and costly efforts of the Church (in money, time, talents, and lives). In his grace and mercy, God has provided his fallen creatures with a redeemer, Jesus Christ, with the goal of bringing them into a loving relationship with their Creator.

Humans can either reject the offer of salvation and persist in their claims of God's non-existence, or they can choose to be reconciled to him through Christ's sacrifice and substitution on the cross. In his desire for true love, the benevolent God does not coerce anyone to love

---

1. Timothy Keller, *The Reason for God*, 27.

him. Whatever choice people make, they will have to live with the consequences, whether good or evil.

For those who are willing to acknowledge their Creator and follow him, he promises to cause "all things to work together for good"[2] and pledges to help them solve their problems.[3] Through the faithful work of the Holy Spirit and the Church, the all-wise God endeavors to bring his followers to maturity and Christlikeness.[4] In his justice and compassion, the sovereign Lord blesses believers with good things, and redeems the pain and torment done to his suffering people.

The many troubling questions raised by sufferers in this fallen realm were cogently answered. People who accept Christ's gift of substitution and eternal life are considered children of God[5] and given much comfort and many promises of support and protection.[6] In his grace and mercy, God uses the existing evils in this world as tools for good,[7] *without* condoning the wrongdoings perpetrated by peccable humans. Sadly, God cannot create humans with free will who never commit evil (impeccable humans) since the uncreated God cannot create uncreated Gods. Hence, various evils (moral, natural . . .) can come from our own actions or other people's twisted deeds and can be used by God for the purpose of Rehabilitation, Edification, Shielding, and Training (REST). The evils we suffer in this realm will be redeemed by the rewards God will bestow on us in heaven.[8] We will be united with Christ, enjoy the marriage feast as the bride of the heavenly groom,[9] attain impeccability and immortality, and reign with him forever.[10] With this knowledge and hope in the future, we can successfully manage the evils in our lives (RECAP) and help others in their sufferings (DARES and HELPS), i.e., the Religious Problem of Evil.

Concerning non-believers, God disapproves of humans claiming that he does not exist. In his disapproval and tough love (a morally justifying reason), the disavowed God does not intervene to prevent all

2. Rom 8:28
3. Ps 50:15
4. Eph 4:13
5. John 1:12
6. Rom 8:28, Heb 4:16
7. Gen 50:20
8. Rev 21:4-5
9. Rev 19:7-9, Eph 5:31-32
10. Rev 22:5

moral and natural evils, gratuitous or otherwise. Thus, contrary to Epicurus's paradox and the contemporary Logical and Evidential Problems of Evil, God and evil coexist in this fallen realm!

In love, through Jesus the Savior,[11] the omnibenevolent Father provides for his errant creatures a way of escape from this world of evil and death to a blessed hope of eternal life, "an inheritance which is imperishable and undefiled and will not fade away, reserved in heaven,"[12] an offer still available to all comers who may yet respond to God's unceasing calls!

> It was the worst news I could get as an atheist: my agnostic wife had decided to become a Christian. Two words shot through my mind. The first was an expletive; the second was "divorce." I thought she was going to turn into a self-righteous holy roller. But over the following months, I was intrigued by the positive changes in her character and values. Finally, I decided to take my journalism and legal training (I was legal editor of the Chicago Tribune) and systematically investigate whether there was any credibility to Christianity. Maybe, I figured, I could extricate her from this cult. I quickly determined that the alleged resurrection of Jesus was the key. Anyone can claim to be divine, but if Jesus backed up his claim by returning from the dead, then that was awfully good evidence he was telling the truth. For nearly two years, I explored the minutia of the historical data on whether Easter was myth or reality. I didn't merely accept the New Testament at face value; I was determined only to consider facts that were well-supported historically. As my investigation unfolded, my atheism began to buckle . . . In the end, after I had thoroughly investigated the matter, I reached an unexpected conclusion: it would actually take more faith to maintain my atheism than to become a follower of Jesus.[13]

In response to the trouble and suffering in his marriage, Lee Strobel accepted the benevolent God's timeless call to follow Jesus.

Yet, other sufferers are undecided, perplexed by the coexistence of a good God and heinous evil. It is our prayer that this work has answered their heart-wrenching questions in this "vale of suffering," brought them comfort in their many trials, provided them with some practical means to help others in their afflictions, and equipped them to make a reasoned assessment of the hope that we share in Christ.

11. John 14:6
12. 1 Pet 1:4
13. Lee Strobel, "How Easter Killed My Atheism." https://stream.org/easter-killed-atheism/?platform=hootsuite

Concerning a successful philosophical and theological argument, Dr. van Inwagen affirmed: "An argument . . . is a success just in the case that it can be used, under ideal circumstances, to convert an audience of ideal agnostics . . . in the presence of an ideal opponent."[14] With its logical, deductive reasoning, its well-supported premises, and its many practical applications, it is our hope that the Tough Love Theodicy successfully rises to Dr. van Inwagen's challenge and cogently resolves our agonizing enigma "Vicious evil! Virtuous God?"

---

14. Peter van Inwagen, *The Problem of Evil*, 47.

# Bibliography

Adams, Marilyn McCord. *Horrendous Evils and the Goodness of God*. Ithaca: Cornell University Press, 1999.
———. "The Problem of Hell: A Problem of Evil for Christians," in *Reasoned Faith*, ed. Eleonore Stump, 301–27. Ithaca: Cornell University Press, 1993.
Aeschylus. "Agamemnon," in *Oresteia*, trans. Peter Meineck, 2–67. Indianapolis: Hackett, 1998.
Ahern, M. B. *The Problem of Evil*. London: Routledge, 1971.
Alcorn, Randy. *If God Is Good: Faith in the Midst of Suffering and Evil*. Colorado Springs: Multnomah, 2009.
Ali, Abdullah. *The Quran in English*. Pakistan: Madina, 2020.
Almeida, Michael. "On Necessary Gratuitous Evils." *European Journal for Philosophy of Religion* 12/3 (2020), 117–35.
Alston, William. "The Inductive Argument from Evil and the Human Cognitive Condition." *Philosophical Perspectives* 5 (1991), 29–67.
Altman, Nathaniel. *Ahimsa: Dynamic Compassion, A Nonviolence Anthology*. Brooklyn: Gaupo, 2020.
Anselm. *Basic Writings*, trans. Thomas Williams. Indianapolis: Hackett, 2007.
———. *Cur Deus Homo*. http://www.ewtn.com/library/christ/curdeus.htm
Aquinas, Thomas. *Summa Theologica*. https://www.ccel.org/ccel/aquinas/summa.i.html
Aristotle, *Physics*. http://classics.mit.edu/Aristotle/physics.1.i.html
Ashby, Stephen. "A Reformed Arminian Response to Michael S. Horton," in *Four Views on Eternal Security*, eds. Stanley Gundry and J. Matthew Pinson, 48–54. Grand Rapids: Zondervan, 2002.
Ashton, W. G. *Shinto: The Way of the Gods*. New York: Longmans, Greens, and Co., 1905.
Athanasius, *On the Incarnation*, 2nd ed., trans. Archibald Robertson. London: D. Nutt, 1891.
Augustine. *Concerning the City of God, Against the Pagans (De Civitate Dei Contra Paganos)*. https://erenow.com/common/city-of-god/
———. *The Enchiridion on Faith, Hope, and Love (Enchiridion ad Laurentium de Fide et Spe et Caritate)*. http://www.tertullian.org/fathers/augustine_enchiridion_02_trans.htm#C11

———. *Exposition on the Psalms (Enarrationes in Psalmos)* https://www.newadvent.org/fathers/1801.htm

———. *The Problem of Free Choice, (De Libero Arbitrio)*, trans. Dom Mark Pontifex. New York: Newman, 1955.

Bailey, Kenneth. *The Cross & the Prodigal*, 2nd ed. Downers Grove: IVP, 2005.

Barnes, Albert. *Notes, Explanatory and Practical, on the Epistle to the Romans*, 9th ed. New York: Harper & Brothers, 1846.

Basinger, Erin et al. "Grief Communication and Privacy Rules: Examining the Communication of Individuals Bereaved by the Death of a Family Member." *Journal of Family Communication* 16/4 (2016), 285–302.

Bauckham, Richard. "Universalism, a Historical Survey." *Themelios* 4/2 (1978), 47–54.

Bavinck, Herman. *Reformed Dogmatics, Vol. 2*. Grand Rapids: Baker Academic, 2004.

Beebe, James. "Logical Problem of Evil," *Internet Encyclopedia of Philosophy*, 2024. http://www.iep.utm.edu/evil-log/

Bergmann, Michael. "Skeptical Theism and the Problem of Evil," in *Oxford Handbook to Philosophical Theology*, eds. Thomas Flint and Michael Rea, 374–99. Oxford: Oxford University Press, 2009.

———. "Skeptical Theism and Rowe's New Evidential Argument from Evil." *Noûs* 35/2 (2001) 278–96.

Bergson, Henri. *The Two Sources of Morality and Religion (Les Deux Sources de la Morale et de la Religion)*, trans. R. Ashley Audra and Cloudesley Brereton. Notre Dame: University of Notre Dame Press, 1977.

Berkhof, Louis. *Systematic Theology*. Grand Rapids: Eerdmans, 1941.

Berkovich, Izhak and Yael Grinshtain, "Typology of 'Tough Love' Leadership in Urban Schools Facing Challenging Circumstances." *Urban Education* (2018), 10.1177/0042085918801883.

Bernáth, László and Daniel Kodaj, "Evil and the God of Indifference." *International Journal for Philosophy of Religion* 88 (2020), 259–72.

Bishop, John. "On Identifying the Problem of Evil and the Possibility of Its Theist Solution," in *The Problem of Evil: Eight Views in Dialogue*, ed. Nick Trakakis, 42–54. Oxford: Oxford University Press, 2018.

———. "Response to Trakakis," in *The Problem of Evil: Eight Views in Dialogue*, ed. Nick Trakakis, 110–12. Oxford: Oxford University Press, 2018.

———. "Response to Oppy," in *The Problem of Evil: Eight Views in Dialogue*, ed. Nick Trakakis, 82–84. Oxford: Oxford University Press, 2018.

Blackmore, John. *Ludwig Boltzmann: His Later Life and Philosophy, 1900-1906, Book Two, The Philosopher*. Boston: Kluwer, 1995.

Blanchette, Kyle and Jerry Walls. "God and Hell Reconciled," in *God and Evil: The Case for God in a World Filled with Pain*, eds. Chad Meister and James Dew, 243–58. Downers Grove: IVP, 2013.

Blockmans, Steven. *Tough Love: The European Union's Relations with the Western Balkans*. The Hague, Netherlands: T.M.C. Asser Press, 2007.

Bonhoeffer, Dietrich. *Letters and Papers from Prison*, ed. Eberhard Bethge. New York: Macmillan, 1968.

Bougheas, Spiros et al. "Tough-love or Unconditional Charity?" *Oxford Economic Papers* 59/4 (2007), 561–82.

Bouhours, Dominique. *The Life of St. Francis Xavier of the Society of Jesus, Apostle of India*. Philadelphia: Eugene Cummiskey, 1841.

Boyd, Gregory. *God at War: The Bible & Spiritual Conflict*. Downers Grove: IVP Academic, 1997.
———. *Satan and the Problem of Evil: Constructing a Trinitarian Warfare Theodicy*. Downers Grove: IVP Academic, 2001.
Brody, Paul. *Son of Sam: A Biography of David Berkowitz*. Anaheim: BookCaps, 2013.
Brown, F., S. Driver, and C. Briggs. *The Brown-Driver-Briggs Hebrew and English Lexicon*. Peabody: Hendrickson, 1997.
Brümmer, Vincent. *Brümmer on Meaning and the Christian Faith: Collected Writings of Vincent Brümmer*, ed. John Hinnells. Burlington: Ashgate, 2006.
———. *The Model of Love: A Study in Philosophical Theology*. Cambridge: Cambridge University Press, 1993.
Buckareff, Andrei and Yugin Nagasawa, eds., *Alternative Concepts of God: Essays on the Metaphysics of the Divine*. Oxford: Oxford University Press, 2016.
——— and Allen Plug. "Hell and the Problem of Evil," in *The Blackwell Companion to the Problem of Evil*, eds. Justin P. McBrayer and Daniel Howard-Snyder, 128-43. West Sussex, UK: John Wiley & Sons, 2013.
Buddha, *The Middle Length Discourses of the Buddha*, trans. Bhikkhu Bodhi. Somerville: Wisdom, 2015.
Bultmann, Rudolf. *Rudolf Bultmann: Interpreting Faith for the Modern Era*, ed. Roger Johnson. Minneapolis: Fortress, 1991.
Bunch, Ted et al. "A Tunguska Sized Airburst Destroyed Tall El-Hammam, a Middle Bronze Age City in the Jordan Valley near the Dead Sea." *Scientific Reports* 11 (2021), 18632.
Burns Stacey and Mark Peyrot. "Tough-love: Nurturing and Coercing Responsibility and Recovery in California Drug Courts." *Social Problems*, 50/3 (2003), 416-38.
Butler, Joseph. *The Analogy of Religion Natural and Revealed, to the Constitution and Course of Nature*. Miami: HardPress, 2017.
Cacciatore, Joanne et al. "What Is Good Grief Support? Exploring the Actors and Actions in Social Support After Traumatic Grief." *PLoS ONE* 16/5 (2021), e0252324.
Calvin, John. *Commentaries on the Catholic Epistles*, trans. John Owen. Edinburgh: Calvin Translation Society, 1855.
———. *Commentary on Psalms Vol 1*. https://www.ccel.org/ccel/calvin/calcom08.html
———. *Institutes of the Christian Religion*, ed. John Mitchell, trans. Ford Lewis Battles. Louisville: Westminster John Knox, 1960.
Camus, Albert. *The Plague (La Peste)*, trans. Stuart Gilbert. New York: Vintage, 1991.
Candari, Christine et al. *Assessing the Economic Costs of Unhealthy Diets and Low Physical Activity: An Evidence Review and Proposed Framework*. Copenhagen: European Observatory on Health Systems and Policies, 2017.
Care, Norman. *Decent People*. New York: Rowman & Littlefield, 2000.
Carnegie, Dale. *How to Win Friends and Influence People*. New York: Pocket, 1976.
Carr, Deborah et al. "Bereavement in the Time of Coronavirus: Unprecedented Challenges Demand Novel Interventions." *Journal of Aging & Social Policy* 32 (2020), 425-31.
Cary, Phillip. "A Classic View," in *God and the Problem of Evil*, eds. Chad Meister and James Dew, 13-36. Downers Grove: IVP Academic, 2017.
Cawley, John et al. "Direct Medical Costs of Obesity in the United States and the Most Populous States." *Journal of Managed Care & Specialty Pharmacy* 27/3 (2021), 354-66.

Center for Behavioral Health Statistics and Quality. *"Behavioral Health Trends in the United States: Results from the 2014 National Survey on Drug Use and Health."* HHS Publication No. SMA 15-4927, 2014.
Chafer, Lewis. *Systematic Theology, Vols 3&4*. Grand Rapids: Kregel, 1976.
Cheney, Johnston. *The Life of Christ in Stereo*. Portland: Multnomah, 1969.
Chisholm, Roderick. "The Defeat of Good and Evil," in *The Problem of Evil*, eds. Marilyn McCord Adams and Robert Merrihew Adams, 53–68. Oxford: Oxford University Press, 1990.
Clark, Claire. "Tough love: A Brief Cultural History of the Addiction Intervention." *History of Psychology* 15/3 (2012), 233-46.
Clement of Alexandria. *The Sacred Writings of Clement of Alexandria, Volume 1*. Charleston: Verlag, 2017.
Clendenin, Daniel. "Partakers of Divinity: The Orthodox Doctrine of Theosis." *Journal of the Evangelical Theological Society* 37/3 (1994), 365–79.
Coelho, Paulo. *The Witch of Portobello (A Bruxa de Portobello)*, trans. Margaret Costa. New York: Harper Collins, 2007.
Cohen, Abraham. "Theology and Theodicy: On Reading Harold Kushner." *Modern Judaism*, 16/3 (1996), 229–61.
Cohn-Sherbok, Dan. "The Jewish Doctrine of Hell," in *Beyond Death*, eds. Dan Cohn-Sherbok and Christopher Lewis, 54–65. London: Palgrave Macmillan, 1995.
Coleridge, Henry. *The Life and Letters of St. Francis Xavier, vol 2*. London: Burns and Oates, 1872.
Collins, Paul. *Partaking in Divine Nature: Deification and Communion*. London: T&T Clark, 2010.
Colman, Richard. "The Role of the Doctor –Tough Love." *British Medical Journal* (2007), 335.
Colson, Charles. *Born Again*. Peabody: Hendrickson, 1995.
Constable, Thomas. "2 Thessalonians," in *The Bible Knowledge Commentary New Testament*, eds. John F. Walvoord and Roy B. Zuck, 713–25. Colorado Springs: David Cook, 1983.
Conway, John. "The Political Theology of Martin Niemöller." *German Studies Review* 9/3 (1986), 521–46.
Cottingham, John. "Evil and the Meaning of Life," in *The Cambridge Companion to the Problem of Evil*, eds. Chad Meister and Paul Moser, 11–26. Cambridge: Cambridge University Press, 2017.
Craig, William Lane. "Diversity, Evil, and Hell," in *God and Evil: The Case for God in a World Filled with Pain*, eds. Chad Meister and James Dew, 227–42. Downers Grove: IVP, 2013.
———. "A Molinist View," in *God and the Problem of Evil*, eds. Chad Meister and James Dew, 37–55. Downers Grove: IVP Academic, 2017.
———. "The Molinist Response," in *God and the Problem of Evil*, eds. Chad Meister and James Dew, 143–50. Downers Grove: IVP Academic, 2017.
Crenshaw, James. *Defending God: Biblical Responses to the Problem of Evil*. Oxford: Oxford University Press, 2005.
Crummett, Dustin. "Sufferer-Centered Requirements on Theodicy and All-Things Considered Harms," in *Oxford Studies in Philosophy of Religion, Volume 8*, ed. Jonathan Kvanvig, 71–95. Oxford: Oxford University Press, 2017.

Cyril of Alexandria, *Commentary on John*, trans. T. Randell. http://www.tertullian.org/fathers/cyril_on_john_11_book11.htm

Dahlke, Paul et al., *The Five Precepts: Collected Essays*. Sri Lanka: Buddhist Publication Society, 1975.

Dalin, David. *The Myth of Hitler's Pope: How Pope Pius XII Rescued Jews from the Nazis* Washington, DC: Regnery, 2005.

Dawkins, Richard. *The God Delusion*. New York: Houghton Mifflin, 2006.

———. "Is Science a Religion?" *The Humanist* 57 (1997), 26–29.

———. *River Out of Eden: A Darwinian View of Life*. New York: Basic, 1995.

De Caussade, Jean-Pierre. *Abandonment to Divine Providence (L'Abandon à la Divine Providence)*, trans. E. J. Strickland. New York: Cosimo, 2007.

Dennett, Daniel. *Breaking the Spell: Religion as a Natural Phenomenon*. New York: Viking, 2006.

De Sales, Francis. *Treatise on the Love of God (Traité de l'Amour de Dieu)*, trans. Henry Benedict Mackey. New York: Cosimo, 2007.

De Spinoza, Benedict. *Ethics (Ethica Ordine Geometrico Demonstrata)*, trans. William White and Amelia Stirling. New York: Hafner, 1949.

Descartes, René. *Meditations on First Philosophy, in Which the Existence of God and the Immortality of the Soul Are Demonstrated (Meditationes de Prima Philosophia, in qua Dei Existentia et Animæ Immortalitas Demonstratur)*. https://corescholar.libraries.wright.edu/cgi/viewcontent.cgi?article=1008&context=philosophy

———. *The Method, Meditations and Philosophy of Descartes*, trans. John Veitch. London: M. Walter Dunne, 1901.

Diller, Kevin. "Are Sin and Evil Necessary for a Really Good World?" in *The Problem of Evil: Selected Readings*, 2nd ed., ed. Michael Peterson, 390–409. Notre Dame: University of Notre Dame Press, 2017.

Dinkmeyer, Don and Lewis Losoncy. *The Skills of Encouragement: Bringing Out the Best in Yourself and Others*. New York: St. Lucie Press, 1996.

Dobson, James. *Love Must Be Tough: New Hope for Marriages in Crisis*. Carol Stream: Tyndale, 2007.

Dodes, Lance, and Zachary Dodes. *The Sober Truth: Debunking the Bad Science Behind Twelve Steps Program and the Rehab Industry*. Boston: Beacon, 2014.

Donne, John. *Devotions Upon Emergent Occasions and Death's Duel*. New York: Vintage, 1999.

Dostoevsky, Fyodor. *The Brothers Karamazov*, trans. David Magarshack. Baltimore: Penguin, 1958.

Dranseika, Vilius, "Moral Responsibility for Natural Disasters." *Human Affairs* 26 (2016), 73–79.

Draper, Paul. "Pain and Pleasure: An Evidential Problem for Theists." *Noûs* 23 (1989), 331–50.

———. "Review: Providence and the Problem of Evil by Richard Swinburne." *Noûs* 35/3 (2001), 456–74.

Drew, A. J. *A Wiccan Bible: Exploring the Mysteries of the Craft from Birth to Summerland*. Franklin Lakes: Career, 2003.

Dyson, Michael. *Pride: The Seven Deadly Sins*. Oxford: Oxford University Press, 2006.

Edwards, Jonathan. *The Works of President Edwards, Vol IV*. New York: Leavitt, Trow & Co., 1844.

Eggerichs, Emerson. *The 4 Wills of God*. Nashville: B&H, 2018.

Ekstrom, Laura. "A Christian Theodicy," in *The Blackwell Companion to the Problem of Evil*, eds. Justin McBrayer and Daniel Howard-Snyder, 266–80. West Sussex, UK: John Wiley & Sons, 2013.

———. "The Cost of Freedom," in *Free Will & Theism: Connections, Contingencies and Concerns*, eds. Kevin Timpe and Daniel Speak, 62–78. Oxford: Oxford University Press, 2016.

———. *Evil and Theodicy*. Cambridge: Cambridge University Press, 2023.

Erickson, Millard. *Christian Theology*, 3rd ed. Grand Rapids: Baker Academic, 2013.

Evans, Jeremy. *The Problem of Evil: The Challenge to Essential Christian Beliefs*. Nashville: Broadman & Holman, 2013.

Exline, Julie and Margaret Early. "Anger Toward God: A Brief Overview of Existing Research." *Psychology of Religion Newsletter* 29/1 (2004), 1–8.

——— and Alyce Martin. "Anger Toward God: A New Frontier in Forgiveness Research," in *Handbook of Forgiveness*, ed. Everett Worthington Jr., 73–88. New York: Routledge, 2005.

Fairbairn, Donald. *Life in the Trinity, An Introduction to Theology with the Help of the Church Fathers*. Downers Grove: IVP Academic, 2009.

Fales, Evan. "Theodicy in a Vale of Tears," in *The Blackwell Companion to the Problem of Evil*, eds. Justin P. McBrayer and Daniel Howard-Snyder, 349–62. West Sussex, UK: John Wiley & Sons, 2013.

Farrar, Frederic William. *The Gospel According to St. Luke, with Maps, Notes and Introduction*. Cambridge: Cambridge University Press, 1891.

Feinberg, John. *The Many Faces of Evil: Theological Systems and the Problem of Evil*. rev. ed. Wheaton: Crossway, 2004.

Fénelon, François. *Spiritual Progress (Avis Chrétiens)*, ed. James Metcalf. New York: M. W. Dodd, 1853.

Fierstein, Harvey. *Torch Song Trilogy*. New York: New American Library, 1988.

Fischer, John Martin, Robert Kane, Derk Pereboom, and Manuel Vargas, *Four Views on Free Will*. Oxford: Blackwell, 2007.

Ford, Elizabeth, and Deborah C. Mitchell. *Apocalyptic Visions in 21st Century Films*. Jefferson: McFarland & Co., 2018.

Frame, John. "Second Chance," in *Evangelical Dictionary of Theology*, 3rd ed., eds. Daniel Treier and Walter Elwell, 792–93. Grand Rapids: Baker Academic, 2017.

Freud, Sigmund. *The Future of an Illusion (Die Zukunft Einer Illusion)*, trans. W. D. Robson-Scott. London: Horace Liveright, 1928.

Fung, Joey, and Anna Lau. "Tough Love or Hostile Domination? Psychological Control and Relational Induction in Cultural Context." *Journal of Family Psychology* 26/6 (2012), 966–75.

Gaine, Simon Francis. *Will there Be Free Will in Heaven? Freedom, Impeccability and Beatitude*. London: T & T Clark, 2003.

Galura, Sandra. "Combating Burnout in Health Care Providers." *Journal of Psychosocial Nursing* 60/2 (2022), 3–4.

Gardiner, Eileen (ed.) *Buddhist Hell: Visions, Tours, and Descriptions of the Infernal Otherworld*. New York: Italica, 2012.

Gardner, Martin. *The Whys of a Philosophical Scrivener*. New York: St. Martin's Press, 1999.

Gaventa, Beverly, "God Handed Them Over: Reading Romans 1:8–32 Apocalyptically." *Australian Biblical Review* 53 (2005), 42–53.

# BIBLIOGRAPHY

Gavrilyuk, Paul. "An Overview of Patristic Theodicies," in *Suffering and Evil in Early Christian Thought*, eds. Nonna Harrison and David Hunter, 1–6. Grand Rapids: Baker Academic, 2016.

Geach, Peter. *Providence and Evil*. Cambridge: Cambridge University Press, 1977.

Geisler, Norman, ed. *If God, Why Evil?* Grand Rapids: Bethany, 2010.

———. *Inerrancy*. Grand Rapids: Zondervan, 1980.

Geivett, R. Douglas. "Augustine and the Problem of Evil," in *God and Evil: The Case for God in a World Filled with Pain*, eds. Chad Meister and James K. Dew, 65–79. Downers Grove: IVP, 2013.

Gerdes, Karen, and Elizabeth Segal. "Importance of Empathy for Social Work Practice: Integrating New Science." *Social Work* 56/2 (2011), 141–48.

Gheorghita, Radu. *The Role of the Septuagint in Hebrews*. Heidelberg, Germany: Mohr Siebeck, 2003.

Giberson, Karl, and Francis Collins. *The Language of Science and Faith: Straight Answers to Genuine Questions*. Downers Grove: IVP, 2011.

Glasser, Robert. *Preparing for the Era of Disasters*. Barton: ASPI, 2019.

Grebe, Matthias and Johannes Grössl (eds.). *T&T Clark Handbook of Suffering and the Problem of Evil*. New York: Bloomsbury, 2023.

Griffin, David Ray. "Creation Out of Chaos and the Problem of Evil," in *Encountering Evil: Live Options in Theodicy*, ed. Stephen T. Davis, 101–18. Atlanta: John Knox, 1973.

Grössl, Johannes. "Introduction," in *T&T Clark Handbook of Suffering and the Problem of Evil*, eds. Matthias Grebe and Johannes Grössl, 1–10. New York: Bloomsbury, 2023.

Grudem, Wayne. *Systematic Theology, An Introduction to Biblical Doctrine*, 2nd ed. Grand Rapids: Zondervan Academic, 2020.

Gundry, Stanley and Dennis Jowers, eds. *Four Views on Divine Providence*. Grand Rapids: Zondervan, 2011.

Harris, Sam. *The End of Faith: Religion, Terror, and the Future of Reason*. New York: W. W. Norton, 2005.

Harrison, Peter. "Theodicy and Animal Pain." *Philosophy* 64 (1989), 79–92.

Hasker, William. "An Adequate God," in *Searching for an Adequate God: A Dialogue Between Process and Free Will Theists*, eds. John B. Cobb Jr. and Clark H. Pinnock, 215–45. Grand Rapids: Eerdmans, 2000.

———. "God and Gratuitous Evil," in *The Problem of Evil: Selected Readings*, 2nd ed., ed. Michael Peterson, 473–87. Notre Dame: University of Notre Dame Press, 2017.

———. "An Open Theist View," in *God and the Problem of Evil*, eds. Chad Meister and James Dew, 57–76. Downers Grove: IVP Academic, 2017.

———. "The Open Theist Response," in *God and the Problem of Evil*, eds. Chad Meister and James Dew, 151–62. Downers Grove: IVP Academic, 2017.

Hawking, Stephen. *Brief Answers to the Big Questions*. New York: Bantam, 2018.

Haybron, Daniel. "Moral Monsters and Saints." *The Monist* 85/2 (2002), 260–84.

Helm, Paul. "God's Providence Takes No Risks," in *The Problem of Evil: Selected Readings*, 2nd ed., ed. Michael Peterson, 344–62. Notre Dame: University of Notre Dame Press, 2017.

Henderson, Luke. "Heaven," in *The Palgrave Handbook of the Afterlife*, eds. Yujin Nagasawa and Benjamin Matheson, 177–96. London: Palgrave Macmillan, 2017.

Hess, Frederick. *Tough Love for Schools: Essays on Competition, Accountability, and Excellence.* Washington D.C.: American Enterprise Institute, 2006.

Hewish, Antony. "Science and God," in *The Missing Link: A Symposium on Darwin's Framework for a Creation-Evolution Solution,* ed. Roy Varghese, 173. Lanham: University Press of America, 2013.

Hick, John. *Evil and the God of Love.* London: MacMillan, 1985.

———. *An Interpretation of Religion: Human Responses to the Transcendent,* 2nd ed. New Haven: Yale University Press, 2004.

———. "An Irenaean Theodicy," in *Encountering Evil: Live Options in Theodicy,* ed. Stephen T. Davis, 39–52. Atlanta: John Knox, 1973.

———. *Philosophy of Religion.* Englewood Cliffs: Prentice-Hall, 1990.

———. "Soul-Making Theodicy," in *The Problem of Evil: Selected Readings,* 2nd ed., ed. Michael Peterson, 262–73. Notre Dame: University of Notre Dame Press, 2017.

Hickson, Michael. "A Brief History of Problems of Evil," in *The Blackwell Companion to the Problem of Evil,* eds. Justin P. McBrayer and Daniel Howard-Snyder, 3–18. West Sussex, UK: John Wiley & Sons, 2013.

Hiers, Richard. "Reverence for Life and Environmental Ethics in Biblical Law and Covenant." *Journal of Law & Religion* 13 (1996), 127–88.

Hitchens, Christopher. *God Is Not Great: How Religion Poisons Everything.* New York: Twelve, 2007.

Hitler, Adolf. *Hitler's Table Talk, 1941-1944, His Private Conversations (Tischgespräche im Führerhauptquartier),* 3rd ed., ed. Gerhard Weinberg, trans. Norman Cameron and R. H. Stevens. New York: Enigma, 2000.

Hocknull, Mark. *Pannenberg on Evil, Love and God: The Realisation of Divine Love.* New York: Routledge, 2016.

Hodge, Charles. *Systematic Theology, Vol. 1.* Woodstock: Devoted Publishing, 2016.

———. *Systematic Theology, Vol. 3.* Grand Rapids: Eerdmans, 1940.

Hodgson Peter and Robert King (eds.) "Luther: Sin and Grace," in *Readings in Christian Theology,* 180–84. Minneapolis: Fortress, 1985.

Hoffman, Richard. *An Environmental History of Medieval Europe.* Cambridge: Cambridge University Press, 2014.

Hoppe, Silke. "A Sorrow Shared Is a Sorrow Halved: The Search for Empathetic Understanding of Family Members of a Person with Early-Onset Dementia." *Culture, Medicine, and Psychiatry* 42 (2018), 180–201.

Horton, Michael. "A Classical Calvinist View," in *Four Views on Eternal Security,* eds. Stanley Gundry and J. Matthew Pinson, 23–42. Grand Rapids: Zondervan, 2002.

Howard-Snyder, Daniel. "Theism, the Hypothesis of Indifference, and the Biological Role of Pain and Pleasure." *Faith and Philosophy* 11/3 (1994), 452–66.

Hume, David. *Dialogues Concerning Natural Religion,* ed. Norman Kemp Smith. New York: Thomas Nelson & Sons, 1947.

———. *The Philosophical Works of David Hume.* London: Fenton and Strand, 1824.

Hunt, David and Linda Zagzebski, "Foreknowledge and Free Will," *The Stanford Encyclopedia of Philosophy* (Summer 2022 Edition), Edward N. Zalta (ed.), URL = <https://plato.stanford.edu/archives/sum2022/entries/free-will-foreknowledge/>.

Ignatius of Loyola, *Ignatius of Loyola: The Spiritual Exercises and Selected Works,* ed. George Ganss. New York: Paulist, 1991.

———. *The Spiritual Exercises of St Ignatius: Based on Studies in the Language of the Autograph,* trans. Louis Puhl. Westminster: Newman, 1951.

Irenaeus, *Against Heresies*, ed. Anthony Uyl. Woodstock: Devoted Publishing, 2018.
———. *On the Apostolic Preaching*. New York: St. Vladimir Seminary Press, 1997.
Jacobsen, Knut. "Three Functions of Hell in the Hindu Traditions." *Numen* 56 (2009), 385–400.
Javorcik, Beata and Mariana Spatareanu. "Tough-love: Do Czech Suppliers Learn from Their Relationships with Multinationals?" *The Scandinavian Journal of Economics*, 111/4 (2009), 811–33.
Jordan, Bill, and Charlie Jordan. *Social Work and the Third Way: Tough-love as Social Policy*. London: Sage, 2000.
Josephus, Flavius. *Antiquities of the Jews*. https://www.gutenberg.org/files/2848/2848-h/2848-h.htm
Kane, G. Stanley. "The Failure of Soul-Making Theodicy." *International Journal for Philosophy of Religion* 6/1 (1975), 1–22.
Kant, Immanuel. *Grounding for the Metaphysics of Morals (Grundlegung zur Metaphysik der Sitten)*, 3rd ed., trans. James W. Ellington. Indianapolis: Hackett, 1993.
———. *Kant's Critique of Practical Reason (Kritik der Praktischen Vernunft)*, trans. Thomas Abbott. New York: Longmans, Green and Co. 1898.
———. *Religion Within the Limits of Reason Alone (Die Religion Innerhalb der Grenzen der Bloßen Vernunft)*, trans. Theodore M. Greene and Hoyt H. Hudson. New York: Harper & Row, 1960.
Keathley, Kenneth. *Salvation and Sovereignty: A Molinist Approach*. Nashville: B&H, 2010.
Kekes, John. *The Roots of Evil*. Ithaca: Cornell University Press, 2005.
Keller, Helen. *We Bereaved*. London: Forgotten, 2018.
Keller, James. *Problems of Evil and the Power of God*. Burlington: Ashgate, 2007.
Keller, Timothy. *The Reason for God: Belief in an Age of Skepticism*. New York: Dutton, 2008.
Kelman, Steven and Sounman Hong (2012). "*Hard, Soft, or Tough-love: What Kinds of Organizational Culture Promote Successful Performance in Cross-Organizational Collaborations?*" Harvard Kennedy School Faculty Research Working Paper Series, RWP12-005. John F. Kennedy School of Government, Harvard University.
Kershnar, Stephen. "The Injustice of Hell." *International Journal for Philosophy of Religion*, 58/2 (2005), 103–23.
Kierkegaard, Søren. *The Sickness unto Death (Sygdommen til Døden)*, trans. Walter Lowrie. Princeton: Princeton University Press, 1941.
Koenig, Harold. "Religion, Spirituality, and Health: The Research and Clinical Implications." *ISRN Psychiatry* (2012), 278730.
Kraay, Klaas. "God and Gratuitous Evil (Part I)." *Philosophical Compass* 11 (2016), 905–12.
———. "God and Gratuitous Evil (Part II)." *Philosophical Compass* 11 (2016), 913–22.
Kreeft, Peter. *Fundamentals of the Faith: Essays in Christian Apologetics*. San Francisco: Ignatius, 1988.
Kushner, Harold. *When Bad Things Happen to Good People*. New York: Random House, 1981.
Kvanvig, Jonathan. *The Problem of Hell*. Oxford: Oxford University Press, 1993.
Lactantius. *The Works of Lactantius, Vol. 2*, trans. William Fletcher. Edinburg: T & T Clark, 1871.
LaHaye, Tim. *The Popular Handbook on the Rapture*. Eugene: Harvest, 2011.

Lamb, Randas. "Tough Love: Prisons, Hinduism, and Spiritual Care," in *Hindu Approaches to Spiritual Care: Chaplaincy in Theory and Practice*, eds. Vineet Chander and Lucinda Mosher, 201–12. London: Jessica Kingsley, 2020.
Lange, Christian (ed.). *Locating Hell in Islamic Traditions*. Leiden: Brill, 2015.
Lawrence, Brother. *The Practice of the Presence of God*. Nashville: Thomas Nelson, 1999.
Leibniz, Gottfried. *Leibniz Selections*. New York: Charles Scribner's Sons, 1951.
Levine, Michael. "The Positive Function of Evil?" *Philosophical Papers* 41/1 (2012), 149–66.
Lewis, C. S. *The Great Divorce*. New York: Harper One, 1946.
———. *A Grief Observed*. San Francisco: Harper One, 2001.
———. *The Problem of Pain*. New York: Harper One, 2001.
Leyton, Elliott. *Hunting Humans: The Rise of the Modern Multiple Murderer*. New York: Carroll & Graf, 2001.
Lind, Jennifer et al. "Infant and Maternal Characteristics in Neonatal Abstinence Syndrome — Selected Hospitals in Florida, 2010-2011." *Morbidity and Mortality Weekly Report* 64/8 (2015), 213–16.
Little, Bruce. *God, Why This Evil?* New York: Rowman & Littlefield, 2010.
Livingston, Alexander. "Tough Love: The Political Theology of Civil Disobedience." *Perspectives on Politics* 3/18 (2020), 851-66.
Luther, Martin. *On the Bondage of the Will (De Servo Arbitrio)*. https://www.monergism.com/thethreshold/sdg/pdf/luther_arbitrio.pdf
Lynch, Joseph. "Theodicy and Animals." *Between the Species* (2002), 1–10.
Mackie, J. L. "Evil and Omnipotence." *Mind* 64 (1955), 200–12.
Maguire, Jack. *Essential Buddhism: A Complete Guide to Beliefs and Practices*. New York: Pocket, 2001.
Maitzen, Stephen. "The Moral Skepticism Objection to Skeptical Theism," in *The Blackwell Companion to the Problem of Evil*, eds. Justin P. McBrayer and Daniel Howard-Snyder, 444–57. West Sussex, UK: John Wiley & Sons, 2013.
Malatesta, Edward. *Interiority and Covenant*. Rome: Biblical Institute Press, 1978.
Maller, Mark. "Animals and the Problem of Evil in Recent Theodicies." *Philosophy Scholarship* (2009), 1–33.
Markham, Ian S. *Understanding Christian Doctrine, 2nd ed*. Hoboken: Wiley Blackwell, 2017.
Marrus, Michael. "Pius XII and the Holocaust: Ten Essential Themes," in *Pope Pius XII and the Holocaust*, eds. Carol Rittner and John Roth, 43–55. New York: Bloomsbury Academic, 2016.
Mavromatis, Mary. "Serial Arson: Repetitive Firesetting and Pyromania," in *Serial Offenders: Current Thought, Recent Findings*, ed. Louis Schlesinger, 67–102. New York: CRC, 2000.
McCloskey, H. J. "God and Evil." *Philosophical Quarterly* 10 (1960), 97–114.
McIntyre, Alison. "Doctrine of Double Effect." *The Stanford Encyclopedia of Philosophy* (Winter 2023 Edition), Edward N. Zalta & Uri Nodelman (eds.), URL = <https://plato.stanford.edu/archives/win2023/entries/double-effect/>.
McMahon, Keith. "The Institution of Polygamy in the Chinese Imperial Palace." *The Journal of Asian Studies*, 72/4 (2013), 917–36.
Meister, Chad and James Dew, eds. *God and the Problem of Evil*. Downers Grove: IVP Academic, 2017.

Mickolus, Edward, and Susan Simmons. *The 50 Worst Terrorist Attacks.* Santa Barbara: Praeger, 2014.

Miele, Frank. "Darwin's Dangerous Disciple: An Interview with Richard Dawkins." *Skeptic* 3/4 (1995), 80–85.

Miley, John. *Systematic Theology, Vol. 1,* New York: Eaton & Mains, 1892.

Milliken, Bill. *The Last Dropout: Stop the Epidemic!* Carlsbad: Hay House, 2007.

Moffitt, Phillip. *Dancing with Life: Buddhist Insights for Finding Meaning and Joy in the Face of Suffering.* New York: Rodale, 2008.

Molesky, Mark. *This Gulf of Fire: The Great Lisbon Earthquake, or Apocalypse in the Age of Science and Reason.* New York: Knopf, 2015.

Moloney, Daniel. *Mercy: What Every Catholic Should Know.* San Francisco: Ignatius, 2020.

Moltmann, Jürgen. *The Crucified God (Der Gekreuzigte Gott),* trans. R. A. Wilson and John Bowden. Minneapolis: Fortress, 1993.

———. "Talk-back Session with Jürgen Moltmann." *The Ashbury Theological Journal* 48/1 (1993), 39–47.

———. "Theodicy," in *A New Dictionary of Christian Theology,* ed. A. Richardson and J. Bowden, 564–66. London: SCM, 1983.

———. *Theology of Hope (Theologie der Hoffnung),* trans. James Leitch. Minneapolis: Fortress, 1993.

Montefiore, Simon. *Young Stalin.* London: Weidenfeld & Nicolson, 2007.

Munn, Jonathan. *Whom Seek Ye?* UK: Anglican Catholic Church, 2019.

Murray, John. *Redemption Accomplished and Applied.* Grand Rapids: Eerdmans, 1984.

Nagasawa, Yujin. "The Problem of Evil for Atheists," in *The Problem of Evil: Eight Views in Dialogue,* ed. Nick Trakakis, 151–63. Oxford: Oxford University Press, 2018.

Nagel, Thomas. *The Last Word.* Oxford: Oxford University Press, 1997.

Neumann, Henry. "Manichaean Tendencies in the History of Philosophy." *The Philosophical Review* 28/5 (1919), 491–510.

Ngor, Haing. *Survival in the Killing Fields.* New York: Carroll & Graf, 1987.

Nietzsche, Friedrich. *The Gay Science (Die Fröhliche Wissenschaft),* trans. Walter Kaufmann. New York: Vintage, 1974.

Oates, Julianne, and Patricia Maani-Fogelman. *Nursing Grief and Loss.* Treasure Island: StatPearls, 2021. https://www.ncbi.nlm.nih.gov/books/NBK518989/

O'Connor, Timothy. "The Problem of Evil: Introduction," in *Philosophy of Religion: A Reader and Guide,* ed. William Lane Craig, 303–16. New Brunswick: Rutgers University Press, 2002.

Oden, Thomas. *The Living God.* San Francisco: Harper and Rowe, 1987.

O'Grady, Kary et al. "Earthquake in Haiti: Relationship with the Sacred in Times of Trauma." *Journal of Psychology & Theology* 40/4 (2012), 289–301.

Olson, Roger. *The Mosaic of Christian Belief: Twenty Centuries of Unity and Diversity,* 2nd ed. Downers Grove: IVP Academic, 2016.

Oord, Thomas Jay. "An Essential Kenosis View," in *God and the Problem of Evil,* eds. Chad Meister and James Dew, 77–97. Downers Grove: IVP Academic, 2017.

———. "The Essential Kenosis Response," in *God and the Problem of Evil,* eds. Chad Meister and James Dew, 163–72. Downers Grove: IVP Academic, 2017

———. *God Can't: How to Believe in God and Love after Tragedy, Abuse, and Other Evils.* Grasmere: SacraSage, 2019.

Oppy, Graham. "Rowe's Evidential Arguments from Evil," in *The Blackwell Companion to the Problem of Evil*, eds. Justin P. McBrayer and Daniel Howard-Snyder, 49–66. West Sussex, UK: John Wiley & Sons, 2013.

Origen. *Contra Celsum*. https://www.newadvent.org/fathers/04166.htm

Otte, Richard. "A Carnapian Argument from Evil: Welcome Back, Skeptical Theism," in *The Blackwell Companion to the Problem of Evil*, eds. Justin P. McBrayer and Daniel Howard-Snyder, 83–97. West Sussex, UK: John Wiley & Sons, 2013.

———. "Transworld Depravity and Unobtainable Worlds." *Philosophy and Phenomenological Research* 78 (2009), 165–77.

Packer, J. I. *Evangelism and the Sovereignty of God*. Downers Grove: IVP, 1961.

Pannenberg, Wolfhart. *Systematische Theologie 1*. Göttingen: Vandenhoeck & Ruprecht, 1988.

Parkes, Colin. "Coping with Loss: Bereavement in Adult Life." *British Medical Journal* 316 (1998), 856–59.

Pascal, Blaise. *The Thoughts of Blaise Pascal (Pensées)*, trans. C. Kegan Paul. London: George Bell and Sons, 1901.

Paul, Norman, and Kenneth Beernink. "The Use of Empathy in the Resolution of Grief." *Perspectives in Biology and Medicine* 11/1 (1967), 153–69.

Pawl, Timothy and Kevin Timpe, "Incompatibilism, Sin, and Free Will in Heaven." *Faith and Philosophy*, 26/4 (2009), 398–419.

Peckham, John. *Theodicy of Love: Cosmic Conflict and the Problem of Evil*. Grand Rapids: Baker Academic, 2018.

Pereboom, Derk. "A Defense Without Free Will," in *The Blackwell Companion to the Problem of Evil*, eds. Justin McBrayer and Daniel Howard-Snyder, 411–25. West Sussex, UK: John Wiley & Sons, 2013.

Peterson, Michael. "Christian Theism and the Evidential Argument from Evil," in *The Problem of Evil: Selected Readings, 2nd ed.*, ed. Michael Peterson, 166–92. Notre Dame: University of Notre Dame Press, 2017.

———. "Introduction," in *The Problem of Evil: Selected Readings, 2nd ed.*, ed. Michael Peterson, 1–13. Notre Dame: University of Notre Dame Press, 2017.

Pietersma, Albert. "Text-Production and Text-Reception: Psalm 8 in Greek." in *Die Septuaginta - Texte, Kontext, Lebenswelten*. eds. Martin Kasser and Wolfgang Kraus, 487–501. Tübingen: Mohr Siebeck, 2008.

Pinnock, Clark. "God Limits His Knowledge," in *Predestination and Free Will*, eds. David and Randall Basinger, 143–62. Downers Grove: IVP Academic, 1986.

Plantinga, Alvin. *God, Freedom, and Evil*. Grand Rapids: Eerdmans, 1977.

———. "Self-Profile," in *Alvin Plantinga*, eds. James E. Tomberlin and Peter van Inwagen, 3–100. Dordrecht: D. Reidel, 1985.

———. "Supralapsarianism or 'O Felix Culpa,'" in *The Problem of Evil: Selected Readings, 2nd ed.*, ed. Michael Peterson, 363–89. Notre Dame: University of Notre Dame Press, 2017.

Plato. *Plato: Complete Works*, eds. John Cooper and D. S. Hutchinson, Cambridge: Hackett, 1997.

Plemmons, Gregory et al. "Hospitalization for Suicide Ideation or Attempt: 2008–2015." *Pediatrics* 141/6 (2018), e20172426.

Plotinus, *Enneads*. https://www.sacred-texts.com/cla/plotenn/index.htm

Polkinghorne, John. *Science and Providence*. Boston: Shambhala, 1989.

Poole, Matthew. *Annotations Upon the Holy Bible, Vol 3*. London: James Nisbet &Co., 1853.
Pope, Alexander. *An Essay on Man*. Farmington Hills: Gale, 2018.
Pope Francis, *The Joy of the Gospel: Evangelii Gaudium*. Dublin: Veritas, 2013.
Pope Paul VI. *Dignitatis Humanae*. New York: St Paul, 1965.
Posner, Gerald, and John Ware. *Mengele: The Complete Story*. New York: McGraw-Hill, 1986.
Poston, Ted. "Social Evil," in *Oxford Studies in Philosophy of Religion vol. 5*, ed. Jonathan Kvanvig, 209–33. Oxford: Oxford University Press, 2014.
Puntel, Lorenz. *Struktur und Sein: Ein Theorierahmen für eine Systematische Philosophie*. Mohr Siebeck, 2006.
Pusey, Edward. *The Minor Prophets*. London: Walter Smith, 1883.
Radhakrishna et al. "Are Father Surrogates a Risk Factor for Child Maltreatment?" *Child Maltreatment* 6/4 (2001), 281–89.
Rae, Michael. "Skeptical Theism and the 'Too Much Skepticism' Objection," in *The Blackwell Companion to the Problem of Evil*, eds. Justin P. McBrayer and Daniel Howard-Snyder, 482–506. West Sussex, UK: John Wiley & Sons, 2013.
Ragland, C. P. "Hell" *Internet Encyclopedia of Philosophy*, 2024. https://www.iep.utm.edu/hell/
Rakestraw, Robert. "Becoming Like God: An Evangelical Doctrine of Theosis." *Journal of the Evangelical Theological Society* 40/2 (1997), 257–69.
Rausch, Thomas. *Systematic Theology: A Roman Catholic Approach*. Collegeville: Liturgical Press, 2016.
Reichenbach, Bruce. *Evil and a Good God*. New York: Fordham University Press, 1982.
Roth, John K. "A Theodicy of Protest," in *Encountering Evil: Live Options in Theodicy*, ed. Stephen T. Davis, 7–22. Atlanta: John Knox, 1973.
Rothaupt, Jeanne and Kent Becker. "A Literature Review of Western Bereavement Theory: From Decathecting to Continuing Bonds." *The Family Journal: Counseling and Therapy for Couples and Families* 15/1 (2007), 6–15.
Rousseau, Jean-Jacques. *Discourse on the Origin of Inequality (Discours sur L'origine et les Fondements de L'inégalité Parmis les Hommes)*, trans. Donald Cress, Indianapolis: Hackett, 1992.
———. "Rousseau to Voltaire, 18 August 1756," in *Correspondence Complète de Jean Jacques Rousseau, vol. 4*, ed. J. A. Leigh, trans. R. Spang. 37– 50. Geneva: Institut et Musée Voltaire, 1967.
Rowe, William. "The Evidential Argument from Evil: A Second Look," in *The Evidential Argument from Evil*, ed. Daniel Howard-Snyder, 262–85. Bloomington: Indiana University Press, 1996.
———. "Evil and the Theistic Hypothesis: A Response to Wykstra." *International Journal for Philosophy of Religion* 16 (1984), 95–100.
———. "Evil and Theodicy." *Philosophical Topics* 16/2 (1988), 119–32.
———. "Paradox and Promise: Hick's Solution to the Problem of Evil," in *Problems in the Philosophy of Religion: Critical Studies of the Work of John Hick*, ed. Harold Hewitt, Jr., 111–24. New York: St. Martin's Press, 1991.
———. "The Problem of Evil and Some Varieties of Atheism," *American Philosophical Quarterly* 16/4 (1979), 335–41.
———. *William L. Rowe on Philosophy of Religion: Selected Writings*, ed. Nick Trakakis. Burlington: Ashgate, 2007.

———, Daniel Howard-Snyder, and Michael Bergmann. "Evil, Evidence, and Skeptical Theism—A Debate," in *The Problem of Evil: Selected Readings, 2nd ed.*, ed. Michael Peterson, 130–65. Notre Dame: University of Notre Dame Press, 2017.

Russell, Bertrand. *Why I Am Not a Christian, and Other Essays in Religion and Related Subjects.* New York: Simon & Schuster, 1957.

Ryrie, Charles. *Basic Theology.* Wheaton: Victor Books, 1986.

Sanders, John. "God, Evil, and Relational Risk," in *The Problem of Evil: Selected Readings, 2nd ed.*, ed. Michael Peterson, 327–43. Notre Dame: University of Notre Dame Press, 2017.

Sartre, Jean Paul. *Being and Nothingness (L'Etre et le Néant)*, trans. Hazel Barnes. New York: Citadel, 1956.

———. *No Exit (Huis Clos) and Three Other Plays*, trans. Stuart Gilbert. New York: Vintage, 1989.

Schellenberg, J. L. *Divine Hiddenness and Human Reason.* Ithaca: Cornell University Press, 1993.

———. "A New Logical Problem of Evil," in *The Blackwell Companion to the Problem of Evil*, eds. Justin P. McBrayer and Daniel Howard-Snyder, 34–48. West Sussex, UK: John Wiley & Sons, 2013.

Schleiermacher, Friedrich. *Christian Faith: A New Translation and Critical Edition, (Der Christliche Glaube Nach den Grundsätzen der Evangelischen Kirche im Zusammenhange Dargestellt)*, eds. Catherine Kelsey and Terrence Tice, trans. Terrence Tice, Catherine Kelsey, and Edwina Lawler. Louisville: Westminster John Knox, 2016.

Schopenhauer, Arthur. *Schopenhauer Selections*, ed. DeWitt Parker. New York: Charles Scribner's Sons, 1956.

Scott, Mark. "Suffering and Soul-Making: Rethinking John Hick's Theodicy." *The Journal of Religion* 90/3 (2010), 313–34.

Sedlak, Andrea et al. (2010). *Fourth National Incidence Study of Child Abuse and Neglect (NIS-4): Report to Congress.* Washington, DC: U.S. Department of Health and Human Services.

Sempangi, F. Kefa. *A Distant Grief.* Glendale: Regal, 1979.

Service, Robert. *Lenin: A Biography.* London: MacMillan, 2004.

Shore, W. Teignmouth. "The First Epistle to the Corinthians," in *The Commentary for Schools*, ed. C. J. Ellicott, 1–170. London: Castle, Petter, Galpin & Co., 1879.

Smith, Jacqui, and Jacqueline Goodnow. "Unasked-for Support and Unsolicited Advice: Age and the Quality of Social Experience." *Psychology and Aging* 14/1 (1999), 108–21.

Solzhenitsyn, Aleksandr. *The Gulag Archipelago, Vol 1.* New York: Harper Collins, 1974.

Sommers-Flanagan, John, and Rita Sommers-Flanagan. *Counseling and Psychotherapy Theories in Context and Practice: Skills, Strategies and Techniques, 3rd ed.* Hoboken: John Wiley and Sons, 2018.

Sorensen, David. "Power Tends to Corrupt." *Carlyle Studies Annual* 29 (2013), 81–114.

Soulé, Michael. "What is Conservation Biology?" *BioScience* 35/11 (1985), 727–34.

Søvik, Atle. *The Problem of Evil and the Power of God.* Boston: Brill, 2011.

Speak, Daniel. *The Problem of Evil.* Malden: Polity, 2015.

Speight, R. Marston. "The Practical Moral Values of Karbala," in *Unique Sacrifice of Imam Hussain for Humanity*, ed. S. Manzoor Rizvi, 151–55. Bloomfield: Message of Peace, 2014.

Spurgeon, Charles. *The Complete Sermons of C. H. Spurgeon, Book 1*, ed. David Attebury. Louisville: Lulu, 2015.
Stausberg, Michael. "Hell in Zoroastrian History." *Numen* 56 (2009), 217–53.
Stenger, Victor. *God: The Failed Hypothesis: How Science Shows That God Does Not Exist*. Amherst: Prometheus, 2007.
Stiepock, Lisa, Amy Lorio, and Lori Gottlieb, eds. *Tough Love, Raising Confident, Kind, Resilient Kids: 18 Top Experts Share Proven Parenting Strategies*. New York: Simon & Schuster, 2016.
Stiffman et al. "Household Composition and Risk of Fatal Child Maltreatment," *Pediatrics* 109/4 (2002), 615–21.
Strobel, Kyle. "Jonathan Edwards's Reformed Doctrine of Theosis." *The Harvard Theological Review* 109/3 (2016), 371–99.
Strobel, Lee. *The Case for Faith*. Grand Rapids: Zondervan, 2000.
Stump, Eleonore. *The Image of God: The Problem of Evil and the Problem of Mourning*. Oxford: Oxford University Press, 2022.
———. "The Problem of Evil." *Faith and Philosophy* 2/4 (1985), 392–423.
———. *Wandering in Darkness: Narrative and the Problem of Suffering*. Oxford: Oxford University Press, 2010.
Sturgis, Gary. *Grief: Hope in the Aftermath*. Trenton: BookLocker, 2021.
Swinburne, Richard. *Providence and the Problem of Evil*. Oxford: Oxford University Press, 1998.
Taber, Tyler. "Divine Hiddenness and the Problem of Evil," in *Evil and a Selection of its Theological Problems*, eds. Benjamin Arbour and John Gilhooly, 14–30. Newcastle upon Tyne, UK: Cambridge Scholars Publishing, 2017.
Tatian. *Oratio ad Graecos and Fragments*, ed. Molly Whittaker. Oxford: Clarendon, 1982.
Ten Boom, Corrie. *The Hiding Place*. Uhrichsville: Barbour, 1971.
———. *Tramp for the Lord*. Fort Washington: CLC, 1974.
Tennyson, Lord Alfred (2003). *In Memoriam A. H. H.* 2nd ed. New York: W.W. Norton.
Tertullian, *Against Marcion (Adversus Marcionem)*. https://www.newadvent.org/fathers/03122.htm
Thai, Lee. *Boundaries of Freedom: The Quantum Proposal of Divine Sovereignty and Human Responsibility*. Eugene: Resource, 2019.
——— and Jerry Pillay. "Can God Create Humans with Free Will Who Never Commit Evil?" *HTS/Theological Studies* 76/1 (2020), a6102.
———. (2020). The Tough-love Proposal: A Novel Theodicy [Doctoral Dissertation, University of Pretoria]. https://repository.up.ac.za/bitstream/handle/2263/75028/Thai_Tough_2020.pdf?sequence=4&isAllowed=y
Thayer, Joseph. *A Greek-English Lexicon of the New Testament*. New York: American Book Company, 1889.
The Catholic Church, *Catechism of the Catholic Church*, 2nd ed. Vatican City: Libreria Editrice Vaticana, 2019.
Thompson, Amanda et al. "A Qualitative Study of Advice from Bereaved Parents and Siblings." *Journal of Social Work in End of Life & Palliative Care* 7 (2011), 153–72.
Tillich, Paul. *Theology of Culture*, ed. Robert Kimball. Oxford: Oxford University Press, 1959.
Timpe, Kevin, Meghan Griffith, and Neil Levy, eds. *The Routledge Companion to Free Will*. New York: Routledge, 2017.

Tooley, Michael. "Inductive Logic and the Probability That God Exists: Farewell to Skeptical Theism," in *Probability in the Philosophy of Religion*, eds. Jake Chandler and Victoria Harrison, 144–64. Oxford: Oxford University Press, 2012.

———. "The Problem of Evil," *The Stanford Encyclopedia of Philosophy* (Winter 2021 Edition), Edward N. Zalta (ed.), URL = <https://plato.stanford.edu/archives/win2021/entries/evil/>.

———. *The Problem of Evil*. Cambridge: Cambridge University Press, 2019.

Trakakis, Nick. "Anti-theodicy," in *The Problem of Evil: Eight Views in Dialogue*, ed. Nick Trakakis, 94–107. Oxford, Oxford University Press, 2018.

———. "The Evidential Problem of Evil." *Internet Encyclopedia of Philosophy*, 2024. http://www.iep.utm.edu/evil-evi/

———. *The God Beyond Belief: In Defense of William Rowe's Evidential Argument from Evil*. Dordrecht: Springer, 2007.

———. "Response to Bishop," in *The Problem of Evil: Eight Views in Dialogue*, ed. Nick Trakakis, 58–60. Oxford: Oxford University Press, 2018.

Twain, Mark. *The Devil's Race-Track: Mark Twain's Great Dark Writings*, ed. John Tuckey. Berkeley: University of California Press, 1980.

———. *Mark Twain's Notebook*. New York: Harper & Brothers, 1935.

United Nations Office on Drugs and Crime, *Drug Counsellor's Handbook*. https://www.unodc.org/pdf/report_2000-05-01_1.pdf

US Department of Justice, "'Boot Camp' Drug Treatment and Aftercare Interventions: An Evaluation Review." https://www.ojp.gov/pdffiles/btcamp.pdf

van Inwagen, Peter. "The Magnitude, Duration, and Distribution of Evil: A Theodicy," in *Philosophy of Religion: A Reader and Guide*, ed. William Lane Craig, 370–93. New Brunswick: Rutgers University Press, 2002.

———. *The Problem of Evil*. Oxford: Oxford University Press, 2006.

van Woudenberg, René. "A Brief History of Theodicy," in *The Blackwell Companion to the Problem of Evil*, eds. Justin P. McBrayer and Daniel Howard-Snyder, 177–91. West Sussex, UK: John Wiley & Sons, 2013.

Vitale, Vince. *Non-Identity Theodicy: A Grace-Based Response to the Problem of Evil*. Oxford: Oxford University Press, 2020.

Voltaire, *Poèmes sur le Désastre de Lisbonne, et sur la Loi Naturelle, avec des Préfaces*. Paris: Hachette, 2018.

von Der Luft, Eric. "Sources of Nietzsche's 'God is Dead!' and its Meaning for Heidegger." *Journal of the History of Ideas* 45/2 (1984), 263–76.

von Hildebrand, Dietrich. *Transformation in Christ: On the Christian Attitude (Die Umgestaltung in Christus)*. Manchester: Sophia, 1990.

Ware, Bruce. "Defining Evangelicalism's Boundaries Theologically: Is Open Theism Evangelical?" *Journal of the Evangelical Theological Society* 45/2 (2002), 193–212.

Wesley, John. *The Works of the Rev. John Wesley, vol. 5*. New York: J. J. Harper, 1826.

White, Heath. *Fate and Free Will: A Defense of Theological Determinism*. Notre Dame: University of Notre Dame Press, 2020.

Wiesel, Elie. *The Night Trilogy: Night Dawn Day*, trans. Marion Wiesel. New York: Hill and Wang, 2008.

Wilde, Oscar. *The Duchess of Padua*. Charleston: Nabu, 2010.

Willows, Adam. "Augustine, The Origin of Evil, and The Mystery of Free Will." *Religious Studies* 50/2 (2014), 255–69.

Wolterstorff, Nicholas. *Lament for a Son*. Grand Rapids: Eerdmans, 1987.

Wright, N. T. *Evil and the Justice of God*. Downers Grove: IVP, 2006.
Wuthnow, Sara. "Healing Touch Controversies." *Journal of Religion and Health* 36/3 (1997), 221–29.
Wykstra, Stephen. "Rowe's Noseeum Arguments from Evil," in *The Evidential Argument from Evil*, ed. Daniel Howard-Snyder, 126–50. Bloomington: Indiana University Press, 1996.
———. "A Skeptical Theist View," in *God and the Problem of Evil*, eds. Chad Meister and James Dew, 99–127. Downers Grove: IVP Academic, 2017.
Yasumaro, Ō no. *The Kojiki: An Account of Ancient Matters,* trans. Gustav Heldt. New York: Columbia University Press, 2014.
Zodkevitch, Ron. *The Tough Love Prescription*. New York: McGraw-Hill, 2006.

# Name and Subject Index

Abba, 6, 9n43, 22
Abraham, xii, 200
Abraham and Isaac, xii
accept trials, 103
Adams, Marilyn McCord, 27n10, 33n46, 77, 135n65
advise others, 107, 109
Aeschylus, 129
Ağca, Mehmet, 13, 14
age of evil, 9, 196, 199, 200, 201, 206
Alcorn, Randy, 159
Allen, Steven, 187
Almeida, Michael, 180
Amin, Idi, 48, 191, 192
Ananias and Sapphira, 68
animal suffering, 49, 91
Anselm, 41, 80, 81
Aquinas, 30, 33n43, 41, 43, 80, 81, 87n108, 130, 134, 142n30
Archbishop of Canterbury, 171
Aristotle, 129
Ashby, Stephen, 89
Athanasius, 86
Augustine, 30, 41, 42n23, 77n6, 80, 81, 86n100, 129, 130n18
Auschwitz-Birkenau, 127

bailing out, 140, 145, 150, 157, 170, 183, 188, 207
"Bambi," 172, 173
Barnes, Albert, 5, 72n125
Bauckham, Richard, 77n9

Bavinck, Herman, 85n79
Bayesian probabilistic argument, 132n40
Beebe, James, 42n24
Beernink, Kenneth, 116
Bergmann, Michael, 132n40
Berkhof, Louis, 41n17, 133n50, 135n64, 136, 139n11
Bezzegoud, Mourad, 175
bigotry, 66
Bishop Chrysostomos, 36
Bishop, John, 28, 77, 136, 183, 184n13
Boltzmann, Ludwig, 142
Bonhoeffer, Dietrich, 3
Brockovich, Erin, 154, 155
Brother Lawrence, 97
Brothers Karamazov, 162
Brümmer, Vincent, 40, 88n109
Buddha, 24, 41, 92, 101, 187
Buffett, Warren, 149, 202
Bultmann, Rudolf, 95
Bush, George H. W., xi
Bush, George W., 4, 5
Butler, Joseph, 133n41

Cacciatore, Joanne, 115
Calvin, John, 24, 42n20, 77n6, 86n100, 130
Camus, Albert, 202
car towed, 73
carnapian construction, 132n40
Carnegie, Dale, 142

Carter, Jimmy, 26
Cary, Phillip, 44n34
change, 95, 99, 101, 107, 124
Cheney, Johnston, 61n63
Chesterton, G. K., 79n25
children, gifts from God, xii
Chisholm, Roderick, 27n10
Clary, Johnny Lee, 52, 53, 98
Clement of Alexandria, 87n108
Clendenin, Daniel, 86n100
Coelho, Paulo, 151
Cohen, Abraham, 147
Collins, Francis, 79, 170n9
Collins, Paul, 86n95
Colman, Richard, 184
Colson, Chuck, 205, 206
compatibilists, 149n10
Cottingham, John, 161
COVID-19, 23, 28, 49, 92, 115, 117, 121, 124, 133, 169, 170, 171
crab legs, 100
Craig, William Lane, 44n34, 81, 135n65
creation of humans, 38, 42
Crosby, Fanny, 102
Crummett, Dustin, 33n46, 152
Cyril of Alexandria, 86

Dahmer, Jeffrey, 31
DARES, 107, 114, 124, 208
Darwin, 147
Dawkins, Richard, 47n4, 90, 92, 144n43, 150, 151n22
de Caussade, Jean-Pierre, 157
de Sales, Francis, 181
defeat concept, 27n10
deism, 156, 207
Descartes, René, 40, 133n42
Dew, James, 47n3
distribution of evil, 202
divorce, Church of England, 67n100
Dobson, James, 182n8, 187
Dodes, Lance, 157
Dostoevsky, Fyodor, 162
double effect principle, 33n43
downplay, 107, 109, 114, 124
Dranseika, Vilius, 54
Draper, Paul, 132n40, 134n52, 154n34
drug overdose, 12, 69, 153, 183, 198

Eden, 40, 43, 44, 82, 87, 91, 176, 177
Edwards, Elizabeth, 205
Edwards, Jonathan, 27n6, 86n100
Ekstrom, Laura, 107, 113, 132, 135n65, 137n74
Eleggua, 187
Elliot, Jim, 201
empathy, 114, 116, 117, 118, 119, 124
enabling, 140, 145, 150, 153, 157, 170, 183, 188, 207
enabling path, 193
Epicurus, 128, 137, 188n39, 190, 209
Erickson, Millard, xiii, 84, 133n50, 135n64, 136, 169n8
epistemic distance, 154n33
escape, way of, 11, 13, 22, 53, 73, 92, 95, 98, 107, 124, 190, 192, 195, 206, 209
eternal punishment, 80
Eucken, Rudolf, 199
Evans, Jeremy, 49n9, 50n13
evaporate, 107, 111, 113
evidential argument from evil, 132, 137, 152
evidential problem of evil, 132, 135, 189
evil,
    definition, 47
    (moral) from one's own actions, 51
    (natural) from one's own actions, 54
    (moral) from other people's actions, 56, 58
    (natural) from other people's actions, 58
    (moral) for the rehabilitation of believers, 60
    (natural) for the rehabilitation of believers, 62
    (moral) for the edification of believers, 64
    (natural) for the edification of believers, 66
    (moral) for the shielding of believers, 68
    (natural) for the shielding of believers, 70
    (moral) for the training of believers, 71
    (natural) for the training of believers, 74

NAME AND SUBJECT INDEX 231

gratuitous, 9, 33, 38, 48, 132ff, 141, 148ff, 164ff, 209
moral, definition, 48
natural, definition, 49
not a functional good, 27
social, 47n2
systemic, 47n2
used by God, 60

factual premise, 135, 152n26
Fairbairn, Donald, 86
Fales, Evan, 162
Feinberg, John, 49n10, 94n2, 135n65
felix culpa, 134, 153n29
Fénelon, François, 27
Fierstein, Harvey, 108
forgive and forget path, 193
four Ps, 95ff, 107, 124
Francis of Assisi, 120
Franzese, Michael, 57, 98
free will,
    and God's sovereignty, 44n35
    defense, 131, 132
    serious, 133
    compatibilist, 149n10
    libertarian, 149n10
Freud, Sigmund, 150

Gates, Bill, 202
general-policy theodicy, 153n30
genocides, 36, 45, 48, 54, 131, 197
Genscher, Hans-Dietrich, 195
God,
    answers prayers, 7, 22
    cannot create uncreated Gods, 43, 45, 86, 208
    does not cause people to commit evil, 23, 29, 37
    does not need evil, 23, 28n13, 37
    forgives sins, 5ff, 13ff, 22, 26, 42, 155, 193
    impeccability, 40ff, 84ff, 93, 208
    intimate presence, 5ff, 22, 64, 80, 179
    matures believers through suffering, 15ff, 33, 71ff, 101, 203
    pledge, 9
    redeems evil, 27, 29, 31, 53, 152, 192n5, 208
    rejection of, 80, 88, 103, 144, 149n10, 155
    restrains evil, 34, 37
    simplicity, 40, 41, 43
    sovereignty and human free will, 44n35
    submission to, 105, 106
    triune, 6
    uses evil as a tool, 30ff, 37, 60ff, 68ff, 71, 75, 194, 208
    way of escape, 11ff, 92, 98, 107, 124, 190, 206, 209
Graham, Billy, 4, 35, 98, 149
greater good theodicy, 27n9, 149n10, 153, 162
Grudem, Wayne, 9, 28n13, 41n16, 133n50, 135n64, 136

Haiti earthquake, 54, 55, 66, 134
Hamilton, Bethany, 10
Hasker, William, xivn6, 27n9, 113, 134n59, 135n60, n62, 137n76, 152n27, 153n30, 155, 169, 173n28
heaven, 76, 82ff, 93, 96, 133, 153n29, 161n73, 196
Hefner, Hugh, 78ff, 95
hell, 76ff, 92
HELPS, 114, 124, 208
Henderson, Luke, 40n7, 85n90
Hewish, Antony, 90
Hick, John, 40, 44n39, 77, 133, 154n33
hiddenness, divine, 26, 37, 154n33
hijackers, 191
Hitchens, Christopher, 95, 144n43
Hitler, 36, 133, 150, 202
Hodge, Charles, 82n49, 156n51
Holy Spirit, 5ff, 9, 18, 22, 34ff, 68ff, 189ff, 206ff
Horton, Michael, 89
hostage, 191ff, 194ff
Howard-Snyder, Daniel, 132n40
human
    fall, 38, 44, 82, 87, 91ff, 134, 192ff
    impeccability, 43, 84ff, 93, 208
    peccable, 42, 45, 84, 89, 208
    state of innocence, 44, 89
Hume, David, 47, 128, 130ff

hurricane,
    Harvey, 58
    Katrina, 49, 58, 66, 124
    Paul's, 55

Ignatius of Loyola, 130
indirect inductive approach, 132n40
Irenaeus, 43, 86, 87, 129, 133

Job, 32ff, 37, 60, 64, 106, 202ff
Jonah, 17, 62
Joseph, 23, 27, 29
Josephus, Flavius, 69
Julian of Norwich, 67

Kant, Immanuel, 149, 162
Keathley, Kenneth, xiiin4
Keller, Helen, 94
Keller, James, 4
Keller, Timothy, 207
Kershnar, Stephen, 80
Khmer Rouge, 50
Kierkegaard, Søren, 79
killing fields, 194
king
    Ahab, 73ff
    David, 29n23, 72, 74, 97, 145
    Herod Agrippa, 69
    Jehoshaphat, 72ff
    Solomon, 96
    Uzziah, 74
Kligler, Jonathan, 187
Koenig, Harold, 150
Krauss, Kurt, 108
Kreeft, Peter, 128
Ku Klux Klan, 51
Kushner, Harold, 139n10
Kvanvig, Jonathan, 76

LaHaye, Tim, 191
Lamb, Randas, 187
lawsuit, medical malpractice, 101
legitimation, 114, 119, 124
Leibniz, Gottfried, xivn6, 27n9, 45n42, 174n33
Lenz, Frederick, 47n4
letter from the Father, 17
Levine, Michael, 27n9

Lewis, C. S., ix, 67, 76ff, 79, 170n13, 193, 206
libertarians, 149n10
Lisbon earthquake, 173ff
logical argument from evil, 28, 131
logical problem of evil, 40n5, 42n24, 131n26, 137, 190
Lord Acton, 95
Luther, Martin, 130
Lutzer, Erwin, 62
Lynch, Joseph, 172

Mackie, J. L., 39, 131ff, 188n39
Mafia, the, 14, 56ff, 98
Maguire, Jack, 187
Manicheans, the, 129
Mao Zedong, 176
Markham, Ian S., 162
marriage of Christ and the Church, 83ff, 86, 93, 208
martyrs, Christian, 156
Mary, mother of Jesus, 96
Masamune, Gorō Nyūdō, 203
mass shootings, 113, 131, 197ff
McIntyre, Alison, 33n43
Meir, Golda, 36, 194
Meister, Chad, 47n3
Mengele, Josef, 127ff
Molesky, Mark, 174
molinism, 153n29
Moloney, Daniel, 187
Moltmann, Jürgen, 163n79, 174
Moon, Sun Myung, 39ff, 45
Mother Teresa, 35, 133
mystery, xiii, 85, 135ff

Nabal, 145ff
Nagasawa, Yujin, 47n2
Nagel, Thomas, 138
nature red in tooth and claw, 92, 177
neonatal abstinence syndrome, 59
Netanyahu, Benjamin, 191
Netanyahu, Yonatan, 191
Niemöller, Martin, 36
Nietzsche, Friedrich, 139n5, 154n36
Nixon, Richard, 98, 100, 205

Oord, Thomas Jay, 135n66, 136, 139n10, 152n27
open heart operation, xii
open theism, 135, 139
Oppy, Graham, 158, 190n55
Origen, 88, 129, 133n45
Orlando, Michael Anthony (Tony), 63
Orthodox Ecumenical Patriarch, 171
Ossefort-Russell, Candyce, 112
Otte, Richard, 132n40

Pannenberg, Wolfhart, 134n59
Parkes, Colin, 109
path/world of death, 45, 87, 92, 178, 192, 207
Paul, Norman, 116
Peter's denials, 60ff
Peterson, Michael, 28n12, 132n34, 135n60, 143n39
physical presence, 112, 120ff
Plantinga, Alvin, 88n114, 131, 134, 136
Plato, 129
Plotinus, 129
Pol Pot, 194
Polycarp, 13
Poole, Matthew, 86n99
Pope Francis, 35, 166, 171ff, 176
Pope Gregory, 95
Pope John Paul II, 14, 77
Pope Paul VI, 26n3
Pope Pius XII, 36
Poston, Ted, 47n2
Praise (God), 17, 66, 68, 95, 105ff, 124, 202
Presley, Elvis, 100
Princess Diana, 183
problem of evil,
    evidential, 132, 135, 137, 152, 189, 209
    logical, 131n26, 137, 190
    religious, 94, 124, 208
Prodigal Son, the, 46, 52, 75, 141, 149n9, 156, 164, 165ff, 188, 207
Pusey, Edward, 11n62

Ragland, C. P., 76n5
Rakestraw, Robert, 86n100
rebuke, 60, 107, 110, 111

RECAP, 95, 107, 124, 208
reconciliation, 31, 37, 53, 81, 111, 140, 153, 155ff, 166ff, 170, 192
refocus, 95ff, 107, 124
REST, 60, 75, 203, 208
Roberts, Charlie, 180
Roser, Max, 199
Roth, John K., 132
Rousseau, Jean-Jacques, 174
Rowe, William, 26n4, 88n110, 132ff, 137n77, 158, 172n22, 181n4, 202n57
"Ryan," 117
Ryrie, Charles, 81, 133n50, 135n64, 139n10

saints or sinners, 202, 206
Sartre, Jean Paul, 79, 88
Satan, 60, 68, 70, 83, 89, 134, 177, 189
Schellenberg, J. L., 40n5, 154n33
Schleiermacher, Friedrich, 163n79
Sempangi, Kefa, 48
sermonize, 107, 113
Sheeran, Ed, 122ff
shipwreck, Paul's, 55ff
Shore, W. Teignmouth, 11
skeptical theism defense, 133ff
Smedes, Lewis, 11n63
Sodom and Gomorrah, 60, 70
"Son of Sam," 163ff
soul making, 40n4, 133, 153n29, 154n33
Søvik, Atle, 44n36
Spafford, Horatio, 67
Speak, Daniel, 137
specific-benefit theodicy, 153n30
Speight, R. Marston, 187
Sproul Jr., R. C., 81
Spurgeon, Charles, 101
Staines, Graham and Gladys, 15ff
Stalin, 147ff
Stoics, the, 129
strengthening, 114, 122, 124
strip club, 12, 13, 98, 99
Strobel, Kyle, 86n100
Strobel, Lee, 209
Stump, Eleonore, 33n46, 134, 135n65, 137, 157, 161n73, 183, 192n5

substitution, 31, 92, 194ff, 200, 206, 207ff
"Sue," 158ff, 160, 161
sufferer-centered requirements, 33n46, 152n28
suffering, definition, 50.
suicide, 6, 24, 28, 30, 52, 69, 111, 113, 142, 180, 198ff
Swinburne, Richard, 88n115, 133ff
sword, samurai, 203

Tada, Joni Eareckson, 7ff
Tatian, 85
temptation,
    definition, 95
    of our own doing, 95
    from other people, 98
ten Boom, Corrie, 33, 38, 105ff
Tennant, Robert, 169
Tertullian, 129
Thai, Lee, 43n31, 44n35, 82n46, 91n138
theodicy, definition, xivn6, 134n59
theological premise, 135, 137n77, 148n8
thorn in the flesh, 70, 99
Tillich, Paul, 143
Tooley, Michael, 132n40, 170n11, 172, 173n27, 184
tough love,
    definition, 139
    deductive argument of theodicy, 141
Trakakis, Nick, 9n50, 28n19, 32, 49n8, 132n37, 132n39, 133n34, 136, 158n59, 183, 189n52, 189n53, 189n54
transworld depravity, 131n29
trial,
    definition, 99
    of our own making, 99
    from other people and from God, 101
    for a little while, if necessary, 102

tsunami, 49, 168ff, 173ff
Turner, Ted, 103ff, 106
Twain, Mark, 159

union with Christ, 85, 87, 93
universal salvation, 77, 133
unsolicited advice, 110

van Inwagen, Peter, 44, 131, 141n23, 153, 193, 194n15, 202, 210
van Woudenberg, René, 160
Vietnam, South, 24ff, 203
Voltaire, 174

Warren, Rick, 6, 97
water damage, 102
weightlifting, 74
Wesley, John, 156n51
Westminster Confession of Faith, 40
White, Heath, 80n29
Whittaker, Jack, 12
Wiesel, Elie, 136
Wilde, Oscar, 47
Wolsterstorff, Nicholas, 48
Wright, N. T., 127
Wuthnow, Sara, 121
Wykstra, Stephen, 48, 81n35, 133

Xavier, Francis, 130

Yancey, Philip, 183
Yehoshua, 192

www.ingramcontent.com/pod-product-compliance
Lightning Source LLC
Chambersburg PA
CBHW070310230426
43663CB00011B/2074